The Rhetoric of American Exceptionalism

Critical Essays

Edited by Jason A. Edwards
and David Weiss

McFarland & Company, Inc., Publishers
Jefferson, North Carolina, and London

LIBRARY OF CONGRESS CATALOGUING-IN-PUBLICATION DATA

The rhetoric of American exceptionalism : critical essays / edited by Jason A. Edwards and David Weiss.
    p.   cm.
    Includes bibliographical references and index.

    ISBN 978-0-7864-5970-4
    softcover : 50# alkaline paper ∞

    1. National characteristics, American — Political aspects.
    2. National characteristics, American — Social aspects.
    3. Exceptionalism — United States. 4. Rhetoric — Political aspects — United States. 5. Rhetoric — Social aspects — United States. 6. Communication — Political aspects — United States. I. Edwards, Jason A., 1973– II. Weiss, David.
    E169.1 .R497   2011
    327.73 — dc22   2011007776

BRITISH LIBRARY CATALOGUING DATA ARE AVAILABLE

© 2011 Jason A. Edwards and David Weiss. All rights reserved

No part of this book may be reproduced or transmitted in any form or by any means, electronic or mechanical, including photocopying or recording, or by any information storage and retrieval system, without permission in writing from the publisher.

Cover photograph by Patrick Rolands
Front cover by TG Design

Manufactured in the United States of America

McFarland & Company, Inc., Publishers
  Box 611, Jefferson, North Carolina 28640
  www.mcfarlandpub.com

The Rhetoric of
American Exceptionalism

Acknowledgments

We have many people to thank for this volume. We would like to extend thanks to our family and friends for putting up with us as we put this project together over the past two years.

Jason would like to thank Bridgewater State University for providing him a CART Summer Grant in 2010 to help finish production of this book. Moreover, he thanks his colleagues in the Department of Communication Studies at Bridgewater State for providing a conducive work environment for completing this book. Special thanks go to Maria Hegbloom, Bjorn Ingvoldstad, Melanie McNaughton, and Nancy Van Leuven. Additionally, Jason thanks his parents, Jim and Paulette Edwards, for their continual support of his scholarly endeavors. His brother Jeff, sister Robin, sister-in-law Pia, and brother-in-law Lee helped keep him constantly laughing and sane throughout this process. Finally, Jason thanks Amber Luckie, who has given him a new direction in life and daily dosages of inspiration. This acknowledgment is a small payment on a debt that can never be fully repaid.

David would like to thank Dean Tasneem Khaleel, the Montana State University–Billings Foundation, and his colleagues in the MSU-B Communication and Theatre Department for their support and constant encouragement throughout the planning, editing, and writing processes; special thanks are due to Sue Balter-Reitz, Steve Coffman, Dan Gross, Sarah Keller, Randy Pugh, Kathy Sabe, and Melinda Tilton. Additional thanks go to David's parents, Aaron and Gladys Weiss, his sister and sister-in-law, Amy Weiss and Mindy Walwer, and his aunt, Gert Sirkin, who never fail to express their unconditional love and their pride in his accomplishments even when he's not actually accomplishing anything. It would not have been possible for David to stay grounded, throughout the duration of this project or at almost any other point during the past 30 years, without the companionship and good humor of friends Anthony Barone, Mike Bufton, Donna Cohn, Susan

Busch & Richard DiNardo, Gary Ensana & David Vickrey, Mike Ettlinger, Lynda Finn & Emily Jones, Debby Geis, Susan & Dan Kahn, Colleen Kaleda & Thad McCracken, Ed Ku, Marylou Lane & Gary Hill, Kathy Moore & Josh Chaiken, Ken Norz, Franny Osman & Bill Freeman, Janet Pennisi & David Jacobs, Lloyd Roberts, Lorisa Seibel & Ron Grunwald, Chari Smith & Ira Diamant, Illana Saraf & James Tulsky, Steve Wells, Regina & Joe Wilmes, and Beth Zemsky. Finally, David would like to thank and acknowledge Karen Foss for being not only a mentor and advisor but also a valued friend.

We would also like to thank our contributors to this project. Editing this book has been a challenge as well as a labor of love. We appreciate each author's openness to our suggestions as we guided this book to its completion. We hope they enjoy the final product as much as we do.

Table of Contents

Acknowledgments v

Introduction: American Exceptionalism's Champions and Challengers
    DAVID WEISS *and* JASON A. EDWARDS 1

Part I. Champions of American Exceptionalism

1. The Rhetoric in the Modern Presidency: A Quantitative Assessment
   RICO NEUMANN *and* KEVIN COE 11

2. Resolving Rhetorical Tensions
   M. KAREN WALKER 31

3. One Nation Under God: Mormon Theology and the American Continent
   BRETT LUNCEFORD 48

4. Re-Contextualizing Americanism: The National Association of Manufacturers' Jeremiad for Free Enterprise During the Roosevelt Era
   BURTON ST. JOHN, III 63

5. The Redeem Team Saves USA Basketball: An Analysis of the U.S.-China 2008 Olympic Games
   KATHERINE L. LAVELLE 82

Part II. Challengers to American Exceptionalism

6. Mormonism and America as Promised Land in Joseph Smith's Letter from Liberty Jail
   DAVID CHARLES GORE 101

7. Henry Cabot Lodge and the Rhetorical Trajectory
   MICHAEL J. HOSTETLER ... 118

8. Discursive Characterization as Embodiment and Critique: The Divergent Rhetorical Trajectories of Pat Tillman as an American Hero
   ARTHUR W. HERBIG ... 132

9. The Sand Creek Massacre National Historic Site: Challenge to and Reification of American Exceptionalism
   LINDSAY R. CALHOUN ... 153

10. Those Who Bear the Heaviest Burden: Warfare and American Exceptionalism in the Age of Entitlement
    CHRISTINA M. KNOPF ... 171

11. Promoting America: U.S. Public Diplomacy and the Limits of Exceptionalism
    CRAIG HAYDEN ... 189

About the Contributors ... 211

Index ... 215

Introduction: American Exceptionalism's Champions and Challengers

DAVID WEISS *and* JASON A. EDWARDS

American exceptionalism is the distinct belief that the United States is unique, if not superior, when compared to other nations (McCartney, 2006; McCrisken, 2003; Rodgers, 2004). Champions of American exceptionalism hold that because of its national credo, historical evolution, and unique origins, America is a special nation with a special role — possibly ordained by God — to play in human history. The belief in American exceptionalism is a fundamental aspect of U.S. cultural capital and national identity (Lipset, 1996; Madsen, 1998). It is an essential part of America's political, cultural, and social DNA. Deborah Madsen has argued that American exceptionalism has always "offered a mythological refuge from the chaos of history and the uncertainty of life" (1998, p. 166). For Americans, exceptionalism projects a certain telos where the United States continues to progress, ever attempting to create a "more perfect union," and never succumbing to the forces of decay (McCrisken, 2003). To believers in American exceptionalism, the United States continues to move in a constant upward pattern, remaining the beacon of light in the darkness and the defender of the rights of man as long as the nation exists. Moreover, America and Americans are exceptional because they are charged with saving the world from itself; at the same time, America and Americans must maintain a high level of devotion to this destiny. Ultimately, champions of American exceptionalism argue that American exceptionalism functions to order Americans' universe and define their place in it (Hunt, 1988).

The rhetoric of American exceptionalism permeates every period of

American history. As early as 1630, Puritan leader John Winthrop declared that the Massachusetts Bay Colony held the promise to be a "new Israel," a "shining city upon a hill" for the world to emulate (quoted in McCrisken, 2003, p. 5). On the eve of the American Revolution, Thomas Paine wrote in *Common Sense* that together the colonies had the power to "begin the world over again" because of their providential heritage (1776/1995, p. 32). In *Democracy in America*, Alexis de Tocqueville (1830/1956) declared the United States to be truly exceptional and exhorted all democratic nations to emulate the example it had set. Herman Melville wrote in his novel *White Jacket* that "we Americans are the peculiar, chosen people — the Israel of our time; we bear the ark of the liberties of the world" (1850/2006, p. 189). Loren Baritz (1985), Thomas Hietala (2003), and Paul McCartney (2006) each chronicled the ways in which American exceptionalism has been fundamental to political rhetoric, serving as the foundation for the doctrine of Manifest Destiny, which was used to justify the Mexican, Spanish-American, and Vietnam wars as well as the westward expansion of U.S. sovereignty across the American continent. Jason Edwards (2008), Trevor McCrisken (2003), and Siobhan McEvoy-Levy (2001) explored American exceptionalism's influence over political arguments regarding the United States's role in the world.

American Exceptionalism: In Politics and Beyond

Although most scholarship on American exceptionalism focuses on its place in political discourse, expressions of exceptionalist sentiment are not limited to the political arena. The belief in American uniqueness and superiority can be found in the rhetoric of religious institutions, works of great literature, newspaper editorials, coverage of sporting events, and the content of television programming and other popular culture texts (Lipset, 1996; Madsen, 1998; Rojecki, 2008; Stephenson, 1996). Based on this evidence, it can be easily said that American exceptionalism is a fundamental, perhaps even primary, characteristic of U.S. political and social culture.

However, there are critics who challenge American exceptionalism's desirability, relevance, and even the validity its continuing existence. For example, sociologist Daniel Bell (1975) asserted that American exceptionalism ended with the Vietnam War. According to Bell, the negative experiences associated with Vietnam made Americans realize that they were a nation like all other nations. Loren Baritz (1985) concurred, arguing that American exceptionalism, our belief in our own moral superiority, and the ability to transform the destiny of nations as the protector of the "free world" were what led us to fight in Vietnam — and that it was this very arrogance that ultimately led to our defeat there. British historian Paul Kennedy (1989) predicted that the United States, having reached the apex of its power, was on a slow and steady decline, its exceptional global leadership now certain to be replaced as other powers rose to counter American hegemony.

More recently, challengers to exceptionalism have become more vocal. In his 2008 presidential campaign, U.S. Representative Ron Paul (R–Texas) constantly questioned and criticized America's role in the world, charging that America's current exceptionalist mission of intervention and leadership had betrayed the foreign policy of the founding fathers. Paul excoriated Democrats and Republicans alike, advocating that the U.S. return to a foreign policy of non-interventionism, which would allow our country to rebuild and rejuvenate itself domestically. Political scientist Andrew Bacevich (2009) put forth a similar argument, asserting that there is a crisis of our own making within the United States. In our pursuit of freedom, we have grown a penchant for empire. Americans, believing that our values are universal, have pursued the global projection of those values at the cost of our domestic well-being. We have tried to shape the world in our image, but have only imperiled our own existence with growing debt. Moreover, Americans have grown complacent, feeling entitled to things, where they once had to work. The penchant for empire, the feeling of entitlement, and the racking up of debt threaten the very existence of the U.S. system, warned Bacevich. America's desire to remake the world in its own image has led us to risk losing our exceptionalist soul and tarnishing the once shining city upon a hill.

Political scientist David Mason (2009) maintained that the United States's decline has begun and that American exceptionalism will hold little currency in the future. Mason cited several factors to support his argument, the most important of which are the growing deficit and the degree of debt accumulated over the last thirty years. The United States has been spending beyond its means and relying on foreign nations to finance the debt, giving it less influence over the rest of the world. Additionally, America lags in its investments in health care, science, technology, infrastructure, and education, falling behind every major industrial power in these areas. Moreover, Mason has argued, our foreign policy, particularly that practiced during the Bush administration, has diminished American prestige as a result of a tendencies to isolate ourselves against a rapidly globalizing world and to pursue a militaristic foreign policy in support of a war endorsed by few other countries. In failing to invest, innovate, or create ties in order to keep its role as world leader, the United States has imperiled its ability to serve as an example for the world to emulate.

Godfrey Hodgson (2009) wrote in *The Myth of American Exceptionalism* that the United States is not as exceptional as it has claimed to be over the years. Hodgson demonstrated that the evolution of American history, particularly its exceptionalism, is actually tied to a broader history, one not shaped by divine providence, but rather by a confluence of factors, many of them international. Hodgson did maintain that America is exceptional, but not necessarily in ways that are exclusively good. (We are the only major developed nation that does not cover its entire people with health care; we have the highest murder rate, the highest gun ownership rate, and one of the highest illiteracy rates among developed nations.) Ultimately, Hodgson argued that American exceptionalism is by and large dangerous for Americans because it disconnects us from larger global movements. American exceptionalism does not allow us to be truly part of the solution to global problems; rather, we come up with a patchwork of solutions that merely forestall but do not prevent or solve greater problems down the road. America is certainly a global leader as a nation-state, but is not a country anointed by God to lead the world to a better tomorrow. Believing otherwise is hubristic and dangerous. Ultimately, all of these critics have argued that our military missteps in Vietnam, Afghanistan, and Iraq, the decline of American power abroad, and continuing domestic problems among races, religions, ethnicities, and classes provide evidence that America is not exceptional, but is, rather, like every other country in the world.

Overview of the Book

This book is situated against the backdrop of two conflicting motifs — the championing of American exceptionalism and the simultaneous challenge to that notion. We offer a collection of essays that explore and analyze the rhetoric of American exceptionalism as it is manifested across a range of contexts and forms including the discourses of the American presidency, U.S. foreign policy, religion, economics, and the mass media's coverage of news and sports. Our specific purpose is to interrogate the notion of American exceptionalism in the words of both its champions and its challengers. By studying how the principles of American exceptionalism have been alternately used, adapted, challenged, and even rejected, this volume demonstrates the continued importance of exceptionalism to the mythology, sense of place, direction, and identity of the United States, both within and outside of the realm of politics.

In Part I, we present essays by authors who write about past and present champions of American exceptionalism. Chapter 1 examines how presidents have used basic themes of American exceptionalism over the last seventy-five years. Rico Neumann and Kevin Coe use a content-analytic approach to illustrate how modern American presidents have been the most vocal champions of our exceptionalist ethos, emphasizing America's leadership in a stable world order and the nation's unique role of teacher, leader, and sometimes global policeman.

In Chapter 2, M. Karen Walker considers how American exceptionalism has been used in presidential inaugural addresses. She asserts that pride of nation is a universal appeal for collective identity and action and asks what makes America's claims unique to our nation. She argues that an axiom of American exceptionalism is the covenant between a providential land and a chosen people, and explores how presidential inaugural addresses use two complementary strands of exceptionalism: the exemplarist and interventionist modes.

Chapter 3 analyzes how American exceptionalism is championed from a religious perspective. Specifically, Brett Lunceford investigates Mormon theology, arguing that members of the Latter-day Saints church find America's exceptional ethos not merely in the nation's political and social system, but in the land itself. American territory, "from sea to shining sea," is not only a "new Israel" proverbially but also literally. Thus, Lunceford shows, America is a sacred site where true believers will have the ability to carry out God's covenant and where Mormons are fundamental keepers of that covenant.

In Chapter 4, Burton St. John, III, examines the rhetoric of the National Association of Manufacturers (NAM) during the New Deal era. St. John argues that the NAM grew increasingly worried that New Deal policies were poisoning Americans' attitudes toward business, and thus undercutting the exceptionalist values of individual freedom and unfettered private enterprise that had long been hallmarks of the American ethos. To combat this trend, the NAM used the rhetorical form of the jeremiad to assail New Deal policies, convincing people to return to the virtues of individualism and free-market capitalism that would ultimately redeem and renew America's exceptionalist credo.

In Chapter 5, Katherine L. Lavelle interrogates how American exceptionalism was employed in the 2008 Beijing Olympics, specifically in the NBC broadcast of the American men's basketball game against China. Lavelle argues that exceptionalism was a prominent aspect of USA Basketball's attempt to "redeem" itself after its disastrous performances in international competitions in 2002, 2004, and 2006 — and that this exceptionalism marked the U.S.–based sports media's coverage of the U.S.-China match-up. Lavelle breaks down how both the players and broadcasters promoted America's "superiority" over the Chinese basketball team and explores the impact of such coverage on American sports culture.

Part II presents essays on challenges to various aspects of America's exceptionalist credo. Chapter 6 explores Joseph Smith's letter from Liberty Jail which, as David Charles Gore argues, was used as a defense of religious liberty and Mormonism through an appeal to a unique vision of American exceptionalism that aimed to discredit the Mormons' persecutors. The letter, framing the wrongs against the Mormons as wrongs against the country, tied the treatment of the then small Mormon sect to the ultimate destiny of the nation. In doing so, Smith's letter painted a powerful vision of American religious liberty, simultaneously defending and attacking America in the best tradition of American civil rights rhetoric. Gore's essay reinforces the idea that American exceptionalism is not monolithic; indeed, there are American exceptionalisms, just as there are Mormonisms, each sufficiently distinct to justify further study.

In Chapter 7, Michael J. Hostetler investigates the foreign policy rhetoric of U.S. Senator Henry Cabot Lodge (1850–1924) of Massachusetts as that rhetoric related to debates over the Philippines and the League of Nations. Hostetler demonstrates that Lodge was initially a staunch advocate of the subjugation and colonization of the Philippines by American forces yet later became an ardent opponent of President Wilson's plan to join the League of Nations. Hostetler argues that this can be explained by the trajectory of American exceptionalism. According to Hostetler's analysis, the interventionist strain of American exceptionalism flows from East to West. Accordingly, Cabot Lodge could approve of America's expansion and intervention westward into the Philippines, but not eastward into European politics. As Hostetler demonstrates, Cabot Lodge's foreign policy discourse both championed and challenged American exceptionalism's interventionist mission at the turn of the last century.

In Chapter 8, Arthur W. Herbig explores how the image of Pat Tillman's death was used in mass-mediated arguments about the propriety of the Iraq War. As Herbig shows, American heroes, regardless of their walk of life, are important embodiments of American exceptionalism as they represent everything that the United States is and could be. However, the images of these heroes are malleable. Illustrating how aspects of American exceptionalism can be used for opposing purposes, Herbig examines the rhetoric of Senator John McCain and MSNBC commentator Keith Olbermann, two public figures who exploited the memory of Tillman to bolster their own starkly contrasting positions on the Iraq War and, by extension, their positions on American exceptionalism itself.

Chapter 9 explores Colorado's Sand Creek Massacre Site as a text that itself interrogates the paradox that is American exceptionalism. In her chapter, Lindsay R. Calhoun argues that this paradox stems from America's celebration of its unique degree of diversity and its simultaneous tendency to (strive to) unite all Americans under one identity banner. Through an analysis of the narratives of the Sand Creek site, Calhoun reveals the attempt by the majority U.S. culture to include Native Americans in the story of America while at the same time ensuring that they stand apart. She concludes that it is this paradoxical disjunctive synthesis that makes American exceptionalism such a pervasive and powerful cultural paradigm.

In Chapter 10, Christina M. Knopf argues that America's ideas of an exceptionalist ethos have evolved from early sentiments of hard work and sacrifice to the currently pervasive emphasis on ease, privilege, and narcissism. Knopf maintains that this ethos of entitlement can be seen not only in the marketplace, where one might expect it, but also in attitudes toward and rhetoric surrounding more important matters, namely America's justifications for war. Ordinary Americans are no longer asked to sacrifice; rather, we ask others to do so for us. As Knopf's chapter demonstrates, the evolving logic of American exceptionalism may actually endanger the nation's exceptionalist ethos.

Finally, in Chapter 11, Craig Hayden examines the contours and influences of American exceptionalism in public diplomacy discourse since the Cold War. He argues that American exceptionalism has been a fundamental part of U.S. public diplomatic efforts over the past sixty years, but that this discourse has often been counterproductive. Exceptionalism has actually been a constraint upon America's public diplomatic efforts, particularly with the Muslim world, because it precludes the development of public diplomatic strategies that are pragmatic when dealing with various regions of the globe. Recent reconfigurations of public diplomacy may point the way to a reconceptualization of the use of American exceptionalism in public diplomacy.

Paradoxically, as interest in (and the number of publications investigating) American exceptionalism and its manifestations has exploded in recent years, the parameters of the study of American exceptionalism have barely widened. Scholarly work has remained limited to the investigation of American exceptionalism's role in and implications for political campaigning, governance, policy formation, and diplomacy, fields often inaccessible to "ordinary people" and others not working directly in these fields. Further, for the most part, the growing body of work on American exceptionalism has approached its object from only one evaluative standpoint; namely, that of endorsement. Missing from most of this otherwise exemplary scholarship is any extended exploration of the many actual or possible challenges to American exceptionalism's core tenets or the advocates of those tenets. Also overlooked is a serious consideration of the diffusion of this once rarefied philosophical notion into realms of American life beyond the explicitly political. In compiling this volume, we aim not only to extend the body of American exceptionalism literature but also to broaden its scope, showing how the rhetorics of American exceptionalism, as offered by both challengers and champions, have become woven into the fabric of the social, cultural, recreational, and spiritual pursuits — that is to say, the daily lives — of a wide variety of Americans.

References

Bacevich, A. (2009). *The Limits of Power: The End of American Exceptionalism.* New York: Macmillan.
Baritz, L. (1985). *Backfire: A History of How American Culture Led Us Into Vietnam and Made Us Fight the Way We Did.* New York: William Morrow.
Bell, D. (1975). "The End of American Exceptionalism." *Parameters: Journal of the U.S. Army War College, 10,* 1–18.
Edwards, J. A. (2008). *Navigating the Post-Cold War World: President Clinton's Foreign Policy Rhetoric.* Lanham, MD: Lexington.
Hietala, T. R. (2003). *Manifest Design: American Exceptionalism and Empire* (rev. ed.). Ithaca: Cornell University Press.
Hodgson, G. (2009). *The Myth of American Exceptionalism.* New Haven: Yale University Press.
Hunt, M. H. (1988). *Ideology and U.S. Foreign Policy.* New Haven: Yale University Press.
Kennedy, P. (1989). *The Rise and Fall of the Great Powers.* New York: Vintage.
Lipset, S. M. (1996). *American Exceptionalism: A Double-Edged Sword.* New York: W.W. Norton.
Madsen, D. L. (1998). *American Exceptionalism.* Oxford: University of Mississippi Press.
Mason, D. S. (2009). *The End of the American Century.* Lanham, MD: Rowman and Littlefield.
McCartney, P. T. (2006). *Power and Progress: American National Identity, the War of 1898, and the Rise of American Imperialism.* Baton Rouge: Louisiana State University Press.
McCrisken, T. B. (2003). *American Exceptionalism and the Legacy of Vietnam: U.S. Foreign Policy Since 1974.* New York: Palgrave.
McEvoy-Levy, S. (2001). *American Exceptionalism and U.S. Foreign Policy: Public Diplomacy at the End of the Cold War.* New York: Palgrave.
Melville, H. (2006). *White Jacket.* New York: Aegypan. (Original work published 1850.)
Paine, T. (1995). *Common Sense.* New York: Barnes and Noble. (Original work published 1776.)
Rodgers, D. T. (2004). "American Exceptionalism Revisited." *Raritan, 24,* 21–47.
Rojecki, A. (2008). "Rhetorical Alchemy: American Exceptionalism and the War on Terror." *Political Communication, 25,* 67–88.
Stephenson, A. (1996). *Manifest Destiny: American Expansionism and the Empire of Right.* New York: Hill and Wang.
Tocqueville, A. de (1975). *Democracy in America.* New York: Vintage. (Original work published 1830.)

PART I
Champions of American Exceptionalism

CHAPTER 1

The Rhetoric in the Modern Presidency
A Quantitative Assessment

RICO NEUMANN *and* KEVIN COE

In April of 2009 President Barack Obama traveled to Strasbourg, France, to attend the twenty-first NATO summit and mark the organization's sixtieth anniversary. While there, a reporter asked Obama if he believed in American exceptionalism, to which the president replied:

> I believe in American exceptionalism, just as I suspect that the Brits believe in British exceptionalism and the Greeks believe in Greek exceptionalism.... Now, the fact that I am very proud of my country and I think that we've got a whole lot to offer the world does not lessen my interest in recognizing the value and wonderful qualities of other countries, or recognizing that we're not always going to be right.[1]

Predictably, Obama's view of American exceptionalism garnered its fair share of criticism from U.S. pundits. Monica Crowley, for example, complained in the *Washington Times* that Obama's rhetoric revealed a "kaleidoscopic ... view [that] no nation is better than any other" and that "every nation is great in its own way" (Crowley, 2009, p. A19), while James Kirchick of the *Los Angeles Times* had this to say: "If all countries are 'exceptional' then none are, and to claim otherwise robs the word, and the idea of American Exceptionalism, of any meaning" (Kirchick, 2009, p. 23A).

Such criticisms seem to reflect the belief that Obama's nuanced view of American exceptionalism is at odds with a more common understanding of the concept — one that suggests America is entirely unique in the world because of its founding principles and the success and stability of its democracy (see

Lipset, 1997; Shafer, 1991). Whether Obama's definition truly is different from his predecessors, of course, depends on precisely how past presidents defined American exceptionalism. Scholarship on the language of American exceptionalism in the presidency (e.g., Edwards, 2008; McCrisken, 2003; McEvoy-Levy, 2001; Rojecki, 2008) provides some clues about this history, but typically has not looked at many presidents over time in a way that allows for the drawing of broad conclusions. This chapter attempts to draw such conclusions by taking a quantitative content-analytic approach to the study of exceptionalism—a departure from the extant research. Although such an approach is clearly limited in the rhetorical nuances it can capture, it has the advantage of facilitating direct and precise comparisons across time periods, political parties, and individual presidents. This study should therefore nicely complement the body of qualitative work on the rhetoric of American exceptionalism, while also contributing more broadly to the scholarship on presidents' foreign policy rhetoric (e.g., Bostdorff, 1994; Stuckey, 1995; Wander, 1984) and national identity rhetoric (e.g., Beasley, 2004; Domke and Coe, 2008; Stuckey, 2004).

Exceptionalism in the American Presidency

American exceptionalism has long been a part of the American ethos. If the idea of exceptionalism was first given voice in Puritan settler John Winthrop's memorable 1630 description of America as a "city on a hill" (itself a reference to the New Testament's Gospel of Matthew), its cultural relevance was solidified in the work of Alexis de Tocqueville, the French political philosopher and historian who in 1831 came to the United States to study the penal system. Tocqueville's resulting book, *De la démocratie en Amérique* (*Democracy in America*, 1835/1948), highlighted various aspects of American social and political life. Drawing comparisons to his home country, Tocqueville sought to explain why the American concept of representative democracy had been failing in France and many other developed countries on the European continent, many of which were emerging from monarchies and experimenting with democratic reform. By emphasizing the differences between the young American nation and the socio-political structures in Europe at the time, Tocqueville presented America as the exception to the international rule. The idea of American exceptionalism has since become a common way of describing the nation's identity, values, and history, and suggesting the United States is an exemplar for the rest of the world (see Malone and Khong, 2003; McCrisken, 2003). Indeed, exceptionalist values can be found in virtually every period of U.S. history (Madsen, 1998).

The bulk of the scholarship on American exceptionalism has focused on defining the concept and identifying its historical causes and consequences. Shafer (1991), for example, describes exceptionalism via the "American model," which builds from the interaction of "populism and individualism at the personal level, democratization and market-making at the institutional level" (p. 223). Lipset (1997), meanwhile, explains the tenets of the "American creed," adding liberty, egalitarianism, and a laissez-faire ethic to the understanding of American exceptionalism. Lipset further identifies three consistent themes in the growing body of research on American exceptionalism. The first theme follows the Tocquevillean tradition that regards the United States as a considerable outlier from other nation states. This includes literature that emphasizes topics such as religion (Greeley, 1991), economics (Temin, 1991), education (Trow, 1991), and political structures/policies (Rose, 1991; Wildavsky, 1991). The second theme, often emphasized by historians or in American literature, focuses on the founding myth of America — its revolutionary beginning and emphasis of key values, such as liberty and equality (e.g., Hodgson, 2009; Johnson, 1999; Lockhart, 2003; Madsen, 1998). Finally, a third, more particular theme in the research deals with the difference of class hierarchies in the United States compared to those nations that were slowly liberated from long-lasting monarchies. Specifically, inspired by the writings of German socialist Werner Sombart (1906/1976), various scholars have explored the failure and absence of Communist or Socialist movements in the United States (e.g., Bell, 1996; Fitrakis, 1993; Howe, 1985; Lipset, 1977, 1997, 2000; Lipset and Marks, 2000).

Regardless of which theme the literature takes up, one pattern is consistent: scholars have paid relatively little attention to how presidents employ the rhetoric of American exceptionalism (though this trend is changing, as evidenced by Edwards [2008] and several chapters in the present volume). This omission is surprising given the considerable role presidential rhetoric plays in constructing, shaping, and reinforcing America's image at home and abroad. As Tulis (1987) has pointed out, the modern presidency is a "rhetorical presidency" in that speaking to the public has become a central function — many would say *the* central function — of the office (see also Campbell and Jamieson, 1990, 2008). If, as Windt (1990, p. 3) contends, "political rhetoric creates the arena of political reality within which political thought and action take place," then omnipresent presidential constructions of American exceptionalism might go a long way toward influencing how exceptionalism is thought of and experienced by Americans. Indeed, such constructions may provide for citizens a "para-ideological" vehicle for making sense of America; that is, "a crystallization of a set of related ideas which explain the world and the U.S. role therein" (McEvoy-Levy, 2001, p. 23).

Despite this general pattern, a few noteworthy studies have focused sustained attention on how U.S. presidents have employed exceptionalist themes. McEvoy-Levy (2001) examined various key transitional moments in U.S. history to illustrate how presidents have consistently relied on the rhetoric of exceptionalism. McEvoy-Levy highlights, for example, how as the Cold War ended and a familiar enemy disappeared, Presidents George H. W. Bush and Bill Clinton emphasized exceptionalist themes to foster national pride. The study makes clear that throughout U.S. history the concept of American exceptionalism is pervasive and has regularly been used "to legitimize ... domestic as well as foreign policies" (McEvoy-Levy, 2001, p. 23).

Rojecki (2008) also studied how American exceptionalism can be used to justify foreign policy, focusing on the rhetorical themes of George W. Bush and others in his cabinet, as well as editorial coverage in elite newspapers, during the buildup to the Iraq War. Rojecki found that the rhetoric of American exceptionalism promoted by the Bush administration provided "a resonant moral catalyst for elite media support of unilateral U.S. military action" (p. 67).

Further detail into precisely how presidents have employed American exceptionalist rhetoric is provided by McCrisken (2003). Focusing on presidential rhetoric in the post–Vietnam era, McCrisken identifies two major strands of exceptionalist rhetoric. The first is the exemplar form in which the U.S. depicts itself as an example to the rest of the world while nonetheless abstaining from intervention in international conflicts. The second is the interventionist form in which the U.S. intervenes in conflict to highlight its "responsibilities and duties ... to protect the higher values of humanity wherever they are threatened" (p. 183). McCrisken notes that either strand can serve as an effective rhetorical strategy, but that presidents in the post–Vietnam era have tended more toward the exemplar variety as the U.S. has sought to engage only in relatively low-risk conflicts — with notable exceptions such as the lengthy wars in Afghanistan and Iraq.

Edwards (2008) demonstrates how this two-fold distinction in American exceptionalist rhetoric played out in the Clinton presidency, illustrating the "rhetorical flexibility" needed to navigate the post–Cold War environment. Clinton's rhetoric, Edwards shows, continued to highlight America's exceptionalist qualities but took a more active, interventionist stance than that of some of his predecessors. This necessitated that Clinton combine aspects of the exemplar and interventionist forms, depending on the severity of the conflict in question. On one hand, Clinton argued that military intervention was "needed to manage the multitude of threats within the globalization era" (p. 145). On the other hand, Clinton elevated the language of partnership as a way to signal an era of broader cooperation in the post–Cold War era.

Taken together, these four studies demonstrate the enduring position of American exceptionalism in presidential rhetoric and the important implications such rhetoric can have. They also point to the need for continued scholarship in this area. With this in mind, the present study attempts to contribute to the literature in two key ways. First, we analyze a wider range of presidents than have previous studies so that we might provide a broad picture of American exceptionalism in the presidency. Our analysis focuses on the modern presidency, which scholars have generally defined as beginning with the administration of Franklin Roosevelt. During Roosevelt's lengthy term the United States and especially the presidency changed significantly. In particular, presidential, federal, and national power grew substantially, permanently altering America's role in the world and the president's role in national governance (Greenstein, 2004). Therefore, beginning with Roosevelt will allow for multiple presidents to be included in the analysis while still holding roughly constant the cultural position of these presidents. Second, we take a quantitative approach to studying exceptionalism. With very few exceptions, scholarship on American exceptionalism has been qualitative. The value of such work is evident, but adding a quantitative assessment to this body of scholarship will make possible some diachronic analyses and direct comparisons that should usefully expand our understanding of American exceptionalism in the presidency.

Measuring Exceptionalism in the Presidency

It should be stressed that any single quantitative measure of American exceptionalism in presidential rhetoric is likely to be imperfect and incomplete. Given this, our approach is to devise multiple measures, each of which might suggest one way that presidents can signal a commitment to American exceptionalism. Taken together the measures should provide a more adequate and complete picture of presidents' exceptionalist rhetoric.

A useful place to begin is with presidential mentions of the nation. Scholars have noted that American national identity — of which exceptionalism is one element — is based in part upon how presidents talk about the nation when addressing the public (Beasley, 2004; Stuckey, 2004). One specific distinction that presidents can draw is to refer to the nation as *America* or *the United States of America*, rather than simply *the United States* or *our nation* or *country*. The difference, as Domke and Coe (2008) point out, is that "*America* ... brings with it a broader set of cultural mythologies than do any of the other ways of invoking the nation.... The term connotes a set of historical, social, and political images that *nation, country,* and *United States* do not" (pp. 54–55, emphasis added). Most of these historical, social, and political images are consonant with the idea of American exceptionalism. Thus one way that presidents might signal a commitment to American exceptionalism — consciously or not — is to use America more commonly than other terms when invoking the nation.

A second possible measure of exceptionalism also deals with presidential invocations of the nation, but adds invocations of other nations to the equation as well. For various reasons — from their personal style, to the aims of their speech writers, to the state of domestic and international affairs — presidents vary in the extent to which they mention the nation relative to the extent to which they mention other nations. Some of these variations might be happenstance, of course, but over the course of an entire presidency a pattern would likely emerge that would suggest something other than chance variation. We argue that, though every president will likely reference America more than other nations, an especially large ratio between these mentions might signal a commitment to American exceptionalism. After all, presidential speaking patterns represent carefully thought out choices about what to emphasize and deemphasize. Thus presidents who take a less America-centric view of the world would likely have a smaller ratio between their mentions of America and their mentions of other nations, while those more focused on America would have a larger ratio.[2]

A third possible measure of exceptionalism moves from the extent of mentions presidents make to the *kind* of mentions they make. Rojecki's (2008) work on American exceptionalism illustrates that drawing a clear good-versus-evil distinction is common to this type of rhetoric: the United States is presented as a model of success and upholder of virtue in the face of those who might not cooperate with the established world order (as imagined by the United States). This idea is consistent with the notion of the exemplar variety of American exceptionalism (e.g., Edwards, 2008; McCrisken, 2003) as well as the broader scholarship on American foreign policy rhetoric (e.g., Coe et al., 2004; Ivie, 1980; Wander, 1984). To signal a commitment to American exceptionalism, then, presidents might choose to emphasize the stability of the U.S.-led world order by more often talking about the "good" nations (i.e., those who are participating in or benefitting from the order) than the "bad" nations (i.e., those who are challenging or dissenting from the order in some way). As before, we would expect these trends to be intermittently influenced by various factors, but for presidency-length trends to be nonetheless suggestive.

As a fourth and final way to measure American exceptionalism in presidential rhetoric we can consider how presidents position the United States in relation to other nations. Two primary possibilities exist. The first is that presidents would position the United States in some kind of "paternalistic" role (Hunt, 1987)—as a leader, teacher, helper, "referee" or "policeman" of other nations (see Carroll, 1996; MacKinnon, 2000; Zakaria, 2009). This approach, which we would expect to be fairly common, might signal a commitment to American exceptionalism in that it would be consistent with the notion that America is exceptional and therefore worthy of imitation, capable of leading the world, and so on (see Lipset, 1997). Conversely, presidents might position other nations as exemplars from which America could learn. This would position America in a relatively subordinate position to the other nations, demonstrating a reversed appeal to authority and thus perhaps signaling less of a commitment to American exceptionalism. Consequently, we would expect this to be a far less common approach among modern presidents.

Analysis

To explore these four questions and analyze the rhetoric of American exceptionalism in the modern presidency, we focused on State of the Union addresses. This seemed appropriate for two reasons. For one, major addresses like the State of the Union attract much larger audiences and greater media attention than most presidential speeches, which increases the potential for impact (Schaefer, 1997; Zarefsky, 2004). Additionally, State of the Union messages typically have a good mix of both deliberative foreign policy rhetoric and epideictic nation-building rhetoric (Campbell and Jamieson, 1990, 2008), which makes them an ideal site for tracking the rhetoric of American exceptionalism. Our content analysis procedure therefore involved identifying every mention of the United States (i.e., mentions of *America, country, nation, United States, U.S., U.S.A.*) and every mention of a foreign entity (i.e., mentions of any foreign city, nation, region, leader, citizen, or governing body) in presidential State of the Union addresses from Franklin Roosevelt's first (1934) to George W. Bush's last (2008).[3] Mentions of foreign entities were then coded according to two additional categories.

The first category was *relation to world order*. Here, we judged whether presidents were presenting the foreign entity as a *participant* in the U.S.–led world order (those that supported, sustained, or benefitted from the order) or a *dissenter* from it (those that were threatening, or choosing not to participate in, the order).[4] Examples of participant language included "America's partners and friends in Western Europe" and "America and Afghanistan are now allies." Examples of dissenter language included "relentless pressures of the Chinese Communists" and "the unwarranted Iranian quarrel with the United States."

The second category was *relation to the United States*. Here, we judged whether presidents explicitly presented the United States as engaging in *paternalism* (by helping, teaching, or leading the foreign entity) or if the president explicitly presented the foreign entity as an *exemplar* (by citing its example as something America should follow). Examples of paternalism language included "We have proudly supported peace and prosperity and freedom from South Africa to Northern Ireland" and "In Asia, the nations from Korea and Japan to Indonesia and Singapore worked behind America's shield to strengthen their economies." Examples of exemplar language were extremely rare; all instances are presented below in the analysis of Question 4.[5]

Question 1: Invoking the Nation

Our first question deals with the terms presidents have used to invoke the nation. We suggested that using *America* as a primary label for the nation might suggest greater American exceptionalism than would using other, less symbolically charged labels such as *country, nation*, or *United States*. We explored this possibility by determining, for each president, what percentage of their overall mentions of the nation used the term *America* (as opposed to another label).[6] Figure 1 presents the results of this analysis. What the figure makes clear is that over the past seven decades presidents have increasingly invoked *America* specifically rather than the nation generally. Between Roosevelt (30.1 percent) and G. W. Bush (57.3 percent), presidents nearly doubled the regularity with which they opted to call the nation *America*. Nor are these two presidents even the extremes. Truman (9.4 percent) was the lowest of all presidents, whereas Reagan (69.1 percent) was the highest — a truly striking increase over four decades. Reagan's position at the top of this measure is consistent with scholarship that suggests the Reagan presidency was a watershed moment for exceptionalist themes, which led to "supra-partisan use" of those themes since (McEvoy-Levy, 2001, p. 31; see also Domke and Coe, 2008).

Two additional points can be gleaned from Figure 1. The first is the difference that exists between Republican presidents and Democratic presidents. On average, Republican presidents (54.7 percent) noticeably exceeded their Democratic counterparts (35.8 percent) in using *America* as a way to label the nation. This finding runs counter to the work of McEvoy-Levy (2001), who argued that "twentieth-century exceptionalism has been predominantly evoked by Democratic Presidents" (p. 31). A second point, however, is con-

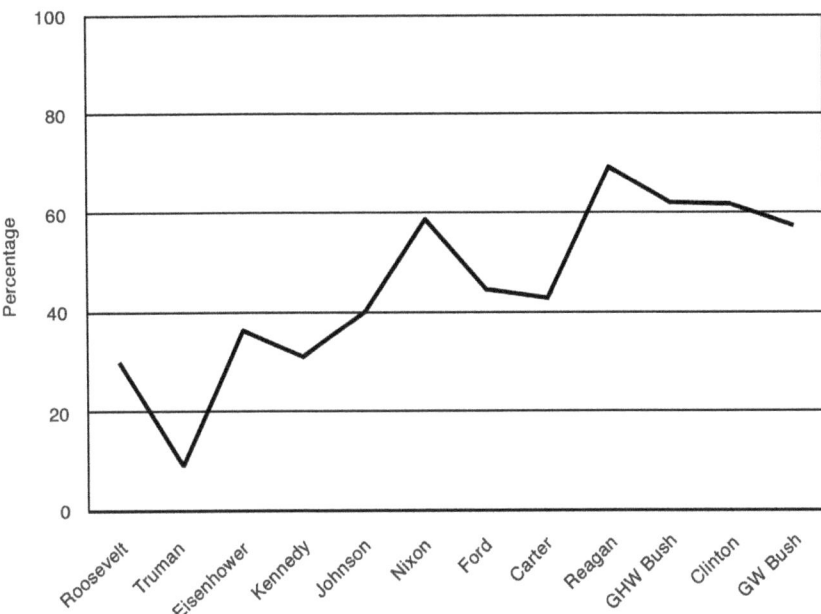

Figure 1. Percentage of "America" Mentions in Presidential Invocations of the Nation

sistent with a different argument made by McEvoy-Levy: that the rhetoric of American exceptionalism can serve "as a tool for community-building during times of transition" (p. 31). Consider that the three largest increases in presidents' invocations of *America* occur between Truman/Eisenhower, Johnson/Nixon, and Carter/Reagan. In all three cases, the nation was making a significant transition—both in international circumstances and in presidential leadership. Harry Truman, largely unpopular by the end of his term, gave way to the very popular Dwight Eisenhower at the dawn of the Cold War era. Lyndon Johnson was taking criticism from all sides over the Vietnam War when he gave way to Richard Nixon. And Jimmy Carter was struggling with the Iran hostage crisis when Ronald Reagan won the presidency. In all cases, Americans were facing an important transition and an uncertain future. The presidential response, it seems, was to emphasize the mythos of America. In doing so, presidents may well have revived or reinforced a sense of American exceptionalism.

Question 2: Foreign vs. Domestic

Our second question continues to consider presidential invocations of the nation, but brings in presidential mentions of foreign nations as a point of comparison. We expected that presidents would fulfill their constitutional obligation and focus primarily on America in their State of the Union addresses. We also argued, however, that the ratio between presidents' mentions of the United States and foreign nations could provide some insight into exceptionalist tendencies, in that a larger ratio would indicate a more America-centric approach to the State of the Union. To be clear, we do not offer a judgment as to the appropriateness or inappropriateness of particular presidents' ratios. We only suggest that the patterns in presidents' speeches represent conscious choices and that, consequently, larger ratios are probably more likely to signify exceptionalism than are smaller ratios.

For each president we tallied the number of times in his State of the Union addresses that he mentioned the nation or its people (via any phrase) or mentioned a foreign nation or its people (again, via any phrase). To control for variation in the length of presidential addresses, we present the findings for each president as a ratio of mentions per 1,000 words. Figure 2 presents the results of this analysis. As expected, every one of the twelve presidents in the analysis mentioned America considerably more often than he mentioned foreign nations. Presidents averaged roughly three times as many mentions of their own nation (13.95 per 1,000 words) as they did of foreign nations (4.66 per 1,000 words). More importantly, there was once again a noticeable difference between Republicans and Democrats. To simplify the comparisons, we calculated each president's ratio of domestic mentions to foreign mentions. For example, Richard Nixon — the president who most often mentioned America and least often mentioned foreign nations — had a domestic-to-foreign ratio of roughly 18:1. On the whole, Republican presidents tended to have higher ratios than did Democrats. Nixon led the way, but Gerald Ford (8:1), Dwight Eisenhower (7:1), and Ronald Reagan (5:1) were also high. Democrats, conversely, were generally lower, with Franklin Roosevelt and John Kennedy both at 2:1, and Harry Truman, Lyndon Johnson, and Jimmy Carter all at 3:1. As with the first measure, then, Republicans proved to be more focused on America than did Democrats.

The exceptions to this rule are worth noting because they all governed in the post–Cold War period. Bill Clinton was uncommonly high for Democrats (5:1), while George H. W. Bush (3:1) and George W. Bush (1.5:1) were surprisingly low for Republicans. Indeed, George W. Bush had the lowest ratio of any president. In his case, this low ratio was the result of often mentioning foreign nations — particularly Afghanistan and Iraq — even as he also often mentioned America. One must be hesitant to generalize from just this single piece of data, but this pattern is consistent with the findings of some comprehensive qualitative works in that the end of the Cold War generated

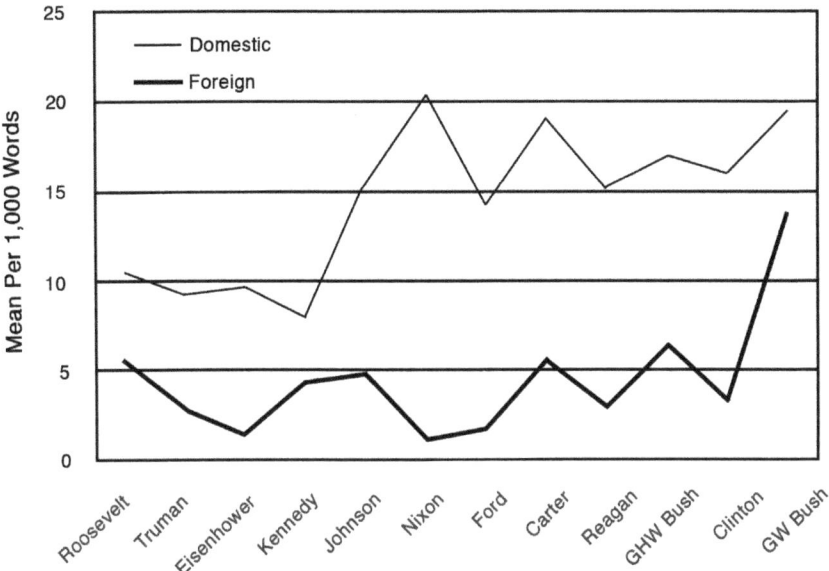

Figure 2. Presidential Mentions of Their Own Nation and Foreign Nations

new rhetorical exigencies for presidents — in terms of both foreign policy rhetoric generally (Edwards, 2008; Stuckey, 1995) and the rhetoric of American exceptionalism in particular (McCrisken, 2003; McEvoy-Levy, 2001).

Question 3: Relation to the World Order

Our third question explores how presidents, when mentioning a foreign entity, fit that foreign entity into the broad, U.S.-led world order that American exceptionalism suggests (see e.g., Rojecki, 2008). We expected that presidents might signal a commitment to American exceptionalism by more often referencing foreign nations as participants in the world order than as dissenters from it. After all, the United States is framed as the leader of the world order, and a stable world order suggests more effective leadership than does a chaotic one. We explored this possibility by examining how often each president positioned a foreign entity as a participant in the world order (as a percentage of their total mentions of foreign entities). Figure 3 presents the results of this analysis. As the figure makes clear, presidents have indeed emphasized participants in the world order rather than dissenters from it. On average, presidents emphasized participants in 76.2 percent of their mentions of foreign entities. No president did so in less than half of his total instances, and 11 of the 12 presidents (all save Franklin Roosevelt) did so at least 60 percent of the

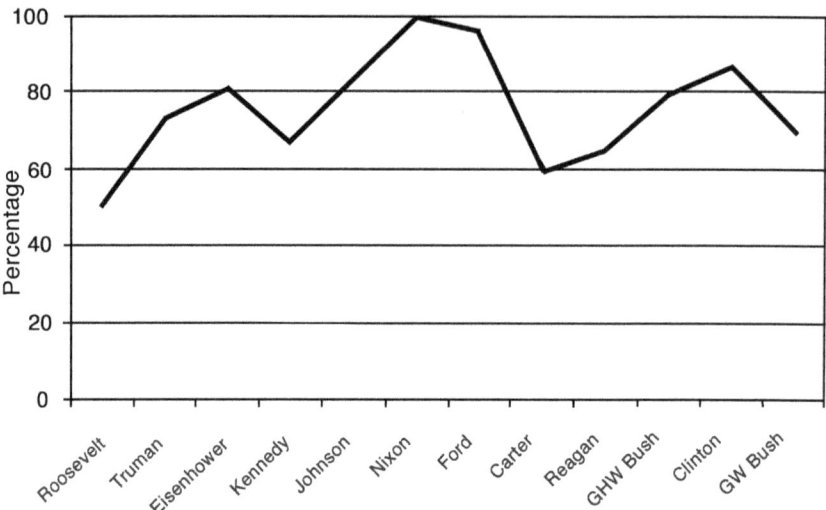

Figure 3. Presidential Positioning of Foreign Entities as Participants in World Order

time. Richard Nixon was especially noteworthy on this measure, discussing foreign entities as participants *every single time* he mentioned one in a State of the Union address over the course of his presidency.

Once again, there also was a difference based on party affiliation. As was the case in the first two parts of the analysis, Republicans were more likely to employ exceptionalist rhetoric than were Democrats. Specifically, Republicans averaged an 82 percent emphasis on participants, with Richard Nixon, Gerald Ford, Dwight Eisenhower, and George H. W. Bush leading the way. The Democrats' average was somewhat lower (70 percent), with Franklin Roosevelt, John Kennedy, and Jimmy Carter those least likely to emphasize participants.

Perhaps more influential than party affiliation in this case, however, was war. Presidents who oversaw the end of a war consistently increased their emphasis on participants over what their immediate predecessor had done. Consider that Truman jumped a remarkable 23 points from where Roosevelt had been (World War II), then Eisenhower moved seven more points from Truman's already-elevated level (Korea). Nixon increased Johnson's usage by 16 points (Vietnam), and G. H. W. Bush moved up 15 points from where Reagan had been (Cold War). It seems that as wars ended, presidents attempted to assure the nation and the international community that the world order was stable and the United States' leadership was steady. To put this in the terms of the extant scholarship on exceptionalism, following an interventionist mission, presidents reverted to a form of American exceptionalism more consistent with the exemplar mission, in which the language of partnership comes to the fore (see Edwards, 2008; McCrisken, 2003). This confirms McEvoy-Levy's (2001) point, discussed above, that the rhetoric of American exceptionalism is an especially important presidential tool in times of uncertainty and transition.

Question 4: Relation to the United States

Our fourth and final question focuses on how presidents positioned other nations in relation to the United States. Two possibilities were considered: that presidents would exhibit paternalism by explicitly positioning the United States as a teacher, leader, or helper of other nations; or, conversely, that presidents would position other nations as an exemplar from which America might learn. Given the tradition of American exceptionalism, we expected to see a fair amount of paternalism and very few instances of presidents explicitly positioning other nations as exemplars. Even taking this expectation into account, the results are astonishing. Out of 2,480 total mentions of foreign entities by presidents in State of the Union addresses from 1934 to 2008, *only three times* did a president explicitly hold up a foreign entity as an exemplar. Given that so few such mentions were made, they are worth quoting directly. The first instance occurred in 1942. Franklin Roosevelt, attempting to galvanize the nation in support of the war effort, looked to the British as examples to follow:

> No matter what our enemies, in their desperation, may attempt to do to us — we will say, as the people of London have said, "We can take it." And what's more we can give it back and we will give it back — with compound interest.

The second such instance came in John Kennedy's 1963 address, when he criticized the state of the U.S. health system by looking to Sweden's superior system:

> I believe that the abandonment of the mentally ill and the mentally retarded to the grim mercy of custodial institutions too often inflicts on them and on their families a needless cruelty which this Nation should not endure. The incidence of mental retardation in this country is three times as high as that of Sweden, for example — and that figure can and must be reduced.

And finally, Ronald Reagan in 1983 presented Japan's educational system as a bar that the United States' own system might seek to reach:

> We Americans are still the technological leaders in most fields. We must keep that edge, and to do so we need to begin renewing the basics — starting with our educational system. While we grew complacent, others have acted. Japan, with a

population only about half the size of ours, graduates from its universities more engineers than we do.

In 74 years, these mentions — by only three presidents, each one only once mentioning a foreign entity as an exemplar for the United States — stand alone.

In contrast, throughout the twentieth century, presidents regularly presented the United States in the role of teacher or leader, helping other nations in myriad ways. In all, 595 of the total mentions (roughly 24 percent) put America in this paternalistic role. In this case, no consistent differences in usage emerged between Republicans and Democrats. Rather, every president used such language, with some standing out for the regularity with which they did so. Bill Clinton led the way, with 43.4 percent of his instances making an explicit claim of paternalism, followed by Richard Nixon (39.5 percent), Lyndon Johnson (30.0 percent), and Harry Truman (34.0 percent). Dwight Eisenhower (14.0 percent), George H. W. Bush (13.6 percent), and Franklin Roosevelt (13.0 percent) were relatively low on this measure. Some quotes illustrating this type of language make concrete the contrast between it and the extremely limited exemplar language.

Truman, for example, in his 1951 State of the Union, said: "In the Near East, in Africa, in Asia, we must do what we can to help people who are striving to advance from misery, poverty, and hunger." Similarly, Johnson, in 1966, offered this message: "[W]e will continue to help the people of South Vietnam care for those that are ravaged by battle, create progress in the villages, and carry forward the healing hopes of peace." And Clinton, who used such language more often than any other president, had this to say in 1995:

> Just think about what our troops have done in the last year, showing America at its best, helping to save hundreds of thousands of people in Rwanda, moving with lightning speed to head off another threat to Kuwait, giving freedom and democracy back to the people of Haiti. We have proudly supported peace and prosperity and freedom from South Africa to Northern Ireland, from Central and Eastern Europe to Asia, from Latin America to the Middle East.

Clearly, the presidential rhetoric of American exceptionalism, represented here by presidents' paternalistic references to other nations, is much more common than the other possibility — presidents looking abroad for exemplars to follow. Indeed, the contrast could hardly be more striking.

Discussion

This chapter attempted to add a new dimension to the literature on American exceptionalism by offering a quantitative assessment of the rhetoric of exceptionalism in the modern presidency. The findings make clear that American exceptionalism has a considerable presence in modern presidential rhetoric. There is a strong and increasing tendency for presidents to refer to the nation as *America* rather than using another term. The symbolic power of the term *America* should not be taken lightly (Domke and Coe, 2008); recent presidents clearly have been attempting to harness that power. Even given the constitutional mandate to regularly report on the state of the union, modern presidents have also been much more likely to refer to their own nation than to other nations — sometimes dramatically so. Indeed, they averaged roughly three times as many references to their own nation as to foreign nations. Further, presidents have emphasized a stable U.S.–led world order by talking primarily about participants in that order rather than dissenters from it. They paired this focus with a considerable emphasis on the paternalistic role the United States plays in the world, as leader, teacher, referee, and sometimes the "world's policeman" (Carroll, 1996). Any one of these trends, taken on its own, perhaps only hints at the presence of American exceptionalism. Taken together, however, they provide a quantitative story consistent with the qualitative story that past research has told: American presidents have a strong impulse toward exceptionalism.

The findings here also show that Republicans have felt this impulse more strongly than have Democrats. On three of the four measures — all except paternalism — Republican presidents noticeably exceeded their Democratic counterparts. This finding runs counter to the claims of some previous scholarship on American exceptionalism (e.g., McEvoy-Levy, 2001), but is consistent with other scholarship that has shown party differences to influence various aspects of presidential rhetoric (e.g., Coe, 2007). It is possible that the difference between our findings and the findings of some other scholars has to do with the fact that we were considering general patterns across all presidents rather than a few specific contexts where presidents clearly employed exceptionalist rhetoric. If that is the case, our findings also confirm that certain presidents are likely to display more exceptionalist rhetoric than are others. Party differences aside, for example, both Richard Nixon and Bill Clinton exhibited a stronger degree of exceptionalism than most of their peers.

Clearly, a variety of factors beyond political party help to determine the quantity and quality of exceptionalist rhetoric a president will use. One of those factors, our study demonstrates, is the time period during which presidents governed. Specifically, consistent with past research (Edwards, 2008; McCrisken, 2003; McEvoy-Levy, 2001), the evidence here shows that presidents highlight exceptionalist themes in times of transition, especially periods of insecurity (e.g., wartime) or uncertainty (e.g., after a long war or interventionist period has ended). It seems that in such times, presidents have found a reliable rhetorical strategy: emphasize exceptionalism to reinforce mythic notions of America as the unquestioned leader of a stable world order. Broadly, such national myths likely help to reinforce the nation's self-confidence and to foster national pride. At the same time, they may sometimes have more dubious outcomes, such as discouraging careful deliberation about serious foreign policy decisions (see Coe et al., 2004; Domke et al., 2006).

Our study also shows, however, that there is one rhetorical tactic presidents almost never employ. Across twelve presidencies and nearly 2,500 mentions of foreign entities, only three times did presidents look abroad to find an exemplar from which America might learn. It is difficult to imagine a more obvious signal of presidents' belief in American exceptionalism. After all, if presidents view America as a "city on a hill," why would they look down the hill for guidance? One hopes this pattern is only a rhetorical phenomenon and not the rule when it comes to the creation of U.S. policy, as some have suggested (Alesina, Glaeser, and Sacerdote, 2001; Brown, 1998; Rose, 1991). Efforts at "cross-national learning" (also frequently referred to as "international learning" or "policy transfer"; Dolowitz and Marsh, 1996, 2000; Knopf, 2003; Padgett, 2003) are not uncommon in Europe, for example, where various nations look to their neighbors as role models for several domestic policy issues. Few would benefit if the tradition of exceptionalism were to keep America from joining such exchanges.

This study was not without its limitations, of course. A quantitative assessment of the rhetoric of American exceptionalism was something we viewed as missing from the extant literature, but it can hardly tell the whole story. The lack of nuance in the patterns that can be captured, along with the various assumptions that must be made when interpreting quantitative trends, both point to the need for more detailed qualitative work that can elaborate on the patterns identified herein. Further, there is a need for additional quantitative studies that might confirm, challenge, or build from preliminary measures considered in this study. Additionally, such research could extend the range of discourse considered here. The State of the Union address, as discussed above, is an appropriate place to begin an assessment of American exceptionalism in the presidency. However, there are numerous other speaking situations in which presidents might employ such rhetoric. And, certainly, political discourse is not restricted to politicians. As Rojecki (2008) has shown, the exceptionalist themes present in presidential discourse can make their way into news coverage. Future research that considers the rhetoric of American exceptionalism, broadly defined, will usefully contribute to our understanding of the topic.

Finally, future research should explore the possibility that the tides of American exceptionalism might be turning. President Obama's view of exceptionalism, mentioned at the outset of this chapter, may well differ from his predecessors, and he may end up sending very different rhetorical signals from those considered here. Indeed, given the president's diverse background and strong international bonds, it seems likely that, at a minimum, his brand of American exceptionalism will feel somewhat different than that of previous decades. Although it is probably too early to point to a single statement as the beginning of a "post-exceptional era" (Steyn, 2009) or a "post–American era" (Glick, 2009; Zakaria, 2009) as some have been eager to do, it may be a sign of what is to come. If so, scholars may come to view Obama's version of exceptionalism as consistent with Lipset's (1997) notion that exceptionalism need not always mean that one thing is better, but rather than it is simply different or unique in its own right.

Notes

1. Texts of presidential speeches, from which all quotations and analyses are drawn, were retrieved from the National Archives' *Public Papers of the Presidents*, the definitive record of presidential communications. Available at: www.americanpresidency.org.

2. We recognize that in State of the Union addresses, our object of analysis, presidents are constitutionally obligated to focus their attention on the state of America, not necessarily the state of other nations. That is why we expect all presidents will focus more attention on America than on other nations. Nevertheless, in the modern presidency, it has become normative for State of the Union addresses to include lengthy treatments of foreign policy as well domestic policy (Campbell and Jamieson, 1990, 2008). Therefore a president who conceives of the State of America's Union as intricately related to the state of the world will likely have a smaller ratio of America mentions to foreign mentions; a president who does not adhere to this conception as strongly will likely have a larger ratio. This is, of course, an imperfect measure of exceptionalism. It should nonetheless provide useful information when considered along with the various other measures included in the study.

3. At the time of this writing, Barack Obama had given only one State of the Union address, which made generalizations difficult to draw. Consequently, he was not included in the study. In all, our analysis included 69 speeches. Those instances where presidents delivered a written rather than spoken State of the Union — Truman 1946 and 1953, Eisenhower 1961, Nixon 1973, and Carter 1981— were excluded from our analysis because these speeches were unlikely to be encountered by many people and therefore had limited chance to influence public perceptions. For the same reason, in the two cases where the speech was written but then a summarized version was delivered to the people (Roosevelt in 1945 and Eisenhower in 1956), the latter was used.

4. Notably, if the foreign entity was talked about as neither a participant nor a dissenter but instead as a victim of the world order, it was excluded from the analysis. This was rare, constituting only 10 percent of the total instances

5. One person completed the content analysis. As a check of reliability, a second person coded approximately 12 percent of the speeches. Agreement scores, corrected for agreement by chance (see Scott, 1955), were all greater than .85 with the exception of paternalism, for which raw agreement was .82, .64 after controlling for agreement by

chance. The relatively low chance-corrected agreement score for paternalism reflects, in part, the fact that Scott's *pi* is a conservative reliability statistic (see Neuendorf, 2002). Nevertheless, the raw agreement score reveals that paternalism was a relatively difficult code to identify consistently, so our findings for this variable should be viewed with more caution than the rest of our results.

      6. For this analysis, *United States of America* was counted as an "America" mention, whereas *United States* was not. The same procedure was used for *U.S.* versus *U.S.A.*

References

Alesina, A. F., E. L. Glaeser, and B. Sacerdote (2001). *Why Doesn't the U.S. Have a European-Style Welfare State?* (Discussion Paper No. 1933.) Cambridge, MA: Harvard University, Harvard Institute of Economic Research.

Beasley, V. B. (2004). *You, the People: American National Identity in Presidential Rhetoric.* College Station: Texas A&M University Press.

Bell, D. (1996). *Marxian Socialism in the United States.* Ithaca: Cornell University Press.

Bostdorff, D. M. (1994). *The Presidency and the Rhetoric of Foreign Crisis.* Columbia: University of South Carolina Press.

Brown, L. D. (1998). "Exceptionalism as the Rule? U.S. Health Policy Innovation and Cross-National Learning." *Journal of Health Politics, Policy, and Law, 23,* 35–51.

Campbell, K. K., and K. H. Jamieson (1990). *Deeds Done in Words: Presidential Rhetoric and the Genres of Governance.* Chicago: University of Chicago Press.

_____, and _____ (2008). *Presidents Creating the Presidency: Deeds Done in Words.* Chicago: University of Chicago Press.

Carroll, E. (1996). "Should the U.S. Be the World's Policeman?" *Peace Review, 8,* 477–484.

Coe, K. (2007). "The Language of Freedom in the American Presidency, 1933–2006." *Presidential Studies Quarterly, 37,* 375–398.

_____, D. Domke, E. S. Graham, S. L., John, and V. Pickard (2004). "No Shades of Gray: The Binary Discourse of George W. Bush and an Echoing Press." *Journal of Communication, 54,* 234–252.

Crowley, M. (2009, July 1). "American Exceptionalism: Without Exception." *The Washington Times,* p. A19.

Dolowitz, D. P., and D. Marsh (1996). "Who Learns What from Whom? A Review of the Policy Transfer Literature." *Political Studies, 44,* 343–57.

_____, and _____ (2000). "Learning from Abroad: The Role of Policy Transfer in Contemporary Policy-Making." *Governance, 13,* 5–24.

Domke, D., and K. Coe (2008). *The God Strategy: How Religion Became a Political Weapon in America.* New York: Oxford University Press.

Domke, D., E. S. Graham, K. Coe, S. L. John, and T. Coopman (2006). "Going Public as Political Strategy: The Bush Administration, an Echoing Press, and Passage of the Patriot Act." *Political Communication, 23,* 291–312.

Edwards, J. A. (2008). *Navigating the Post–Cold War World: President Clinton's Foreign Policy Rhetoric.* Lanham, MD: Rowman and Littlefield.

Fitrakis, R. J. (1993). *The Idea of Democratic Socialism in America and the Decline of the Socialist Party.* New York: Garland.

Glick, C. B. (2009, April 10). "Surviving in a Post-American World." *The Jerusalem Post,* p. 24.

Greeley, A. M. (1991). "American Exceptionalism: The Religious Phenomenon." In B. E. Shafer (Ed.), *Is America Different? A New Look at American Exceptionalism* (pp. 94–115). New York: Oxford University Press.

Greenstein, F. I. (2004). *The Presidential Difference: Leadership Style from FDR to George W. Bush* (2nd ed.). Princeton, NJ: Princeton University Press.
Hodgson, G. (2009). *The Myth of American Exceptionalism.* New Haven: Yale University Press.
Howe, I. (1985). *Socialism and America.* San Diego: Harcourt Brace Jovanovich.
Hunt, M. H. (1987). *Ideology and U.S. Foreign Policy.* New Haven: Yale University Press.
Ivie, R. L. (1980). "Images of Savagery in American Justifications for War." *Communication Monographs, 47,* 279–294.
Johnson, P. (1999). *A History of the American People.* New York: Harper Perennial.
Kirchick, J. (2009, April 28). "Squanderer in Chief." *Los Angeles Times,* p. 23A.
Knopf, J. W. (2003). "The Importance of International Learning." *Review of International Studies, 29,* 185–207.
Lipset, S. M. (1977). "Why No Socialism in the United States?" In S. Bialer and S. Sluzar (Eds.), *Sources of Contemporary Radicalism* (pp. 31–149). Boulder, CO: Westview.
_____ (1997). *American Exceptionalism: A Double-Edged Sword* (2d ed.). New York: Norton.
_____ (2000). "Still the Exceptional Nation?" *Wilson Quarterly, 24,* 31–45.
_____, and G. Marks (2000). *It Didn't Happen Here: Why Socialism Failed in the United States.* New York: W. W. Norton.
Lockhart, C. (2003). *The Roots of American Exceptionalism: Institutions, Cultures and Policies.* New York: Palgrave Macmillan.
MacKinnon, M. G. (2000). *The Evolution of U.S. Peacekeeping Policy Under Clinton. A Fairweather Friend?* London: Frank Cass.
Madsen, D. L. (1998). *American Exceptionalism.* Edinburgh: Edinburgh University Press.
Malone, D. M., and Y. F. Khong (2003). "Unilateralism and U.S. Foreign Policy: International Perspectives." In D. M. Malone and Y. F. Khong (Eds.), *Unilateralism and U.S. Foreign Policy: International Perspectives* (pp. 1–18). Boulder, CO: Lynne Rienner.
McCrisken, T. B. (2003). *American Exceptionalism and the Legacy of Vietnam: U.S. Foreign Policy Since 1974.* New York: Palgrave Macmillan.
McEvoy-Levy, S. (2001). *American Exceptionalism and U.S. Foreign Policy: Public Diplomacy at the End of the Cold War.* New York: Palgrave Macmillan.
Neuendorf, K. A. (2002). *The Content Analysis Guidebook.* Thousand Oaks, CA: Sage.
Padgett, S. (2003). "Between Synthesis and Emulation: EU Policy Transfer in the Power Sector." *Journal of European Public Policy, 10,* 227–245.
Rojecki, A. (2008). "Rhetorical Alchemy: American Exceptionalism and the War on Terror." *Political Communication, 25,* 67–88.
Rose, R. (1991). "Is American Public Policy Exceptional?" In B. E. Shafer (Ed.), *Is America Different? A New Look at American Exceptionalism* (pp. 187–221). New York: Oxford University Press.
Schaefer, T. M. (1997). "Persuading the Persuaders: Presidential Speeches and Editorial Opinion." *Political Communication, 14,* 97–111.
Scott, W. A. (1955). "Reliability of Content Analysis: The Case of Nominal Scale Coding." *Public Opinion Quarterly, 19,* 321–325.
Shafer, B. E. (Ed.). (1991). *Is America Different? A New Look at American Exceptionalism.* New York: Oxford University Press.
Sombart, W. (1976). *Why Is There No Socialism in the United States?* White Plains, NY: International Arts and Sciences Press. (Original work published 1906.)
Steyn, M. (2009, April 25). "The End of the World as We Know It." *National Review Online.* Retrieved from http://article.nationalreview.com/392405/the-end-of-the-world-as-we-know-it/mark-steyn.

Stuckey, M. E. (1995). "Competing Foreign Policy Visions: Rhetorical Hybrids After the Cold War." *Western Journal of Communication, 59,* 214–227.
_____ (2004). *Defining Americans: The Presidency and National Identity.* Lawrence: University Press of Kansas.
Temin, P. (1991). "Free Land and Federalism: American Economic Exceptionalism." In B. E. Shafer (Ed.), *Is America Different? A New Look at American Exceptionalism* (pp. 71–93). New York: Oxford University Press.
Tocqueville, A. de (1948). *Democracy in America.* New York: Alfred A. Knopf. (Original work published 1835.)
Trow, P. (1991). "American Higher Education: 'Exceptional' or Just Different?" In B. E. Shafer (Ed.), *Is America Different? A New Look at American Exceptionalism* (pp. 138–186). New York: Oxford University Press.
Tulis, J. K. (1987). *The Rhetorical Presidency.* Princeton, NJ: Princeton University Press.
Wander, P. (1984). "The Rhetoric of American Foreign Policy." *Quarterly Journal of Speech, 70,* 339–361.
Wildavsky, A. (1991). "Resolved, that Individualism and Egalitarianism Be Made Compatible in America: Political-Cultural Roots of Exceptionalism." In B. E. Shafer (Ed.), *Is America Different? A New Look at American Exceptionalism* (pp. 116–137). New York: Oxford University Press.
Windt, T. O., Jr. (1990). *Presidents and Protestors: Political Rhetoric in the 1960s.* Tuscaloosa: University of Alabama Press.
Zakaria, F. (2009). *The Post-American World.* New York: Norton.
Zarefsky, D. (2004). "Presidential Rhetoric and the Power of Definition." *Presidential Studies Quarterly, 34,* 607–619.

Chapter 2

Resolving Rhetorical Tensions

M. Karen Walker

Pride of nation is a universal appeal for collective identity and action. The distinguishing question, therefore, is not what makes Americans exceptional, but rather, what makes claims to exceptionalism uniquely American? An axiom of *American* exceptionalism is the covenant between a providential land and a chosen people. As a rhetorical resource, the land serves to keep Americans bounded, if not rooted, by geography. The character of a people befitting such a bounty is not easily contained. Associating providence with land entails conservatism; associating providence with character presents an open-ended promise. Tension emanates from the belief that the unbridled projection of America's character jeopardizes the continuity of its blessings. A rhetorical function of American exceptionalism is to resolve this tension by associating the American character with tangible and positive ends: the symbiotic relationship of American genius and American institutions.

Warranting American Exceptionalism

My argument attends to enthymematic constructs that warrant American exceptionalism in domestic and foreign policy argument. I invoke enthymematic reasoning as inventional, situational and based in social consensus (Farrell, 1991). Rhetors rely on social consensus when seeking resonance for argumentative appeals, particularly where identity claims are concerned. Writing in this vein, McCormick (2005) explores post–Cold War foreign policy choices of the transatlantic powers, juxtaposing a resurgent brand of American exceptionalism, associated with George W. Bush's freedom agenda and doctrine of pre-emption, with a new "Europeanism" that captures the European

Union's political, economic, and social distinctiveness. McCormick's essay highlights the rhetorical function of exceptionalism in formation of national — or in this case, continental — identity.

The connection of American exceptionalism with the Global War on Terror is an especially vibrant strain of critique of the Bush Administration's justifications for a unilateralist foreign policy. Rojecki (2008) employs narrative and frames analysis to identify which of the Bush Administration's appeals resonated with media elites, represented by the *New York Times* and the *Washington Post*. Rojecki's analysis surfaces a preponderance of themes that he associates with American exceptionalism, including evil enemies, U.S. virtue, the U.S. as a model of success, and counter-critique of America's allies. The harnessing of a realist argument to appeals to America's exemplar status overpowers the liberal internationalist viewpoint.

Noting that the 2008 presidential campaign created opportunity for a fresh analysis of American exceptionalism, Ivie and Giner (2009) do not disappoint. The authors define American exceptionalism as Americans' habituated imagining of themselves "as a morally elevated people set apart from the rest of the world and living in a land of opportunity that is the envy and aspiration of humankind" (p. 361). The authors cite within President Obama's campaign rhetoric an "American exceptionalism with a democratic inflection," which they describe as "a restorative vision of renewing the nation's leadership by returning to its founding values — of behaving in ways that reflected the decency of the American people, affirmed the equality of all people, and served the common good on a global scale" (p. 361). To individuals sharing in this vision, America remains "the world's last and best hope for promoting freedom and justice over tyranny and despair, but it would operate on the world stage with a democratic attitude of interdependence" (p. 361).

If American exceptionalism warrants foreign policy argument, a precursor question concerns the particular constructs that reify Americans' sense of themselves as special and apart. Such constructs are prominent in unity discourses, more formally recognized by form, context and content as epideictic rhetoric. My appreciation for epideictic rhetoric aligns with Hauser's summation of scholarship that ascribes to epideictic a performative force (see also Beale, 1978; Finkelstein, 1981) and "demonstrates how rhetorical choices of inclusion and omission inscribed contrasting visions of the polis" (Hauser, 1999, p. 5). I concur with Hauser that "examining epideictic provides insight into how a public sphere may serve as the crucible in which a people constitute and validate their tradition" (p. 18). Hauser's public sphere perspective imbues epideictic rhetoric with a constitutive possibility. This possibility may be realized through definition/understanding, shaping and sharing of community, and display or entertainment, three characteristics of "communal definition" that extend the function of epideictic beyond commemorative contexts of praise and blame (Condit, 1985).

A collection of presidential inaugural addresses provides a useful set of texts through which to interrogate the reification of the American self through epideictic discourse. Finkelstein argues convincingly for the existence of an inaugural genre that combines a distinct rhetorical situation with identifiable and substantive responses, with action occurring through "the future power of present discourse" (1981, p. 52). Campbell and Jamieson (1990) formalize the characteristics of the presidential inaugural, e.g., unifying the audience, rehearsing communal values, advancing political principles, demonstrating appreciation of the requirements and limitations of the Office, and urging contemplation rather than action. Applying Campbell and Jamieson's schema in his own analysis, Sigelman (1996) discovers that "over time, presidents have become more and more likely to employ language that is accessible to the masses, have invoked more and more unity symbols, and have done more to establish links with traditional American values" (p. 90). Dudash offers a reminder that inaugurals address the international community, and therefore perform a deliberative as well as epideictic function in the portrayal of the presidency as an international entity (2007, p. 49).

Mining presidential inaugurals as a rhetorical resource for national identity, Beasley "suggests that presidents have not only urged the American people to think of themselves as sharing certain ideals, but also as sharing a particular attitudinal disposition, thus defining American character in terms of both principles and pose" (2001, p. 169). Beasley's objective is to not only name the ideals associated with national identity across time, but also how specific political actors have amplified certain ideals (p. 170). Beasley's critique affirms that newly inaugurated presidents draw upon the "myth of America," attributed to Bercovitch (1981), describing a people driven by divine providence as well as certain rites of assent, and possessing a "characteristically American mental discipline and self-restraint" (p. 177).

Rhetorical Resources of American Exceptionalism

My critique offers insight into the rhetorical resources present in presidential inaugurals that remind Americans of their unique place in the world. My analysis homes in on two qualities in particular: the material and tangible nature of America as a place, and the ideational nature of the American character. Whereas my motivation is straightforward, I offer three caveats regarding my approach to inquiry. First, my reliance on American presidential inaugurals is illustrative rather than probative; my attitude is that of playful musing rather than definitive claim. Second, my approach is contextual rather than analytical, with a primary interest in pulling the two threads of land and character through individual texts. Accordingly, the situational factors that would guide analysis of individual speeches serve as loose mooring rather than textual anchor. Chronology unfolds in broad strokes punctuated by inaugural moments. Third, in the mode of contextualist critique, the propositional content of analysis emanates from points of intersection and tension.

A Bounteous Land

The Puritans' founding of the Massachusetts Bay Colony is a familiar topos within American exceptionalism. An American identity began to emerge concurrent with the founding of new colonies, internal infrastructure, conflict over territorial rights, routes of commerce, and new knowledge produced by land surveys and cartography. Celebration of America's geography and topography reassured colonists-cum-citizens equally desirous of protection and growth. For example, Thomas Jefferson in his first inaugural in 1801 observed that America is "kindly separated by nature and a wide ocean from the exterminating havoc of one quarter of the globe." (quoted in Schlesinger and Israel, 2007, p. 17). With awareness of world events and heeding the government's first directive to avoid entangling alliances, Jefferson describes a "chosen country" with "room enough for our descendants to the thousandth and thousandth generation" (quoted in Schlesinger and Israel, 2007, p. 17). Americans had no need to abandon their new homeland, and indeed would have been foolhardy to do so, a condition the president reaffirmed four years later, celebrating "the favor of that Being in whose hands we are, who led our forefathers, as Israel of old, from their native land, and planted them in a country flowing with all the necessaries and comforts of life" (quoted in Schlesinger and Israel, 2007, p. 25).

Whereas Jefferson's celebration of America's bounty emanated from the tradition of Winthrop, Edwards and the Puritan myth, James Monroe's first inaugural in 1817 took an empirical turn. Monroe described the United States as "situated within the temperate zone, and extending through many degrees of latitude along the Atlantic," such that its people could "enjoy all the varieties of climate, and every production incident to that position of the globe" (quoted in Schlesinger and Israel, 2007, p. 38). Consonant with the clustering of providence and errand, Jefferson's second inaugural kept Americans in a subordinate position, the recipient of God's gifts. Monroe's first inaugural hinted at a people called to make more of what they had been given, associating, however obliquely, nature with man-made infrastructure, and geography with commerce: "Nature has done so much for us by intersecting the country with so many great rivers, bays, and lakes, approaching from distant points so near to each other, that the inducement to complete the work seems to be peculiarly strong" (quoted in Schlesinger and Israel, 2007, p. 41). A third area of iteration from Jefferson to Monroe is Americans' understanding of the sources of their protection. Quoting Monroe: "Possessing as we do all the raw materials, the fruit of our own soil and industry, we ought not to depend in the degree we have done on supplies from other countries. While we are thus dependent the sudden event of war, unsought and unexpected, can not fail to plunge us into the most serious difficulties" (quoted in Schlesinger and Israel, 2007, p. 41). Jefferson's inaugurals implied that geographic separation was sufficient for Americans to husband their pastoral resources; Monroe's inaugural layered self-reliance with a national security imperative.

Inaugurated into office at the mid-century mark, Franklin Pierce gave an address that illustrated the layering of meanings then associated with America as a land: "Our attitude as a nation and our position on the globe render the acquisition of certain possessions not within our jurisdiction eminently important for our protection, if not in the future essential for the preservation of the rights of commerce and the peace of the world" (quoted in Schlesinger and Israel, 2007, p. 123). Pierce's construction reflected Americans' association of physical territory and sovereign rights. Whereas the previous examples emphasized the interior direction of growth and commerce, the directional force of Pierce's words are outward from America's shores to extraterritorial claims. In the same breath, Pierce kept the providential location of the continent as a touchstone, a necessary support to nuance benevolent intent.

The layering of meanings now etched into the American soil aids in our understanding of how Presidential addresses have regenerated the belief that America and her people are exceptional. What one orator may add, another can peel back. The physical defense of America and the sanctity of its borders, which privileges land as the protectorate of ideal, is a representative case. Warren Harding's 1921 inaugural address lauded the "Republic's capacity to emerge from the wreckage of war," rendered easier in the knowledge that "the world's embittered travail did not leave us devastated lands nor desolated cities, left no gaping wounds" (quoted in Schlesinger and Israel, 2007, p. 253). Lyndon Johnson's 1965 inaugural offers a separate example of an orator's choice to reach deep into cultural memory: "They came here, the exile and the stranger, brave but frightened; to find a place where a man could be his own man. They made a covenant with this land. Conceived in justice, written in liberty, bound in union, it was meant one day to inspire the hopes of all mankind; and it binds us still" (quoted in Schlesinger and Israel, 2007, p. 333). Absent the attribution, one might assume these words were uttered by a president when the Republic was at its youngest, rather than at its most mature.

American Character

In the pursuit of independence from Britain, colonial legislators faced the challenge of creating a new governing structure that would nurture and project not only a common purpose but also a binding character of its people. The challenge was resolved in what Lipset (1996) termed the American Creed, containing the ideographic constructs of liberty, egalitarianism, individualism, populism, and laissez-faire. The terms are ideographs as defined by McGee, "interpenetrating systems or 'structures' of public motives [that] influence the shape and texture of each individual's reality" (1980, p. 1). The ideographic nature of the constructs combines material and social reality with the mythologized stories of the colonies' founding, struggles, and military and economic success (McGee, 1980). Taken together, the constructs reflect the tension between morality and pragmatism that appears consistently in rhetoric of the American character (Andrews, 1971). Lipset's (1996) American Creed speaks to the principles guiding a system of governance appropriate to the American character.

Writing with a singular eye toward the makeup of the American character, Steele and Redding (1962) generate a fulsome list based on their independent analyses of the 1952 presidential campaign. Notable characteristics include: puritan and pioneer morality; the value of the individual; achievement and success; change and progress; ethical equality; equality of opportunity; effort and optimism; efficiency, practicality, and pragmatism; rejection of authority; sociality; humor; generosity; and patriotism. These qualities suggest the rhetorical resources of cultural identity and memory that allow candidates to issue appeals customized to segmented audiences. Accordingly, we cannot assume that these characteristics are universally resonant or equally motivating for the majority of Americans. In contrast to the political discourse of the campaign, presidential inaugurals, categorized previously as a genre of epideictic discourse, contain the rhetoric of unification, consensus, and nation building; an orator's selection of characteristics to valorize is an inventional and necessarily reductive choice (Stuckey, 2004).

If seeking an iterative list within the inaugural canon, the tableau offered by George W. Bush in 2001 is both cumulative and comprehensive. The inaugural highlights, in quick succession, civility, good will, respect, fair dealing, forgiveness, courage, purpose without arrogance, resolve, strength, compassion, duty, personal responsibility, generosity, and decency. (quoted in Schlesinger and Israel, 2007, pp. 408–409). Acknowledging that one may mine the inaugural canon for like denotations of the American canon, I limit my points here to a few key themes that presage the tension and reconciliation of Americans' belief that they are worthy of emulation, with the store of cautionary tales against unbridled ambition.

Preternatural wisdom. A reading of American inaugurals highlights a recurrent theme that the people possess a preternatural wisdom, which when exercised in policy ensures the continuance of America's standing in the world. John Adams's 1797 inaugural, for example, suggests a character inbred — a natural state of being evidenced in the "purity of their intentions, the justice of their cause, and the integrity and intelligence of the people" (quoted in Schlesinger and Israel, 2007, p. 8). In revising America's form of government from Confederation to Constitution, the "people of America were not abandoned by their usual good sense, presence of mind, resolution, or integrity" (quoted in Schlesinger and Israel, 2007, p. 9). Adams's observations associate reason with a cautious course of action taken absent haste. Later presidents would use this precedent in valorizing American genius as a reaching, inventive and brash form of the American mind.

James Madison's second inaugural, delivered in 1813, validates America's course in comparison to the rashness of the British government: "Our nation ... is composed of a brave, a free, a virtuous, and an intelligent people. Our country abounds in the necessaries, the arts, and the comforts of life. A general prosperity is visible in the public countenance. The means employed by the British cabinet to undermine it have recoiled on themselves; have given to our national faculties a more rapid development" (quoted in Schlesinger and Israel, 2007, p. 33). In this comparative frame, virtue and intelligence — wisdom — are characteristics that set Americans apart; the exercise of wisdom creates its own reward. James Monroe (1817) iterates the dangers of a people forgetting their first principles and abandoning a wise course. In Monroe's construction, wisdom is passed generationally in acts of citizenship: "Had the people of the United States been educated in different principles, had they been less intelligent, less independent, or less virtuous can it be believed that we should have maintained the same steady and consistent career or been blessed with the same success?" (quoted in Schlesinger and Israel, 2007, p. 39). From Monroe, we sense that the rhetorical resources of American exceptionalism involve not only the named characteristics, but also the reassurance that future generations will recognize and act upon wisdom received.

Virtuous action. Concordance of virtue and action is a second theme evidenced in presidential inaugurals. Drawing from the canon, Woodrow

Wilson's expression of this synergy is among the most direct and most eloquent. Upon first taking office in 1913, Wilson opined that "nowhere else in the world have noble men and women exhibited in more striking forms the beauty and the energy of sympathy and helpfulness and counsel in their efforts to rectify wrong, alleviate suffering, and set the weak in the way of strength and hope" (quoted in Schlesinger and Israel, 2007, p. 241). Four years hence, Wilson reaffirmed the sentiment: The behaviors by which Americans would be recognized in the world were in service to "the principles of a liberated mankind" (quoted in Schlesinger and Israel, 2007, p. 247). Wilson works from a mutually reinforcing if not tautological relationship of character and action; that is, the character of Americans required them to live by certain principles, and in the exercise of those principles, they became more American.

Rhetorical Tension

Does a providential land beget a providential people? Or do a providential people find a providential land? Calvin Coolidge captured the tension between the two in his 1921 inaugural: "The physical configuration of the earth has separated us from all of the Old World, but the common brotherhood of man, the highest law of all our being, has united us by inseparable bonds with all humanity" (quoted in Schlesinger and Israel, 2007, p. 262). In short, the American character and its ideals can be emulated in imaginings of a place and people, absent direct and immersed experience. America's founding documents are governing templates available for replication. Associating providence with land entails conservatism; associating providence with character entails an open-ended promise.

Reliance on Covenant as a Moderating Force

In managing this tension, America's covenant with a providential God has served as a moderating force on America's sphere of influence, in which the bounty of the land is conditional upon right action at home and abroad. George Washington's first inaugural, delivered in 1789, expressed the common view of the period regarding God's intervention in and judgment of the affairs of man on earth: "The propitious smiles of Heaven can never be expected on a nation that disregards the eternal rules of order and right which Heaven itself has ordained" (quoted in Schlesinger and Israel, 2007, p. 4). Washington's first inaugural described a divine partnership unique to the young nation and its inhabitants. Washington asserted the belief that "no people can be bound to acknowledge and adore the Invisible Hand which conducts the affairs of men more than those of the United States" (quoted in Schlesinger and Israel, 2007, p. 3). And yet he also bade Americans to take an active role in charting the way forward: "The sacred fire of liberty and the destiny of the republic model of government [is] staked on the experiment entrusted to the hands of the American people" (quoted in Schlesinger and Israel, 2007, p. 4). The partnership was not among equals, however. America requires providential aid; Man can act, but absent an abiding faith it will falter.

The missionary quality of America's engagement with the world may be found in Jefferson's first inaugural. Delivered in 1801, Jefferson's optimistic expression attuned Americans to the promise of a new century: "A rising nation, spread over a wide and fruitful land, traversing all the seas with the rich productions of their industry, engaged in commerce with nations who feel power and forget right, advancing rapidly to destinies beyond the reach of mortal eye" (quoted in Schlesinger and Israel, 2007, p. 15). In 1813, Madison's second inaugural affirmed America's righteousness through God's favor in what many view as the nation's second war for independence: "The war with a powerful nation, which forms so prominent a feature in our situation, is stamped with that justice which invites the smiles of Heaven on the means of conducting it to a successful termination" (quoted in Schlesinger and Israel, 2007, p. 32).

Yet just a few decades later, Martin Van Buren placed a cautionary brake on America's ambition, warning in his 1837 inaugural address that "position and climate and the bounteous resources that nature has scattered with so liberal a hand ... will avail us nothing if we fail sacredly to uphold those political institutions that were wisely and deliberately formed" (quoted in Schlesinger and Israel, 2007, p. 75). In this inaugural, Van Buren balanced America's growing power with its first principles: "From a small community we have risen to a people powerful in numbers and in strength; but with our increase has gone hand in hand the progress of just principles" (quoted in Schlesinger and Israel, 2007, p. 76). Successors would strike similar notes, including James K. Polk, inaugurated in 1845, who sought God's intercession to "guard this Heaven favored land against the mischiefs which without His guidance might arise from an unwise public policy" (quoted in Schlesinger and Israel, 2007, p. 104); Zachary Taylor, inaugurated in 1849, who encouraged his fellow citizens to "seek to deserve that continuance [of the high state of prosperity] by prudence and moderation in our councils" (quoted in Schlesinger and Israel, 2007, p. 118); and Benjamin Harrison, who in 1889 reminded his fellow citizens that God's gifts are subject to the "condition that justice and mercy shall hold the reins of power and that the upward avenues of hope shall be free to all the people" (quoted in Schlesinger and Israel, 2007, p. 194). Taken together, this progression embosses stewardship with worldly obligation.

Bearing witness. America's role as exemplar to the world implies that the nations and peoples of the world are watching. That others bear witness to America's actions makes a convincing argument for restraint and right action. In some cases, the act of bearing witness places a sanction on behavior. For instance, in his second inaugural in 1805, Thomas Jefferson asserted that "a government ... doing no act which it would be unwilling the whole world should witness, can be written down by falsehood and defamation" (quoted in Schlesinger and Israel, 2007, p. 24). To offer a second example, Andrew Jackson, in his second inaugural in 1833, reminded Americans that "the eyes of all nations are fixed on our Republic" and encouraged Americans to realize the "importance of the attitude in which we stand before the world" (quoted in Schlesinger and Israel, 2007, p. 72).

Other inaugurals employ the act of bearing witness as an imperative to meet world expectations. Sounding this refrain, Franklin Pierce's 1853 address described "the oppressed throughout the world ... [who] have turned their eyes hitherward, not to find those lights extinguished or to fear lest they should wane, but to be constantly cheered by their steady and increasing radiance" (quoted in Schlesinger and Israel, 2007, p. 122). Four years later, James Buchanan would reprise the theme: "Our own country could alone have exhibited so grand and striking a spectacle of the capacity of man for self-government" (quoted in Schlesinger and Israel, 2007, p. 131). Warren G. Harding made the same point not once but twice in his 1921 address, modulating the nation's thematic role from observer to actor: "We have seen the world rivet its hopeful gaze on the great truths on which the founders wrought" (quoted in Schlesinger and Israel, 2007, p. 251); and then, "We have riveted the gaze of all civilization to the unselfishness and the righteousness of representative democracy" (quoted in Schlesinger and Israel, 2007, p. 253).

Words not deeds. If the whole world is watching, how do American presidents inclined toward intervention accomplish their aims while keeping America's covenant intact? In answer to this question, I note that definition by negation is a popular and straightforward tactic contained in inaugural addresses. Franklin Pierce reassured both domestic and foreign audiences that "we have nothing in our history or position to invite aggression; we have everything to beckon us to the cultivation of relations of peace and amity with all nations" (quoted in Schlesinger and Israel, 2007, p. 123). James Buchanan, next in line in 1857, asserted that "it is our glory that whilst other nations have extended their dominions by the sword we have never acquired territory except by fair purchase or, as in the case of Texas, by the voluntary determination of a brave, kindred, and independent people to blend their destinies with our own" (quoted in Schlesinger and Israel, 2007, p. 136).

Taking office in 1889, Benjamin Harrison declared that "we have not sought to dominate or to absorb any of our weaker neighbors, but rather to aid and encourage them to establish free and stable governments resting upon the consent of their own people" (quoted in Schlesinger and Israel, 2007, p. 190). And then in 1897, William McKinley pledged that "our diplomacy should seek nothing more and accept nothing less than what is due us. We want no wars of conquest; we must avoid the temptation of territorial aggression" (quoted in Schlesinger and Israel, 2007, p. 211). Events transpiring during McKinley's first term in Office would necessitate a revision in his second inaugural that nonetheless managed to downplay American ambition. The United States would "demonstrate its fitness to administer any new estate which events devolve upon it, and in the fear of God will take occasion by the hand and make the bounds of freedom wider yet" (quoted in Schlesinger and Israel, 2007, p. 217).

Reliance on definition by negation reappears in the aftermath of the First World War. Warren Harding declared that "we shall give no people just cause to make war upon us; we hold no national prejudices; we entertain no spirit of revenge; we do not hate; we do not covet; we dream of no conquest, nor boast of armed prowess" (quoted in Schlesinger and Israel, 2007, pp. 253–254). Calvin Coolidge described an America that "seeks no earthly empire built on blood and force" and "aware of its might but obedient to its conscience" (quoted in Schlesinger and Israel, 2007, p. 268). Hoover chided "superficial observers [who] seem to find no destiny for our abounding increase in population, in wealth and power except that of imperialism" (quoted in Schlesinger and Israel, 2007, p. 276). Americans had no time or capacity to embark on an imperialistic course because they were "engrossed in the building for themselves of a new economic system, a new social system, a new political system all of which are characterized by aspirations of freedom of opportunity and thereby are the negation of imperialism" (quoted in Schlesinger and Israel, 2007, p. 276).

Blessed be the humble. The capability to self-correct, either to continue favorable providence or regain God's favor, is an early hallmark of the American character. Inheritance and indebtedness is a minor yet representative theme, found for example in John Quincy Adams's inaugural address of 1825: "We now receive [the social compact/Constitution] as a precious inheritance from those to whom we are indebted for its establishment, doubly bound by the examples which they have left us and by the blessings which we have enjoyed as the fruits of their labors to transmit the same unimpaired to the succeeding generation" (quoted in Schlesinger and Israel, 2007, p. 57). Presidential inaugurals also have celebrated and encouraged piety as an assurance of God's continued pleasure with his creation. Piety permits the expression of national pride, illustrated in an atypically direct passage from John Adams's 1797 address: "If national pride is ever justifiable or excusable it is when it springs, not from power or riches, grandeur or glory, but from conviction of national innocence, information, and benevolence" (quoted in Schlesinger and Israel, 2007, p. 10).

Through the nation's evolution from republicanism to progressivism, humility and caution against hubris remain mainstays of Americans' behavior. In his second inaugural in 1893, Grover Cleveland warned against "exaggerated confidence in our country's greatness" (quoted in Schlesinger and Israel, 2007, p. 197). Theodore Roosevelt asked Americans to give thanks "in no spirit of boastfulness in our own strength, but with gratitude to the Giver of good who has blessed us with the conditions which have enabled us to achieve so large a measure of well being and of happiness" (quoted in Schlesinger and Israel, 2007, p. 221) and opined that successes in the past and confidence of success in the future "should cause in us no feeling of vainglory" (quoted in Schlesinger and Israel, 2007, p. 221). Not to be outdone, Woodrow Wilson's first inaugural, in 1913, presented a platform of domestic reforms as correctives to America's "haste to succeed and be great" (quoted in Schlesinger and Israel, 2007, p. 242).

The jeremiad. These leaders' sentiments do not belie America's providential beginnings and exceptionalism among nations. Rather, moderating ambition and demonstrating care for one's own people reifies Americans' faith in themselves and their inheritance, reconnects them with their providential mission, and thus fortifies belief in America's exceptional status. The pattern is decidedly *not* oscillation between greatness and decline, but instead a cycle of dormancy, rebirth, and growth. This pattern of renewal marks presidential orators' reliance on the jeremiad, a sermonic argumentative form that outlines the terms, conditions, and duties of the people's providential and social covenants and accounts for success or failure of the community by its keeping or breaking its covenant (Madsen, 1998). Bormann (2001) calls this particular jeremiad "fetching good out of evil": sufferings and sacrifice are a purging or cleansing experience through which "the chosen people emerge once again free, happy, and right with their God" (p. 227).

Within the canon of presidential inaugurals, Ronald Reagan's addresses illustrate most clearly the linkage of the jeremiad with belief in American exceptionalism. In his first address (1981), Reagan promised that "as we renew ourselves here in our own land, we will be seen as having greater strength throughout the world. We will again be the exemplar of freedom and a beacon of hope for those who do not now have freedom" (quoted in Schlesinger and Israel, 2007, p. 369). Four years later, accounting for his administration's accomplishments and readying the nation to do more, Reagan provides a coda that synopsizes the argument: "My fellow citizens, our Nation is poised for greatness. We must do what we know is right and do it with all our might. Let history say of us, these were golden years, when the American Revolution was reborn, when freedom gained new life, when America reached for her best" (quoted in Schlesinger and Israel, 2007, p. 375).

Reading signs. As a rhetorical resource for conservative restraint, providence has proven to be both reliable and resilient. The comparison of two war-time generals who ascended to highest office deserves further commentary. Ulysses S. Grant's second inaugural, in 1873, presages America's leadership in an era that witnessed dramatic change in commerce, education, communication, and mobility: "I believe that our Great Maker is preparing the world, in His own good time, to become one nation, speaking one language, and when armies and navies will be no longer required" (quoted in Schlesinger and Israel, 2007, p. 159). Pervading Grant's words is the understanding that the one nation would be modeled after America, the one language would be English, and America's duty would be done.

In 1953, General Dwight Eisenhower's first inaugural likewise responded to technological advancement, with a subtext appropriate to the anxiety of the Atomic Age and ideological warfare:

> In the swift rush of great events, we find ourselves groping to know the full sense and meaning of these times in which we live. In our quest of understanding, we beseech God's guidance. We summon all our knowledge of the past and we scan all signs of the future. We bring all our wit and all our will to meet the question. How far have we come in man's long pilgrimage from darkness toward light? Are we nearing the light; a day of freedom and of peace for all mankind? Or are the shadows of another night closing in upon us? [quoted in Schlesinger and Israel, 2007, p. 313].

Like the jeremiad, reading signs harkens to early Puritan traditions. The early settlers of Massachusetts Bay understood that only their ministers, as intercessors and interpreters of God's will in earthly events, could see and accurately interpret events that alternatively allowed the colonists to flounder and flourish (Bormann, 2001). One senses that the reading of signs resonates more deeply with Americans' cultural memory when the country faces an existential threat. In Eisenhower's rhetoric, the prophetic voice "advanced an expansive vision of national 'spiritual' being to which corporeal images could only gesture [and] positioned himself as a kind of priestly mediator" (O'Gorman, 2008, p. 44).

Whereas Eisenhower leads his audience to the right answer, George W. Bush frames and responds demonstrably to an existential threat in promoting his Freedom Agenda. In his 2005 inaugural, Bush progressed from reading signs, "We have seen our vulnerability — and we have seen its deepest source" (quoted in Schlesinger and Israel, 2007, p. 414), to authoritative remedy: "So it is the policy of the United States to seek and support the growth of democratic movements and institutions in every nation and culture, with the ultimate goal of ending tyranny in our world" (quoted in Schlesinger and Israel, 2007, p. 414). In Eisenhower's framing and public persona, the existential threat implies physical destruction; danger resides in a reckless response to external circumstance and the danger is met through internal resolve and wisdom. In Bush's framing and public persona, the existential threat implies a rejection of America's ideology; danger resides in places beyond America's shores. In short, the degree to which an orator points his audience toward self-reflection and self-improvement as a lesson to others, or toward evangelism and intervention in remaking others' systems in America's model, bears greatly on Americans' (and other peoples') comfort with American exceptionalism.

American Genius

American genius, and its companion forms of common sense and American know-how, offers a palatable if not also laudatory vehicle for the expansion of the American character and an interventionist mode of American exceptionalism. In contrast to personal ambition, commercial acquisition, or the projection of force, American genius has few negative connotations. Genius is also a commonplace within the inaugural canon, and therefore a quality that Americans celebrate. In contrast to qualities of character that keep Americans tethered to their providential past, American genius can expand autonomously and with minimal restraint. New presidents who have invoked American genius include Andrew Jackson, who in 1829 spoke of "the lights that flow from the mind that founded and the mind that reformed our system" (quoted in Schlesinger and Israel, 2007, p. 67), pegging internal improvement to the diffusion of knowledge (quoted in Schlesinger and Israel, 2007, p. 66). James K. Polk, inaugurated in 1845, proposed American genius as an alternative repository for Americans' energy: "No longer tasked in devising means to accomplish or resist schemes of ambition, usurpation, or conquest.... Genius is free to announce its inventions and discoveries, and the hand is free to accomplish whatever the head conceives not incompatible with the rights of a fellow being" (quoted in Schlesinger and Israel, 2007, pp. 106–107). Decades would unfold before the American people would reach a workable consensus on notions of fundamental rights, suffrage, and citizenship. Contextually,

Polk's construction not only reaches back, to connect American genius with American benevolence, but also projects American genius toward the realization of universal rights through democratic systems of governance.

The symbiosis of American institutions and American genius dates to the adoption of a constitutional form of government. John Adams's inaugural included his reaction to the completed document from his post overseas: "I read [the Constitution] with great satisfaction, as the result of good heads prompted by good hearts, as an experiment better adapted to the genius, character, situation, and relations of this nation and country than any which had ever been proposed or suggested" (quoted in Schlesinger and Israel, 2007, p. 9). Martin Van Buren, inaugurated in 1837, gave primacy to American institutions as a nurturing source: "The power and influence of the Republic have arisen to a height obvious to all mankind ... new and inexhaustible sources of general prosperity have been opened; the effects of distance have been averted by the inventive genius of our people, developed and fostered by the spirit of our institutions" (quoted in Schlesinger and Israel, 2007, p. 78). The next president, Zachary Taylor, returned institutions and genius to par, touting America's "geographical position, the genius of our institutions and our people, the advancing spirit of civilization" (MFC, p. 117). In this particular phrasing, America's land provides a point of origin; civilization, its telos; and genius, its propellant.

Drawing examples from inaugural addresses in the last half-century, John F. Kennedy proclaimed: "Man holds in his mortal hands the power to abolish all forms of human poverty and all forms of human life" (quoted in Schlesinger and Israel, 2007, p. 327), and William Jefferson Clinton affirmed that "our greatest strength is the power of our ideas, which are still new in many lands. Across the world, we see them embraced, and we rejoice. Our hopes, our hearts, our hands, are with those in every continent who are building democracy and freedom. Their cause is America's cause" (quoted in Schlesinger and Israel, 2007, p. 394). Kennedy's and Clinton's inaugurals espouse a new purpose for American institutions: to translate genius into action.

Conclusion: Blending Exemplarist and Interventionist Designs

In a comprehensive critique of President Clinton's foreign policy rhetoric, Edwards (2008) establishes two rhetorical traditions of American exceptionalism. Exemplarists, as the word implies, believe that America fulfils its destiny by making itself worthy of emulation. Narratives built around metaphors of the "beacon" and "shining city" express exemplarist thought. Exemplarists recognize that tending the flame is a full time job, and therefore limits America's active engagement in the affairs of other states. Rhetorical analysis of presidential inaugural addresses finds that exemplarists have a ready set of inventional strategies to convey their belief in America's mission. These strategies include framing America's natural resources and boundaries as a natural protection; describing characteristics such as humility in a positive light; invocation of America's covenant as a moderating force on actions abroad; crafting appeals in the jeremiad form; and the interpretation of signs. Exemplarists are not inactive; their energies are directed toward internal improvements and continuous striving toward perfection of the American ideal.

The connection of genius and institutions buttresses Edwards's claim that presidents in office after World War II intertwined exemplarist and interventionist thought to justify America's global leadership (2008). Interventionists believe America maintains its exceptional status through direct action and wide-ranging engagement in the economic, political, social and cultural affairs of other nation-states. Whereas exemplarists are drawn into world events, interventionists consider international involvement a standing requirement. In the exemplarist mode, institutions nurture and contain genius; this interaction is a closed loop, with the benefits of American genius fueling innovations ripe for others to emulate. In the interventionist mode, institutions not only contain but carry their own processes of replicating American genius through standing structures of nation-state and multilateral governance.

Institutions alone, without the continuous feeding of ideas, can decay. Ideas alone, without visible and replicable structures to improve the human condition, fade from public memory. The dual framing of American genius and American institutions offers reassurance of permanence; America's story is protected in the perpetuity of her institutions. Working with the illustrative texts within the corpus of American inaugural address, we have come to understand that American exceptionalism is not mere sloganeering, but a term infused with multiple layers of meaning that warrant America's relation to the world. American genius, translated into action through institutions, is elemental to Americans' belief that they are special and apart. American exceptionalism began with the connection between a chosen people and their providential land, and continues in colonizing the world of ideas.

References

Andrews, J. R. (1971). "Reflections of the American Character in National Rhetoric." *Quarterly Journal of Speech, 57,* 316–324.
Beale, W. H. (1978). "Rhetorical Performative Discourse: A New Theory of Epideictic." *Philosophy and Rhetoric, 11,* 221–243.

Beasley, V. B. (2001). "The Rhetoric of Ideological Consensus in the United States: American Principles and American Pose in Presidential Inaugurals." *Communication Monographs, 68*, 169–183.
Bercovitch, S. (1981). "The Rites of Assent." In S. B. Girgus (Ed.), *The American Self: Myth, Ideology, and Popular Culture* (pp. 5–42). Albuquerque: University of New Mexico Press.
Bormann, E. G. (2001). *The Force of Fantasy: Restoring the American Dream.* Carbondale: Southern Illinois University.
Campbell, K. K., and K. H. Jamieson (1990). *Deeds Done in Words: Presidential Rhetoric and the Genres of Governance.* Chicago: University of Chicago Press.
Condit, C. M. (1985). "The Functions of Epideictic: The Boston Massacre Orations as Exemplar." *Communication Quarterly, 33*, 284–299.
Dudash, E. (2007). "International Appeal in the Presidential Inaugural: An Update on Genre and an Expansion of Argument." *Contemporary Argumentation and Debate, 28*, 47–64.
Edwards, J. A. (2008). *Navigating the Post-Cold War World: President Clinton's Foreign Policy Rhetoric.* Lanham, MD: Lexington.
Farrell, T. (1991). "Practicing the Arts of Rhetoric: Tradition and Invention." *Philosophy and Rhetoric, 24*, 183–212.
Finkelstein, L., Jr. (1981). "The Calendrical Rite of the Ascension to Power." *The Western Journal of Speech Communication, 45*, 51–59.
Hauser, G. A. (1999). "Aristotle on Epideictic: The Formation of Public Morality." *Rhetoric Society Quarterly, 29*, 5–23.
Ivie, R. L., and O. Giner (2009). "American Exceptionalism in a Democratic Idiom: Transacting the Mythos of Change in the 2008 Presidential Campaign." *Communication Studies, 60*, 359–375.
Lipset, S. M. (1996). *American Exceptionalism: A Double-Edged Sword.* New York: W. W. Norton.
Madsen, D. L. (1998). *American Exceptionalism.* Jackson: University of Mississippi Press.
McCormick, J. (2005). "American Exceptionalism: The Implications for Europe." *Journal of Transatlantic Studies, 3*, 199–215.
McGee, C. M. (1980). "The 'Ideograph': A Link Between Rhetoric and Ideology." *Quarterly Journal of Speech, 66*, 1–16.
O'Gorman, N. (2008). "Eisenhower and the American Sublime." *Quarterly Journal of Speech, 94*, 44–72.
Schlesinger, A. M., Jr., and F. L. Israel (Eds.) (2007). *My Fellow Citizens: The Inaugural Addresses of the Presidents of the United States, 1789–2005.* New York: Checkmark.
Sigelman, L. (1996). "Presidential Inaugurals: The Modernization of a Genre." *Political Communication, 13*, 81–92.
Steele, E. D., and W. C. Redding (1962). "The American Value System: Premises for Persuasion." *Western Speech, 26*, 83–91.
Stuckey, M. E. (2004). *Defining Americans: The Presidency and National Identity.* Lawrence: University Press of Kansas.

CHAPTER 3

One Nation Under God
Mormon Theology and the American Continent

BRETT LUNCEFORD

The notion that the United States is a unique nation with a particular destiny has long been a staple of American rhetoric; moreover, this notion of American exceptionalism is often couched in religious discourse. The idea that America is a New Jerusalem is especially prominent in discourses surrounding American exceptionalism. As Bellah (1991) put it, "Europe is Egypt; America, the promised land. God has led his people to establish a new sort of social order that shall be a light unto all the nations" (p. 175). Such views of the American continent can be seen in early colonial sermons such as Samuel Danforth's (1670/1995) sermon, "A Brief Recognition of New England's Errand in the Wilderness." The significance of America transcended the events that transpired on that continent; America had a special role to play in the events of the world. As Hietala explains, "Americans believed that their progress provided a beacon light to a world in darkness" (2003, p. 257).

Such discourses are generally metaphorical, but there are some that consider the American continent to be the literal site of the New Jerusalem. Members of the Church of Jesus Christ of Latter-day Saints (LDS), commonly referred to as Mormons,[1] believe that the American continent itself is a choice land, chosen by God. In Mormon theology, American exceptionalism is not a product of the United States government, democracy, or even religion. Rather, American exceptionalism is rooted in the land itself. As O'Dea (1957) observed, "The Mormon church saw in the discovery of this continent and its settlement the preparation for the restoration of which it claimed itself to be the institutional embodiment" (p. 169). N. Eldon Tanner (1977), who served as a member of the Quorum of the Twelve Apostles, proclaimed, "The discovery of the Americas was not an accident. The event had been foreordained in the eternal councils" (p. 36).[2]

The belief that the American continent is a choice land has had implications for the church's theology and its relationship with the government. This essay explores how such a conception of the land has influenced religious discourse in the LDS church up to the present day, examining the intersection of Latter-day Saint theology and space as it relates to the North American continent and the United States government. Considering the land itself, rather than the people on it, as sacred provides an interesting counterpoint to other discourses of American exceptionalism, most of which place the distinction on the people or on the form of government. Foregrounding the role of the land also provides a way to understand more fully the role of religious discourse in constructing the idea of American exceptionalism.

Basic Tenets of Mormon Theology Relating to the American Continent

Unlike most other religions practiced in the United States, Mormonism is a distinctly American religion. Latter-day Saints believe that the *Book of Mormon*, a core book of scripture in Mormon theology, was written by prophets who lived on the American continent. The book was hidden in upstate New York and ultimately given to Joseph Smith, Jr., in 1827 by the angel Moroni, the last prophet to write in the *Book of Mormon*.[3] Smith translated the *Book of Mormon* and, as he organized the church, pronounced many revelations, which are found in the *Doctrine and Covenants*.[4]

According to Latter-day Saint theology, the *Book of Mormon* contains a record of Israelites who were led to the American continent by God through the prophet Lehi. The followers of Lehi consisted mostly of his extended family and were later split into two groups—the Nephites and the Lamanites. The lighter-skinned Nephites were generally more righteous than the Lamanites, who were cursed with a darker skin; both lived together on the continent from approximately 590 B.C. until A.D. 421. In addition to the records of wars and prophecies, the *Book of Mormon* contains an account of Jesus Christ's ministry on the American continent after his resurrection (*BM*, 3 Nephi 11–28). During this time, Christ related many of the teachings found in the biblical Sermon on the Mount (see Matthew 5–7 and *BM*, 3 Nephi 12–14). Around A.D. 421 the Lamanites and the Nephites had a great battle in which the Nephites were completely destroyed (see *BM*, Mormon 1–9; *BM*, Moroni, 1, 9). Mormons believe that the indigenous peoples of North and South America are descendents of the Lamanites.

The followers of Lehi were told that they would be led to a promised land: "And inasmuch as ye shall keep my commandments, ye shall prosper, and shall be led to a land of promise; yea, even a land which I have prepared for you; yea, a land which is choice above all other lands" (*BM*, 1 Nephi 2:20). Similar notions were also held by other groups of people discussed in the *Book of Mormon*. Before Lehi led his family to the American continent, another group, the Jaredites, had also been guided there.[5] Their record, found in the book of Ether, states: "For behold, this is a land which is choice above all other lands; wherefore he that doth possess it shall serve God or shall be swept off; for it is the everlasting decree of God. And it is not until the fulness of iniquity among the children of the land, that they are swept off" (*BM*, Ether 2:10). The notion of freedom is connected with serving the God of the land, who is Jesus Christ (*BM*, Ether 2:12). The book of Ether serves as a cautionary tale for those who would inhabit this land; the Jaredites were eventually destroyed in war amongst themselves when they became wicked.

Modern revelation by the prophet Joseph Smith also describes the American continent as a choice land:

> Hearken, O ye elders of my church, saith the Lord your God, who have assembled yourselves together, according to my commandments, in this land, which is the land of Missouri, which is the land which I have appointed and consecrated for the gathering of the saints. Wherefore, this is the land of promise, and the place for the city of Zion [*D&C*, 57:1–2].

However, the idea of America as a chosen land was not unique to LDS scripture and, in fact, was quite widespread even before the church was founded. Barlow (1989) notes in his study of Joseph Smith's use of the Bible that "he read its narratives with presuppositions about the immutability of truth and the direct relevance of prophecy (the imminent millennium, America as chosen) that were common to his place and time" (p. 741).

Yet few had been so specific concerning why America was a chosen land. For Mormons, Missouri is not only the site of future dealings with the Lord; this land has been foreordained from the beginning of time. In May 19, 1838, Joseph Smith prophesied that "Spring Hill is named by the Lord Adam-ondi-Ahman, because, said he, it is the place where Adam shall come to visit his people, or the Ancient of Days shall sit, as spoken of by Daniel the prophet" (*D&C*, 116:1). Heber C. Kimball, who served as an apostle, reinforces the idea that Adam lived on the American continent after he was cast out of the Garden of Eden (quoted in Whitney, 1945, pp. 208–209). Smith also took this knowledge to the larger public, writing in a letter to the editor of a newspaper in Rochester, New York, "The City, of Zion, spoken of by David in the 102 Psalm shall be built upon the Land of America and the ransomed of the Lord shall return and come to it with songs of everlasting joy upon their heads." (1833/1989, p. 77).

The church has worked to protect the land of Adam-ondi-Ahman that they hold sacred (Gentry, 1973; Matthews, 1972). However, it is not only Spring Hill in Missouri that is held sacred by the Lord. Joseph Smith declared that "the whole of America is Zion itself from north to south, and is described by the Prophets, who declare that it is the Zion where the mountain of the Lord should be, and that it should be in the center of the land" (quoted in Church of Jesus Christ, 1948, vol. 6, pp. 318–319). He later clarifies this and states, "I have received instructions from the Lord that from henceforth wherever the Elders of Israel shall build up churches and branches unto the Lord throughout the States, there shall be a stake of Zion" (quoted in Church of Jesus Christ, 1948, vol. 6, p. 319).

As the church has spread around the world and therefore no longer remains a strictly American religion, there has been an emphasis on the idea that Zion is anywhere the Saints gather, rather than a specific geographical location. For example, in 1972, the apostle Bruce R. McConkie stated,

> The place of gathering for the Mexican Saints is in Mexico; the place of gathering for the Guatemalan Saints is in Guatemala; the place of gathering for the Brazilian Saints is in Brazil; and so it goes throughout the length and breadth of the whole earth. Japan is for the Japanese; Korea is for the Koreans; Australia is for the Australians; every nation is the gathering place for its own people [quoted in *Church History in the Fullness of Times*, 2003, p. 576].

Yet McConkie (1985) also reaffirmed the centrality of the American continent: "Let every land be a Zion to those appointed to dwell there.... But still there is a center place, a place where the chief temple shall stand.... And that center place is what men now call Independence in Jackson County, Missouri" (p. 595). Thus even while expanding the definition of Zion to include all Saints in all lands, the American continent remains the most important, the most blessed — the capital of Zion itself— by virtue of containing within it the land of Adam-ondi-Ahman.

Mormons see themselves as part of a chain of prophecy beginning with Adam, through the prophets of the Old and New Testaments and the *Book of Mormon*, up to the present day. The idea of a restoration makes sense in a new place — this was no mere reformation; rather, this was a completely new movement. Much as America was no longer simply Europe on this continent, the Church of Jesus Christ of Latter-day Saints was not a reformation, but rather a restoration of the one true church that no longer existed. Yet this was still placed within a context of existing religious traditions; as Barlow writes,

> Substantially before the organization of the Mormon church, Smith began to see events in his own life as a continuation of Bible narratives. It was not simply that the canon was to be extended, but that the whole biblical narrative had come to life again, as endings were put on stories that had their beginnings in the scriptural text [1989, p. 752].

Even the Saints' migration to Utah can be seen in biblical terms. Belk (1992) observes, "It was not lost on the Mormons that the ancient Israelites were also cast into a desert wasteland" (p. 343). Yet despite the familiarity of the biblical and social contexts from which the Mormons drew, one cannot help but observe the boldness of the statement found in the first section of the *Doctrine and Covenants*:

> And also those to whom these commandments were given, might have power to lay the foundation of this church, and to bring it forth out of obscurity and out of darkness, the only true and living church upon the face of the whole earth, with which I, the Lord, am well pleased, speaking unto the church collectively and not individually [*D&C*, 1:30].

Few denominations, even today, make the claim of holding absolute truth. This statement radically departs from the commonly held narratives surrounding religion. Mormonism is not merely one possible path to God, but rather the *only* path to God. Moreover, the founding of the church was so important that it could not take place just anywhere — it had to take place in a land divinely appointed by God, the land on which God himself created the first man in the Garden of Eden. This was truly an exceptional church founded in an exceptional land.

The Church and the United States Government

Flake (2004) remarked that "if proto-sociologist Alexis de Tocqueville had lived to see the Mormon kingdom, he probably would have been amused that the nation with the soul of a church had given birth to a church with the soul of a nation" (p. 27). Scholars have noted the inherent tensions in maintaining a theocratic kingdom of God on earth within the confines of a secular democracy. This tension is built into the core beliefs of Mormon theology, whose twelfth Article of Faith states, "We believe in being subject to kings, presidents, rulers, and magistrates, in obeying, honoring, and sustaining the law" (*PGP*, Articles of Faith 1:12). Mormons have attempted to work within the law, much to the dismay of those who opposed them. For example, Joseph

Smith was a candidate for the United States Presidency in 1844 (Church of Jesus Christ, 1948; Hinckley, 1988) and in 1903, Reed Smoot, who was also a member of the Quorum of the Twelve Apostles, was the first Mormon to be elected to the United States Senate and, after a protracted debate, seated in the legislature (Flake, 2004). Mormons also attempted to redress their grievances to the authorities, with Joseph Smith even meeting with President Martin Van Buren regarding the persecution of the Saints in Missouri (Church of Jesus Christ, 1948).

Yet it is this tension between theocracy and democracy that caused many to distrust the Mormons, in much the same way that some opposed John F. Kennedy's candidacy for president because they feared that he would be under the control of the Vatican. Such concerns persist even today; when Mitt Romney, a Mormon who had previously served as governor of Massachusetts, ran for president in 2008, some simply feared his beliefs, while others worried that he would be beholden to the Prophet (see Weisberg, 2007). In some ways, these concerns should come as little surprise. Despite the presence of the First Amendment, which ostensibly grants freedom of religion, Flake (2004, p. 15) notes, "Religious liberty did not come naturally to Americans.... Only gradually did the failure of any one church to dominate convert all churches to the principle of tolerance." Because the political landscape, as well as the religious landscape, of the United States is heterogeneous, people tend to fear those who would reduce the influence of their faction. Thus we can see an uneasy alliance among the adherents of various evangelical Protestant faiths, who, despite their differences, conclude that they have more in common with each other than they do with groups such as Catholics, Mormons, Jews and others who do not fall under their banner.

Even in the face of persecution Mormons have, from the beginning, held fast to the belief that the United States government was ordained of God and established in order to bring forth the restoration of His true church. Orson Hyde (1860) proclaimed,

> With the view of raising up a church pursuant to the doctrine contained in these records of a fallen people, a government has to be established on this *chosen* and *promised* land whose provisions should be liberal enough to allow and tolerate every principle, precept, and doctrine of the new Church which then existed only in prophetic vision. The Constitution of the United States forms the basis of that government, extending protection to all, and showing especial favour to none [p. 108].

For the Mormons, the founding of the United States was necessary for the gospel of Jesus Christ to be restored to the earth. Marion Romney (1980) provides a larger chronology of events that spans two and a half millennia and in which the founding of the Constitution is only one element:

Jesus Christ, the God of this land, led Columbus to it. He led the Pilgrims to Plymouth. He sustained and gave victory to the colonists. He established the Constitution of the United States. Over a period of some twenty-six centuries he directed the writing of the Book of Mormon, which contains the record of the former inhabitants of this land. At his command, Moroni finished the record and hid it up in the Hill Cumorah, where, under his surveillance, it was safely preserved for some fourteen hundred years [p. 6].

In Mormon theology, the founding of the United States is merely one step in a chain of events that were necessary to bring forth the true church. The discovery of the American continent by Columbus and the later arrival of the Pilgrims were simply fulfillments of Lehi's prophecy that "there shall none come into this land save they shall be brought by the hand of the Lord" (*BM*, 2 Nephi 1:6). Indeed, even the Revolutionary War is described by Nephi, another *Book of Mormon* prophet (see *BM*, 1 Nephi 13:17–19), and held up as evidence that the nation established by the hand of God cannot be destroyed except through iniquity.

Mormons have also held the American founding fathers in high regard because they are seen as instrumental in the founding of the LDS church. Wilford Woodruff (1897), then prophet of the church, called the founding fathers "the best spirits the God of heaven could find on the face of the earth" (p. 89). One element in Mormon theology that is considerably different from other strands of Christianity is the idea of vicarious work for the dead. Mormons believe that saving ordinances such as baptism must be done on the earth and cannot be done in the world of spirits (see 1 Corinthians 15:29; *D&C*, 124:29–30, 127:5–9, 128:1–18, 138:32–34). These ordinances are performed by proxy in temples (Packer, 1980). In 1877, Woodruff related the following experience with the spirits of the founding fathers:

> I will here say, before closing, that two weeks before I left St. George, the spirits of the dead gathered around me, wanting to know why we did not redeem them. Said they, "You have had the use of the Endowment House for a number of years, and yet nothing has ever been done for us. We laid the foundation of the government you now enjoy, and we never apostatized from it, but we remained true to it and were faithful to God." These were the signers of the Declaration of Independence, and they waited on me for two days and two nights.... I straightway went into the baptismal font and called upon brother McCallister to baptize me for the signers of the Declaration of Independence, and fifty other eminent men, making one hundred in all, including John Wesley, Columbus, and others; I then baptized him for every President of the United States, except three; and when their cause is just, somebody will do the work for them [1878, p. 229].[6]

Thus, according to Mormon theology, even the signers of the Declaration of Independence ratified the founding of the church from beyond the grave and wished to be a part of it. Such a narrative reinforces the connection between the establishment of the church and that of the United States. Moreover, there is also an explicit connection between the founding of the government and remaining faithful to God. After all, Mormons believed that no one could come to the Promised Land unless they were led by God. Thus, by definition the founders were righteous and inspired men. Moreover, the inclusion of John Wesley places the church within a long line of reformers and truth-seekers.

The Constitution is also held in high regard in Mormonism. Ezra Taft Benson (1987), then prophet of the church, stated, "I reverence the Constitution of the United States as a sacred document. To me its words are akin to the revelations of God, for God has placed His stamp of approval upon it" (p. 4). On July 4, 1854, Brigham Young, second president of the Church, declared that the Constitution "will be held inviolate by this people; and, as Joseph Smith said, 'The time will come when the destiny of this nation will hang upon a single thread. At that critical juncture, this people will step forth and save it from the threatened destruction.' It will be so" (1860, p. 15). Such narratives reinforce the notion that the founding of the United States was God's will and thus link it to the establishment of the church. Young also placed the destiny of the nation in the hands of the Saints as protectors of the Constitution.

Present day church leaders have continued to emphasize connections between the church, the Constitution, and the notion that America is a promised land chosen by God. Shortly after the attacks of September 11, 2001, Gordon B. Hinckley, then president of the church, reported in General Conference that he had met with the President of the United States. Later in his address, he reinforced the connection between theology, the government, and the land:

> Great are the promises concerning this land of America. We are told unequivocally that it "is a choice land, and whatsoever nation shall possess it shall be free from bondage, and from captivity, and from all other nations under heaven, if they will but serve the God of the land, who is Jesus Christ" (Ether 2:12). This is the crux of the entire matter — obedience to the commandments of God. The Constitution under which we live, and which has not only blessed us but has become a model for other constitutions, is our God-inspired national safeguard ensuring freedom and liberty, justice and equality before the law [Hinckley, 2001, p. 73].

Here we see a conflation of the commandments of God and the Constitution, a document that itself is also inspired of God. Yet Hinckley's words also contain an implicit warning that if the nation is *not* righteous, its people will *not* be free from bondage, captivity, and other nations.

Reverence for the United States is always tempered by a knowledge that the nation can only stand so long as it serves the God of the land. In the face of mounting persecution in the early history of the church, whether or not the United States would continue to prosper was sometimes called into question. In 1840, Joseph Smith wrote that "my heart faints within me when I see, by the visions of the Almighty, the end of this nation, if she continues to disregard the cries and petitions of her virtuous citizens, as she has done, and is now doing" (Church of Jesus Christ, 1948, vol. 4, p. 89; see also vol. 6, p. 116). Yet, even in the face of persecution, members of the church continued to believe that the Lord would protect them, not only because they were his chosen people, but also because the government itself had been established chiefly to bring about the establishment of their religion and was thus ordained of God.

An Exceptional Religion in an Exceptional Land

Boyer (2001) observes that Mormonism "offers the distilled essence" of the idea within American Christianity that America is God's chosen land (p. 248). Mulder (1957) likewise argues, "With its central theme of the continent as a favored land providentially preserved for the gathering of a righteous people, [the *Book of Mormon*] improved the American dream with scripture and endowed it with sacred myth" (p. ix). Yet the *Book of Mormon* was viewed with suspicion, and even today many denounce Mormonism as a cult, with some denying that its believers are Christians. Shupe and Heinerman note that "among the various interreligious hostilities in American history, probably none has been so violent or prolonged as that between Mormons ... and assorted Fundamentalist/Baptist (i.e., Independent and Southern) groups" (1985, p. 146). Despite protections under the First Amendment, the Mormons were plagued by mobs that burned their homes and crops, tarred and feathered leaders, murdered their prophet, and eventually drove them into the wilderness.

Tocqueville (1848/2000) remarked, "It was religion that gave birth to the English colonies in America. One must never forget that. In the United States religion is mingled with all the national customs and all those feelings which the word fatherland evokes" (p. 432). It is for this reason that the United States has always had an uneasy relationship with religious pluralism. D'Antonio and Hoge note that the colonists were much less tolerant of other religions and that "after adoption of the First Amendment, disestablishment of denominations proceeded slowly" (2006, p. 346). This provides some perspective concerning why Mormons were not welcomed as fellow Christians.

However, it was not only their difference, but the belief held by Mormons that all other religions were incorrect and that they alone held the true gospel of Christ that was likely jarring to the members of the other denominations (see *PGP*, Joseph Smith — History, 1:19).

Joseph Smith was imprisoned or indicted on many occasions, but the courts did not convict him; he was tried, convicted, and sentenced to death in the court of mob violence. John Taylor of the Council of the Twelve, who was a witness to the murder of Joseph and Hyrum Smith, proclaimed that "their *innocent* blood, with the innocent blood of all the martyrs under the altar that John saw, will cry unto the Lord of Hosts till he avenges that blood on the earth" (*D&C*, 135:7). As with other elements of Mormon theology, they saw the Smiths as just the latest links in a long chain of Christian martyrs who had died in defense of the gospel of Jesus Christ. The Lord had long stated that his people would be a "peculiar people" (see Exodus 19:5; Deuteronomy 14:2, 26:18; Titus 2:4; 1 Peter 2:9–10). Mormons recognized that they were a peculiar people and accepted the fact that they would never be accepted by "a crooked and perverse generation," unless they repented and received the gospel (see *D&C*, 33:2, 34:6). They took solace in the Lord's admonition, "And if they persecute you, so persecuted they the prophets and righteous men that were before you. For all this there is a reward in heaven" (*D&C*, 127:4).

Mormons have woven together strands of prophecy and localized them such that they have re-envisioned the place of both America and themselves in the history of the world. In the Mormon vision, the new world is perhaps the oldest site of humanity's dealings with God. America is the location of the Garden of Eden and the place where Adam will return to visit his people. Christ himself visited the American continent to minister to his "other sheep" spoken of in John 10:16. God inspired Christopher Columbus, the signers of the Declaration of Independence, and the framers of the Constitution in order to ensure that the nation would be fertile ground for the restoration of the gospel of Jesus Christ. Most important, Mormons believe that this land is "choice above all other lands, which the Lord God had preserved for a righteous people" (*BM*, Ether 2:7). Such beliefs are prescriptive in that they significantly influence how Mormons interact with their fellow (non–Mormon) citizens. The tenet that the land is protected by God and that those who find it are led by Him, leads one (at least, if one is a Mormon) to reverence the founders of this nation as righteous men. If one sees the establishment of the Constitution as preliminary to the restoration of the gospel, then the Constitution becomes a sacred document in itself. If one sees the establishment of the government as the fulfillment of prophecy, one is much more likely to attempt to work within the system rather than simply revolt, recognizing the nuances between unjust men within the government and an unjust government in itself, despite the many persecutions heaped upon the church both individually and collectively.

Despite their deep reverence for the land, the founding fathers, and the Constitution, in maintaining the identity of a peculiar people that hold God's absolute truth, they embodied competing narratives of American exceptionalism while reinforcing the idea that America was indeed exceptional. Tuveson (1980, p. 176) notes that Mormons had a "uniquely *American* form of millenarianism," in that they recognized the importance of declaring the land itself as holy. Yet once a theology becomes fixated on a geographic space, it is difficult to alter the constraints of that belief. With a knowledge that the land is both a blessing and a curse, Mormons, perhaps more than others, believe that if the United States becomes too wicked, they shall be "swept off" the land (*BM*, Ether 2:10). Barlow notes that

> the prophesied role of America in the Book of Mormon is hardly the one of unqualified celebration common in the nineteenth century. To the contrary, the overall theme of the book is the destruction that awaits even a chosen people in a promised land if they succumb as a society to evil [1989, p. 76].

Mormons can point to a continual cycle throughout the *Book of Mormon* in which the people enjoy prosperity, followed by pride and wickedness, then destruction, which leads the people to humble themselves and serve the Lord once more. It is because the land itself is blessed above all others that the Saints were compelled to spread the gospel; the survival of the nation was dependent on serving the Lord, and the Saints were the only ones who knew how to truly do so.

The Mormons' belief that they were a peculiar people that held the keys to salvation and absolute truth was at odds with mainstream society's notion of what it meant to be an American. Defining is a rhetorical process; as Black (1970) explains, "In all rhetorical discourse, we can find enticements not simply to believe something, but to *be* something" (p. 119). It is not simply enough to believe in the American system of government; it is clear by their beliefs and their actions that the Mormons held a deep reverence for the founding fathers, the Constitution, and the land itself. But one must also *perform* the role of American and, for better or for worse, mainstream Christian identity was a part of that role. Of course the idea that there was a cohesive Christian identity was, and still is, a historical myth (Boyer, 2001), but there were certainly established mainstream Christian religions whose presence provides at least anecdotal support for such a myth. By maintaining the tenets of their own religion, Mormons violated the American convention of assimilation into the norm — a lesson that has implications for other groups who deviate from the norms of American society.

Conclusion

Religion and American exceptionalism have been intertwined from colonial times, but Mormons, more than any other religion, have continued to promote the idea of America as a chosen land, "choice above all other lands" (*BM*, 1 Nephi 2:20). However, this particular strand of American exceptionalism stands as both a blessing and a curse; America can be great only so long as they serve Jesus Christ, who is the God of the land (*BM*, Ether 2:12). Rooting the idea of exceptionalism in the land, rather than in the people, has had implications for Mormon theology, the relationship between Mormons and the United States government, and Mormons' attitudes toward history. It was the belief in the United States government as divinely inspired that allowed the early church to maintain its faith in the government even in the face of mounting persecution, rather than attempting to circumvent the government or actively fight against it. More important for the building up and protection of the church, the Mormons' belief that they needed to come to Zion provided a reason for European converts to migrate to the United States, and especially the Salt Lake Valley.

Mormon theology still holds to the doctrine that America is a choice land, protected by and ordained of God, yet this is always tempered by a belief that the land will be protected only so long as its people are righteous. Mormons see themselves as an integral part of this proposition and have mounted aggressive missionary efforts to draw people to the truth (*D&C*, 123:12–13). In Mormon theology, the future of America is wrapped up in the future of the church — if the people serve the God of the land, they will prosper, but if they do not, they will be swept off. Mormons believe that they have a great work to do, pronounced by God Himself: "And by your hands I will work a marvelous work among the children of men, unto the convincing of many of their sins, that they may come unto repentance, and that they may come unto the kingdom of my Father" (*D&C* 18:44). This is not simply a theological concern; if the prosperity of the nation depends on the righteousness of its inhabitants, bringing others into the kingdom of God is also a political concern.

Mormon exceptionalism is simply another strand of American exceptionalism. Mormons believe that they are the chosen people of God, placed on His chosen land, with a government established by His hand to bring forth

His one true church. All are interlocked — the United States, the founding fathers, the Constitution, the *Book of Mormon*, and the land itself — into one divinely appointed system. In scripture and in addresses given by the general authorities of the church, Mormons reinforce the idea that America is a chosen land. Thus, even as the Church of Jesus Christ of Latter-day Saints transforms from a quintessentially American faith to a worldwide religion, it continues to maintain its roots in the land that the Lord Himself has ordained as exceptional, a land choice above all others.

Notes

1. In this essay, I will use the terms "Mormon," "LDS," "Saints," and "member of the Church of Jesus Christ of Latter-day Saints" interchangeably. Although there are offshoots, in this essay I refer only to the main church.

2. In the church hierarchy, Apostle is one step below the Prophet, who is the earthly leader of the church. When the Prophet dies, the president of the Quorum of the Twelve Apostles becomes the next Prophet. The Prophet and his two counselors, chosen from the Quorum of the Twelve Apostles, make up the First Presidency of the church. There are other general authorities of the church, such as the Quorum of the Seventy and area representatives. Local leaders, called bishops, are over wards, which consist of members of a congregation that live within specific geographic areas. Groups of wards are called stakes. Each stake is presided over by a stake president. Members of the Quorum of the Twelve and the First Presidency are considered to be "prophets, seers, and revelators," thus, when they speak, they speak for the church as a whole. Members of the Quorum of the Twelve hold the title "Elder," and the Prophet is referred to as "President." For the purposes of this essay, I will omit these titles.

3. The Book of Mormon was first revealed to Joseph Smith in 1823, but he was forbidden to take them until 1827 (see *PGP*, Joseph Smith — History, 1:53).

4. There are four major books of scripture in the Church of Jesus Christ of Latter-day Saints: the King James Version of the *Bible*, the *Book of Mormon*, the *Doctrine and Covenants*, and the *Pearl of Great Price*. I will cite scripture using the standard conventions of book, chapter, and verse. The *Book of Mormon* and the *Pearl of Great Price* follow similar conventions, but I will preface quotes from those texts with the abbreviated titles of the scriptural works (*BM* and *PGP*, respectively), followed by the book, chapter, and verse. The *Doctrine and Covenants* follows similar citation conventions, but rather than books, it is divided by section; these will be cited as *D&C*, followed by the section and verse numbers.

5. The Jaredites were led by the brother of Jared and had come to the American continent shortly after the time of time of the tower of Babel.

6. The three for whom baptism was not performed were James Buchanan, Martin Van Buren, and Ulysses S. Grant. Although there seems to be no authoritative reason, there is speculation that this is because of Van Buren's and Buchanan's actions against the Saints. When seeking protection from mob violence, Joseph Smith reported that Van Buren responded to his entreaties by stating, "Gentlemen, your cause is just, but I can do nothing for you," and "If I take up for you I shall lose the vote of Missouri" (Church of Jesus Christ, 1948, vol. 4, p. 80). Buchanan had ordered troops to Salt Lake City to quell a supposed insurrection and install a secular government by deposing Brigham Young, who was also the prophet at the time, from the governorship (see Mulder, 1957, p. 275). However, baptism and other ordinances were subsequently performed for both Buchanan and Van

Buren (see Newell, 2000, p. 221). Grant was still alive at the time of the speech, and thus would not have been eligible for vicarious work.

References

Barlow, P. L. (1989). "Before Mormonism: Joseph Smith's use of the Bible, 1820–1829." *Journal of the American Academy of Religion, 57,* 739–771.
Belk, R. W. (1992). "Moving Possessions: An Analysis Based on Personal Documents from the 1847–1869 Mormon Migration." *Journal of Consumer Research, 19,* 339–361.
Bellah, R. N. (1991). *Beyond Belief: Essays on Religion in a Post-Traditional World.* Berkeley: University of California Press.
Benson, E. T. (1987, November). "Our Divine Constitution." *Ensign, 17,* 4–7.
Black, E. (1970). "The Second Persona." *Quarterly Journal of Speech, 56,* 109–119.
Boyer, P. (2001). "Two Centuries of Christianity in America: An Overview." *Church History, 70,* 544–556.
Church of Jesus Christ of Latter-day Saints. (1948). *History of the Church of Jesus Christ of Latter-day Saints* (Vols. 1–6). Salt Lake City: Deseret News.
Church History in the Fullness of Times, Student Manual, Religion 341–43 (2nd ed.). (2003). Salt Lake City: Church of Jesus Christ of Latter-day Saints.
Danforth, S. (1995). "A Brief Recognition of New-England's Errand into the Wilderness." In R. F. Reid (Ed.), *American Rhetorical Discourse* (2d ed., pp. 38–52). Prospect Heights, IL: Waveland. (Original work published 1670.)
D'Antonio, W. V., and D. R. Hoge (2006). "The American Experience of Religious Disestablishment and Pluralism." *Social Compass, 53,* 345–356.
Flake, K. (2004). *The Politics of American Religious Identity: The Seating of Senator Reed Smoot, Mormon Apostle.* Chapel Hill: University of North Carolina Press.
Gentry, L. H. (1973). "Adam-ondi-Ahman: A Brief Historical Survey." *BYU Studies, 15,* 553–576.
Hietala, T. R. (2003). *Manifest Design: American Exceptionalism and Empire* (Rev. ed.). Ithaca: Cornell University Press.
Hinckley, G. B. (1988). *Truth Restored and Gospel Principles.* Salt Lake City: Church of Jesus Christ of Latter-day Saints.
_____ (2001, November). "The Times in Which We Live." *Ensign, 31,* 72–74.
Hyde, O. (1860). "Celebration of American Independence." In G. D. Watt, J. V. Long and Others (Eds.), *Journal of Discourses: Vol. 4.* (pp. 107–110). Liverpool: Amasa Lyman.
Matthews, R. J. (1972). "Adam-ondi-Ahman." *BYU Studies, 13,* 1–8.
McConkie, B. R. (1985). *A New Witness for the Articles of Faith.* Salt Lake City: Deseret.
Mulder, W. (1957). *Homeward to Zion: The Mormon Migration from Scandinavia.* Minneapolis: University of Minnesota Press.
Newell, C. (2000). *Latter Days: A Guided Tour Through Six Billion Years of Mormonism.* New York: St. Martin's.
O'Dea, T. F. (1957). *The Mormons.* Chicago: University of Chicago Press.
Packer, B. K. (1980). *The Holy Temple.* Salt Lake City: Bookcraft.
Romney, M. G. (1980, March). "The Message: America's Promise." *New Era,* pp. 4–7.
Shupe, A., and J. Heinerman (1985). "Mormonism and the New Christian Right: An Emerging Coalition?" *Review of Religious Research, 27,* 146–157.
Smith, J. (1989). "Letter to an Editor." In R. L. Millet (Ed.), *Joseph Smith: Selected Sermons and Writings* (pp. 74–78). Mahwah, NJ: Paulist. (Original work published 1833.)
Tanner, N. E. (1977, July). "If They Will but Serve the God of the Land." *New Era,* pp. 36–41.

Tocqueville, A. de (2000). *Democracy in America* (J. P. Mayer, Ed.) (G. Lawrence, Trans.). New York: Perennial Classics. (Original work published 1848.)

Tuveson, E. L. (1980). *Redeemer Nation: The Idea of America's Millennial Role.* Chicago: University of Chicago Press.

Weisberg, J. (2007). "A Mormon President?" *Humanist, 67,* 4–5.

Whitney, O. F. (1945). *Life of Heber C. Kimball* (2d ed.). Salt Lake City: Stevens and Wallis.

Woodruff, W. (1878). "Discourse by Elder Wilford Woodruff." In B. Young, et al. (Eds.), *Journal of Discourses* (Vol. 19, pp. 223–230). Liverpool: William Budge.

Woodruff, W. (1897). "Historical Incidents — Keys of Power from Joseph to the Twelve — Founders of Our Nation Inspired — Afflictions Awaiting the World — Importance of Redeeming the Dead." In *Sixty-Eighth Semi-Annual Conference of the Church Of Jesus Christ of Latter-Day Saints, Held in the Tabernacle, Salt Lake City, October 4th, 5th and 6th, 1897, with a Full Report of the Discourses* (pp. 88–90). Salt Lake City: Deseret News.

Young, B. (1860). "Celebration of the Fourth of July." In G. D. Watt, J. V. Long, and Others (Eds.), *Journal of Discourses* (Vol. 7, pp. 9–15). Liverpool: Amasa Lyman.

CHAPTER 4

Re-Contextualizing Americanism
The National Association of Manufacturers' Jeremiad for Free Enterprise During the Roosevelt Era

BURTON ST. JOHN, III

By the mid–1930s, American business, still struggling with the lingering effects of the Depression, also perceived that the free enterprise system itself was at risk. Economic distress brought increased union activity, the consumer movement, increasingly vocal social reform advocates and the Roosevelt Administration's active approach to addressing the nation's economic challenges. Industry, formerly the benefactors of a widespread *laissez-faire* attitude toward business, was concerned, said Stuart Ewen, that "the long term balance of power seemed to be shifting" (1996, p. 292). Accordingly, during the late 1930s, the National Association of Manufacturers (henceforth, NAM) accelerated a propaganda campaign in defense of industry. "Silence may be golden, but more often than not it is damning in the face of repeated accusation," it said in a pamphlet for its members. "Few groups are more often under attack ... few groups are more misrepresented before the public" (NAM, n.d.a., p. 3). In particular, NAM was concerned that government had stepped forward to assume leadership on economic matters mainly because manufacturers have "not told the facts about industry to the public. They have let others speak to America while they remain silent," the group said (NAM, n.d.a., p. 3). It continued:

> American Industry today must make its position clear and appealing to the American public. Nothing more clearly proves the necessity of reselling to the people the industrial system that has given them by far the highest standard of

living in the world. This is the task before us. It is industry's duty to itself ... its duty to the public [NAM, n.d.a., p. 4].

This document revealed that corporate leaders believed that business still had the leading role in promoting economic and social order, as well as societal advancement. This view was emblematic of long-standing American exceptionalist values that trumpeted a symbiosis of individualism and unfettered private enterprise over the meddling of the state (Ellis, 1993; Lipset, 1996). This conviction had long been widely acknowledged, as evidenced in 1925 when President Calvin Coolidge said,

The chief business of the American people is business. They are profoundly concerned with producing, buying, selling, investing, and prospering in the world. I am strongly of the opinion that the great majority of people will always find these are moving impulses of our life [quoted in Sobel, 1998, pp. 313–314].

NAM's planning documents revealed its own expansive view of this exceptionalist strain. "Our tradition," it said, "is that the individual matters.... Individuals are the end; institutions, even the state, only the means" (NAM, 1941, p. 3). The association's perspective reflected an American exceptionalism that cast *laissez faire* as the progenitor of continued progress; any other system outside of free enterprise (e.g., socialism, communism) was unthinkable and against the natural order of things (Lewis, 1999; Rojecki, 2008; Tedlow, 1979).

However, this convention about the primacy of business interests ran against the grain of events in the Roosevelt era. The widespread financial collapse had called into question the authority of business, and the New Deal's activism emphasized that government should work to protect and restore citizens' economic security against the whims of the marketplace (Wall, 2008). In fact, NAM's own polling data revealed the public's growing disapproval of business. In 1937, the group reported that 66 percent of the public had an unfavorable opinion of industry, with almost half of all Americans believing that industry had not focused enough on addressing unemployment (NAM, 1937a). In contrast, the New Deal offered a series of works projects and labor laws that attempted to address Americans' difficulties with finding employment.

By the mid-to-late 1930s, industry leaders grew increasingly concerned that the state would continue to exert more influence and Americans would become acclimated to a strong government presence in the marketplace. NAM determined that industry could best re-assert itself by extolling how, through free enterprise, business delivered on the promise of progress for every American. Beginning around 1937, NAM formulated a righteous jeremiad that emphasized Americans needed to re-embrace the links between the free enterprise system and American exceptionalist notions of freedom and progress.

NAM's use of the jeremiad was a part of a mass persuasion campaign known as integration propaganda. This kind of propaganda, as identified by Jacques Ellul (1965), speaks to a society's values and beliefs in an attempt to link individuals to the desires of the propagandist. NAM appealed to citizens to look beyond the financial fallout of the Depression toward the American exceptionalist ideal that each individual had the opportunity to reach for progress. Americans should not become dependent on the government for help, it said; instead, said the association, progress could best be realized by Americans holding strong to the covenant with business paternalism, a leadership that had led the country to "health, happiness and conditions of working and living that are best in the world." In fact, America's Depression "is a luxury in any other part of the world," it proclaimed (NAM, n.d.b., p. 1). Essentially, NAM's jeremiad appropriated exceptionalist ideas of achievement, progress, and individualism and linked them to the idea that Americans could continue to trust in business leadership to help citizens endure, and ultimately overcome, economic hard times.

NAM's ability to associate foundational beliefs about America's exceptional nature with the primacy of business has profound implications to this day. At this writing the lingering effects of the recession of 2008 and the country's health care debate of 2009 have severely tested the notion of this covenant with free enterprise in the United States. Still, government officials, business leaders, pundits, and even many economists call upon American society to sustain business, until free enterprise can re-assert its leadership role. However, business's willingness to accept the increasing penetration of the government into the free enterprise sphere (e.g., through bailouts and subsidies) has now strained the credibility of exceptionalist views that trumpet an unsullied symbiosis of individual and marketplace.

American Exceptionalism

In the 1990s, scholars described American exceptionalism as a longenduring ideology that is centered on the fundamental values of liberty, democracy, egalitarianism, equality, individualism, civil liberties, *laissez-faire*, and a belief in the power of the free market (Ellis, 1993; Lipset, 1996; Wilson, 1998). These values, taken individually, are, of course, not unique to the U.S., but, collectively, they operate in a distinctive way. In particular, they serve to orient Americans toward a belief in perpetual progress, taking the "improvement of the human condition as a given" (Rojecki, 2008, p. 69). American exceptionalism evolved from the early puritan model that spoke, in both pragmatic and spiritual terms, of an inimitably non–European sense of self-sufficiency and purpose (Bercovitch, 1978). It stressed that individuals must chart their direction, while also emphasizing that such an entrepreneurial perspective must be in service to the Maker. Accordingly, to find the purpose God had set for him or her, the individual must be in a continual state of striving. Over time, American exceptionalism gradually secularized this impetus, emphasizing that the country's socio-economic progress is propelled uniquely through the discrete acts of citizens; in this way, exceptionalism cast the American implementation of a democratic society as the truly ideal model (Lewis, 1999). Furthermore, over the decades, the country has evolved an American Creed, a view that American society is centered on asserting the rights of the individual against the power of the government. As Lipset noted, America "began and continues as the most anti-statist" nation (1996, p. 20).

At the same time, Americans also experience a sense of conflict about exceptionalism's tendency to pull citizens out of communion with others. Americans are subject to a stress that comes from the inner tensions of "collective individualism"; citizens struggle with the need "to strike a balance between the absence of restraint and the ability to belong" (Kammen, 1972, p. 269). Ellis (1993) pointed to a tension that has been present in America since its colonial days — a strong streak of individualism that stresses opportunity for achievement, in conflict with an egalitarianism that prefers there be no wide disparity in results. Additionally, there is a least one large factor that contributes to citizens' sense of dissonance about the creed. While Americans espouse that their society prizes the ideal of individual advancement against the constraints of cultural, socio-economic, or governmental factors, wealth inequality in the U.S. is pronounced, with one percent of Americans controlling about one-third of the country's net worth (McNamee and Miller, 2009). Therefore, Americans may profess that class distinctions are minimal and that the opportunities for social mobility are abundant, but structural inequalities in wealth distribution make visions of egalitarianism more myth than reality (Wilson, 1998).

The Jeremiad and Integration Propaganda

The jeremiad is a rhetorical form that calls upon members of an audience to understand that they have fallen away from a covenant with their basic values. Furthermore, the jeremiad points to the dangers that await its listeners if they continue on their wayward path, and then calls upon the audience to "come home" to its values to avoid disaster (Bercovitch, 1978; Jones and Rowland, 2005; Owen, 2002). The jeremiad's European origins stressed conformity to authority and "resignation to one's lot in life"; in the American colonies, the Puritans transformed it into a call for "continual striving for improvement and progress" (Ellis, 1993, p. 170). Still, even transformed for American use, the jeremiad is a rhetoric of social control. It is designed, in times of crisis, to present to the public a vision of an America characterized by "a constant movement toward a special destiny, sanctioned by God" (Murphy, 1990, p. 412). In particular, the American jeremiad's spiritual overtone of the valiance of personal striving and self-reliance linked well to capitalism's aura of individual enterprise. Indeed, the American jeremiad built such strong associations between an individual's "faith in process" work orientation and capitalism's entrepreneurship model that it presented the free enterprise system as sanctifying the toils of the individual (Bercovitch, 1978, pp. 22–23). Jones and Rowland have pointed out that the American jeremiad can be adjusted to emphasize this state of grace aspect. They have shown that some rhetors use a variation called the "covenant-affirming" jeremiad, wherein the audience is told that the covenant, although strained, has not been broken. Instead, in times of trial, the audience needs to hold stronger to the blessings of the covenant and realize that problems can be overcome through an "ideological adaptation" (2005, pp. 161–162).

In NAM's case, the covenant-affirming jeremiad was crucial to their integration propaganda campaign to restore the primacy of industry. The term "propaganda" often carries with it pejorative connotations, customarily associated with manipulative campaigns in service of governments, political parties, and corporate entities. However, up until World War I, the term was more neutral, understood as "the spreading of self-interested opinions through publicity" (Sproule, 1997, p. 9), and sometimes even carried reputable connotations as it was linked to the efforts of religious figures (Irwin, 1936). After the propaganda efforts of World War I, critics re-examined propaganda and found that it had manipulated Americans into the war effort. Consequently, from the 1920s on, propaganda has often been studied as a deceitful form of communication (Jowett and O'Donnell, 1992; Sproule, 1997). The present examination situates NAM's use of the jeremiad within a more functional view of propaganda — that is, it features systematically constructed messages designed to move mass audiences toward acceptance of attitudes, predispositions, and behaviors that will benefit a privileged group (Cunningham, 2002; Sproule, 1997). Furthermore, this study explores how NAM used the jeremiad as a rhetorical iteration of integration propaganda, a type of propaganda described by Jacques Ellul as a propaganda of conformity. It is related to the fact ... that in Western society it is no longer sufficient to obtain a transitory political act (such as a vote); one needs total adherence to a society's *truths and behavioral patterns*. As the more perfectly uniform the society ... each member should be ... perfectly adapted and integrated [1965, pp. 74–75; emphasis added].[1]

By 1935, NAM began its propaganda campaign, focusing on how to appeal to the American exceptionalist notions of a symbiotic relationship between individualism and free enterprise. However, NAM archival material reveals that the organization did not begin to make these links more explicit until 1937. The goal, said a NAM PR plan from that year, was to make people aware of the dangers of government intrusion and re-affirm business's covenant with Americans: in exchange for its unfettered place in society, American industry offered unsurpassed material well-being (e.g., payrolls, tax contributions, charitable giving, pension plans) for all classes of citizens (NAM, 1937). To achieve its goal, the group constructed a jeremiad that (1) established a need for vigilance against the rise of the power of the state; (2) warned that creeping statism could fatally undermine private enterprise's ability to provide Americans a uniquely high standard of living; and (3) issued a call for citizens to support free enterprise as essential for the maintenance of both individual liberties and the rewards of the marketplace.

The Need for Vigilance Against the State

NAM was concerned about Americans becoming acclimated to the rise of government activism—especially since the Roosevelt administration was often prodded by labor unions, consumerist movements, and social reformers (Ewen, 1996; Wall, 2008). Its covenant-affirming rhetoric normally accentuated the individualistic values of Americanism rather than make direct accusations against the state. Accordingly, one of the prevailing strands in NAM's messages was reinforcing to Americans that the free enterprise system acted in concert with American beliefs that human liberties were paramount, to be served by the government. In a pamphlet produced about the nation's "system," NAM devoted several of the first pages to delineating constitutionally guaranteed rights. It then stated:

> Nowhere is the individual man more secure in his personal liberty than in the United States. There are, of course, miscarriages of justice. There are even outrageous outbreaks of mob rule—but by and large, as it affects 127,000,000 persons, the American system functions with the greatest liberty for all the people [NAM, 1936, p. 10].

Therefore, said NAM, the American system was based on a belief that individuals should be free of the entanglements of the state. The country's way of life featured a "system of economic individualism [where] the political supremacy of the individual is possible" putting into practice the realization that the "essence of real civilization is the retention and growth of the liberties of the individual" (NAM, 1936, p. 11). This was most apparent in how the individual could enter the free market and produce, buy, and sell materials and services, it said, "securing the greatest good for the greatest number in steadily rising number" (NAM, 1936, p. 16).

In another pamphlet published at approximately the same time, NAM asserted that America's economic individualism allowed citizens to achieve three objectives: "equality of opportunity, a higher standard of living and a classless society." The free market system, the association said, provides "social justice in its highest form." Mass production offered all citizens affordable products, increased employment opportunities and enhanced buying power. (NAM, n.d.c., p. 4). In yet another contemporaneous pamphlet, NAM said the benefits of the American private enterprise system were so extensive that, even though the country had but a small fraction of the world's population and land mass, its "percentage in the worldly goods, [its] enjoyment of comforts and usage of new inventions and achievements is greater than anywhere else" (NAM, n.d.d., p.4). It continued:

> We have produced three times as much wealth as the whole world had been able to produce up to 1776. And this wealth has been so generally distributed that the average man here became a magnet to attract others from all over the world.... Is this a social order worth every protection and safeguard? [NAM, n.d.d., p. 4].

To NAM, this was not a rhetorical question: the group's materials often emphasized the pitfalls of complacency about growing statism. Remarks prepared for a NAM's speaker bureau speech from the late 1930s urged listeners to understand that the government's interventionist policies often attacked industry. In doing so, NAM said, is not the demagogue "attacking your community whose welfare depends on industry?" (NAM, n.d.e., p. 1). It urged citizens to realize that when American industry was attacked, when "exuberant theorists and calculating agitators would destroy our industrial system, such attacks strike home" and should not be ignored (NAM, n.d.e., p. 1). If left unchecked, utopian philosophies, planned economy and interfering regulations would undermine the free enterprise system and contribute to the lingering depression, NAM said.

It was essential that Americans resist adapting to the government's desire to wield more power, said the group. In another undated pamphlet, NAM maintained that what was once a popular expression, "let George do it" was becoming "let the government do it." Where "George" may not have always been willing, "governments through history have been ready to take more and more power, to undertake new activities. And then take more taxes to pay for the extra jobs," it said (NAM, n.d.f., p. 2). Rather than being compliant with an activist government, Americans must become more aware that when they allow the government to increasingly regulate their daily lives, they put their most sacred liberties at risk. Citizens may be mistakenly confident that current office holders will use their increased power judiciously. However, after those officials depart, the rising influence of the government remains, it said. "Governments love power!" said NAM. "Don't give any government the right to dictate where you shall work, when you shall work and what your wages shall be!" the group urged (NAM, n.d.f., p. 4).

Instead, citizens should be aware of how industry made the American way of life possible, it said. In a late-1930s pamphlet, the association provided an overview of how a typical plant in a small city served as an engine for employment, infrastructure, taxes for state and federal services, and payroll spending throughout the community. Town and factory are interdependent, it said, a microcosm of how the free enterprise system allowed individuals to flourish, chart their own directions in life, and develop a standard of living unmatched by any other country. NAM alerted individuals to what they had at stake if they allowed government activism to penetrate too much of the private sphere:

> The town and the factory depend upon each other, and this one small example is repeated and multiplied the country over, until, in great sum total, we have America—the greatest industrial nation in the world, the country with the highest standard of living and the best and happiest communities yet conceived by man [NAM, n.d.g., pp. 2–3].

Of course, the state was not mentioned in this portrait. Instead, NAM chose to illustrate an America that thrived on the hard work of individuals, enabled by a free market that provided the infrastructure and encouragement for personal striving and achievement. With such an approach, NAM attempted to affirm not only a positive link between American individualism and industry, but to also subtly warn about the need for vigilance against the rise of a state that could intrude on the mutual success of citizens and business.

The Ills of Creeping Statism

The second element of NAM's covenant-affirming jeremiad featured a more direct portrayal of the dangers of increasing governmental control over the free enterprise system. In an undated NAM internal memo from the late 1930s, board member George Houston, an executive of a Philadelphia locomotive firm, maintained that the fundamental concern before the country was either acquiescing to the government's desire for national economic planning or upholding the nation's tradition of free enterprise. There was no way to compromise between the two routes, Houston said. He maintained that the government wanted to control the markets by balancing production and consumption and that "free enterprise cannot live in the face of [such] coercion" (NAM, n.d.h., p. 4). The New Deal was jeopardizing the free enterprise system, he said, and that "American institutions in general, built upon individual liberty, are in peril." It was crucial for NAM to make sure this larger, systemic concern did not fall into the realm of abstractions; it "must be made intensely real to the American people," he said (NAM, n.d.h., p. 4).

NAM worked to make clear to the public how government activism could disrupt Americans' personal liberties and diminish each person's quality of life. In a pamphlet from the same period, it claimed that an overweening government was contributing to the nation's struggle to recuperate from the lingering effects of the Depression. While the state believed that a combination of regulations and an infusion of federal funds into the economy would spur recovery, it was actually intervening "in the ordinary process of production and distribution," NAM said. In doing so, the government reduced individual initiative and ingenuity, kept "freedom of opportunity to a minimum" and put "brakes upon human freedom" (NAM, 1936, p. 12). Instead of prizing the liberty of each individual to achieve, the New Deal's activism too often chose to emphasize the needs of particular groups while it placed a "dead hand upon the lives" of others (NAM, 1936, p. 13).

NAM's rhetoric revealed a strong concern about government interventionism furthering the cause of labor unions. The association particularly emphasized to working-class Americans — who ostensibly could readily identify with labor — that an activist state that intervened in workplace concerns was anathema to American individualism. In a 1939 pamphlet, NAM affirmed that the Roosevelt Administration furthered pro-labor laws that moved beyond protecting individual rights and "into the field of affirmative control and direction, [becoming] a serious obstacle to the effective functioning of enterprise" (NAM, 1939a, p. 4). The following year, NAM president Henning Prentiss claimed government's intrusiveness, mostly in the cause of labor, had created a morass that impeded free enterprise. The federal bureaucracy was out of control, he said, evident by its creation of more than 130 commissions and agencies, and a compulsion to keep creating workplace regulations. The government upset economic progress because this jumble of agencies inconsistently applied work rules and, in the process, helped sow confusion and inefficiency, he said (NAM, 1940b).

The government's activism, said NAM, created uncertainty about the markets, dissuading men from putting forth capital to help spur economic recovery. In a 1939 pamphlet about job creation, NAM sent a questionnaire to "thousands of present investors" in the United States and found that 75 percent of respondents had additional monies available but weren't willing to provide funding (NAM, 1939b, p. 3). More than two-thirds of these retrenched investors said that existing and proposed government regulations and taxes and current and possible labor troubles were their reasons for holding back on supplying capital for the markets. NAM pointed out that these hesitant investors saw overheated government spending and intrusive government interventions into private enterprise as driving down potential profits (NAM, 1939b). The association used this data to point out that the New Deal's interventions into the business sphere translated into more than simply lowering the bottom line for industry. As government leveraged more of the tools at its disposal — taxes, regulations, creation of new labor laws, and infusing federal dollars into works projects — NAM maintained that jittery investors perceived that the free marketplace was increasingly subject to the whims of government bureaucrats. An invasive government led to investor reluctance to support new endeavors, said NAM, threatening individuals' opportunities to find work, advance their careers and standards of living, or even create their own enterprise.

All of these signs — state intrusion into free market production and distribution, legislation that disproportionately favored labor over industry, the growth of a government bureaucracy that imposed mounting state prerogatives, and the dampening of investor infusions of capital into the markets — pointed to the danger of the New Deal's attempts to implement a planned economy, said NAM. Such a regime is inflexible and cannot meet the demands required of production, chiefly because "no one central authority attempting to dictate the operating practice in industry has the knowledge required to solve these problems" (NAM, 1939a, p. 3). The association, calling this approach the method of the totalitarian state, described it as an alien system that was repellent to Americans. "It destroys personal liberty, religious freedom and individual initiative," said NAM, because all individual freedoms must be surrendered to make a planned economy work (NAM, 1939a, p. 3). The group's clarion call was clear: The New Deal's approach to business violates American precepts of individual self-determination, putting everyone's liberties at risk.

The Call for Citizens to Support Free Enterprise

The last element of NAM's covenant-affirming jeremiad focused on how free enterprise — powered by American individualism — was the optimal formula to bring about the country's recovery. In a declaration of principles it said that "the American citizen wants an opportunity to earn the necessities of life and the comforts and luxuries that go to make life richer." Free enterprise was the resource that allowed an American the opportunity "to feel secure — in his liberties and for his person, in his job and for his old age, in himself and for his family," the association said (NAM, 1939a, p. 1).

Consequently, NAM's rhetorical appeal exalted America's uniqueness, pointing out to Americans that individualism and free enterprise provided a source of resilience during tough times. In a speakers bureau speech, it said:

> Anyone who has had the opportunity to travel and to live for any extended period in other countries than the one we know and love as the United States of America will undoubtedly reach the conclusion that the land of the stars and stripes is the most prosperous, happy, and developed of them all. Even a depression in America is prosperity in the lands of our neighbors East and West across the seas [NAM, n.d.b., p. 1].

American institutions and social structures point to a happy and healthy people that is unmatched, the group said. American blessings are "the fruits of thrift and free enterprise, freedom and democratic chance for self-expression and growth" (NAM, n.d.b., p. 1). Why would any American want a substitute for a society "wrought by created and instructed minds, thrifty and hard-working bodies, inspired and consecrated souls?" it asked. (NAM, n.d.b., p. 1). NAM answered its own question by asserting that Americans knew that their individualist way of life was best as it was based on God leaving "the world unfinished that we, his immortal sons, might feel its challenge and take the raw material and put the picture puzzle together" (NAM, n.d.b., p. 4).

At the same time, Americans needed to understand that the interventions of government could regulate and inhibit the individual's liberties and initiatives. NAM asserted its opposition to such restrictions and made a link between each citizen's opportunity to achieve and the essentiality of the free market:

> Give freedom to the brains and energy of men. Do not paralyze them with dictatorship, do not cause them to atrophy under regimentation, do not render them impotent with initiative killed. Turn them loose — inspire them ... reward them in good old American free enterprise fashion [NAM, n.d.b., p. 5].

And the rewards of free enterprise for the average American were numerous, said NAM. The association pointed out that the symbiosis between the markets and individualism resulted in not only opportunities for personal achievement, but a high quality lifestyle. The American standard of living — measured in great part by access to electricity, modern plumbing and a wide range of consumer goods — has increased fourfold from 1790 until 1930, it said. Meanwhile, the average number of hours in a work week went from about 60 in 1890 to almost 48 in 1936. The United States "has the highest per capita ownership of wealth on earth," the group said, with the amount of national income paid out in wages and salaries increasing from 38 percent in 1850 to about 65 percent in 1929 (NAM, 1936, p. 20). NAM reminded citizens that their ability to attain such material well-being was rooted in the premium that Americans placed on both individualism and the markets. Such exceptional increases in standard of living are unique to the American system, NAM said, "a system in which the state is the servant of the citizen rather than the citizen being the servant of the state. No other system of the past or present can show such a record" (1936, p. 21).

Finally, Americans needed to know that this ability to chart one's life and acquire material well-being was indicative of the country's unique ability to deliver social justice, said NAM. The American individualist way allowed each person to develop one's abilities and genius without regard to place of birth, race, or religion. "The American economic system, under the Constitution, provides equal opportunity for all," the association said, continuing, "this is social justice in its highest form" (NAM, n.d.c., p. 2). Citizens were also able to achieve a high standard of living because the mass production system provided them affordable products, increased employment and increased buying power. This chain of efficient production and affordable goods and services allowed wealth to be disseminated among all Americans, NAM claimed. Wealth was spread through enhanced buying power; further, citizens could participate in such a flow of economic benefits because America

> is a classless society [where there] can there be equality of opportunity and a rising standard of living for the greatest number. Under the American Economic System, society is classless. All men enjoy equality of opportunity. The door to success is open to any man or woman [NAM, n.d.c., p. 4].

In this third element of the jeremiad, NAM asserted that, rather than succumb to the interventions of the state, citizens needed to more deeply realize the strengths of the American way. Rather than a "big business" argument, NAM offered a "big individualism" appeal. Essentially, NAM told Americans to re-connect with their best selves: the self-propelling, industrious individualist, who was blessed to work in an exceptional country whose matchless economic system allowed people of all stripes to advance both their sense of personal fulfillment and their standard of living. Individuals could indeed open the "door to success," but NAM was also reminding citizens that a distinctly American free enterprise system built that door in the first place.

Implications

NAM's jeremiad in the Roosevelt era attempted to recontextualize traditional American exceptionalist truth and behavior patterns regarding independence, liberty and egalitarianism. As part of this re-contextualization of Americanism, NAM used a jeremiad strategy that bolstered American values that tended to privilege the free market system. Although Lipset (1996) maintained that post–World War II prosperity contributed to the re-ascendancy of free market values, it would appear that NAM had already accomplished some rehabilitation of free enterprise prior to that war. After NAM diffused its jeremiad widely through pamphlets, brochures, speeches and mass media, it commissioned independent polls in the late 1930s that revealed a reverse in public apprehension about industry and an increased concern about the ascendancy of the state in economic affairs. For example, in 1937, as NAM ramped up its propaganda campaign, two-thirds of the public expressed an unfavorable opinion of business, and almost half of Americans believed that industry had done little to address unemployment (NAM, 1937a). However, by the end of 1939, NAM released a nationwide survey that indicated 53 percent of Americans said that recovery would be more rapid if government would leave business alone to increase industrial production. A separate question revealed that 60 percent of respondents believed government should take more advice from business ("Curbs on Industry," 1939).

NAM's use of the covenant-affirming jeremiad played a significant role in achieving this level of support from the public. The association's rhetorical approach worked on several levels to coax Americans into accepting the primacy of business, while simultaneously avoiding strategies that might inadvertently appear to attack working class Americans who had turned to Roosevelt's work and relief programs. First, rather than accuse Americans of abandoning their values, it warned that the public was putting its principles at risk by becoming unconcerned about the nation's overactive government. Second, NAM rhetoric tended to avoid absolutes — it saw a rightful place for a judicious government that clearly defined laws and regulations that allowed business to flourish. By also affirming this idea of a circumspect government in American society, NAM further avoided an overly negative and accusatory tone. Instead, it simply attempted to cajole Americans toward making an ideological adaptation to the state's increased role — be watchful, it said, of the state stepping too much into all arenas and, therefore, impinging on your liberties. Third, NAM often accentuated the positives, stressing that Americans could help constrain an overreaching state by aligning themselves with business as the true engine of recovery for the country. Finally, the association's use of a covenant-affirming jeremiad allowed it to avoid a hectoring quality that would have revealed a fear that it had, indeed, already lost much of its leadership role. By sounding vigilant, yet reassuring, NAM subtly positioned industry as continuing in its rightful pledge to act in concert with America's exceptionalist values of liberty, individualism and entrepreneurship and lead the country out of tough times.

Encouraged by the effectiveness of this rhetorical approach, NAM had greatly solidified their concept of Americanism by early 1940. That year the organization more precisely described the symbiosis between citizens and industry by referring to a "tripod of freedom." NAM president Henning Prentiss described the tripod as an inseparable linking of democratic governance, religious liberty and free enterprise, arguing that

> on that spiritual concept rests the free man's right to participation in government, in other words, representative democracy. On it rests man's right to be free to worship, to read, to think, write and speak, as his conscience directs, and to enjoy other traditional civil liberties. On that concept also rests the right of man to determine for himself the course of his economic life — the right to use his individual initiative in private enterprise. In other words, the spiritual principle of the sanctity of the individual soul is the foundation of our entire American system of government, economics and civil and religious liberty [NAM, 1940b, p. 3].

Americans must be careful, he said, that continued economic hardship did not erode our faith "in the economic system under which America has built, on an industrial foundation, the greatest, the most prosperous, the freest civilization this world has ever known" (NAM, 1940b, p.4). If we doubted our system, Prentiss said, we could fall prey to those who called for national economic planning. When a group of people designed for everyone what they thought was best, they would not abide individuals who put forth views that would upset their plans, he continued. Eventually, planners would seek to control the dissemination of dissenting viewpoints and clamp down on the press, churches and schools. Then, Americans would see the complete collapse of the tripod — all for the desire to have the fleeting security that government would bring, Prentiss warned. Rather than rely on the whims and caprices of the state, Americans should feel confident that business was the better partner for all for two fundamental reasons. First, industry, along with all Americans, cherished a spiritual freedom that recognized "the full social value of individual initiative and enterprise." Second, business worked to support a distinctively American civilization that recognized all men as persons with rights "that no rulers or classes or majorities may annul" (NAM, 1940b, p. 16).

This appeal to American exceptionalism reveals how the propagandist can appropriate what an audience sees as crucial cultural values and convince the audience to bind itself even tighter to those beliefs. NAM's integration propaganda campaign attempted to reinforce the individual's conviction that he or she acts out of self-interest. This is apparent in a NAM jeremiad that worked in three parts. First, it asserted the need for citizens to be watchful about an increasingly activist government. Second, it pointed to specific dysfunctions of the state's intrusions. Third, it called on Americans to assert their values and interests against growing statism by supporting free enterprise. In concert with Jones and Rowland's (2005) concept of the covenant-affirming jeremiad, NAM's rhetoric allowed the group to leverage existing values and ask the audience to avoid state-induced dramatic upheaval in favor of an ideological adjustment. The tripod of freedom — with its equal emphases on representative government, civil liberties, and free-enterprise — served as a vehicle to encourage that ideological adjustment. In particular, the tripod metaphor stressed that Americans should insist upon a more prudent government, one that was essential, but not so active as to imperil American exceptionalist notions of liberty, freedom, and egalitarianism.

Such a covenant-affirming approach, when cast within a larger integration propaganda campaign, subtly called the audience to align itself with the concerns of a privileged interest — an interest whose agenda may not actually have been in concert with the audience's. For example, while it touted individualism, the intent of NAM's propaganda campaign, said one of its early PR plans, was to actually "build up a feeling of closer partnership between management and labor so that both can better fight the very strong tendencies ... in this country toward a more complete bureaucratic political control of our everyday lives" (NAM, 1937, p. 9). However, NAM's jeremiad did not betray this idea of building such an institutional alliance with labor. Instead, its rhetoric consistently evoked the individual as the valiant creator of an America that uniquely excelled on the world stage. Said NAM President Colby Chester:

> Hey, America isn't done! It is just beginning! ... It needs to be reminded that we can run faster, build taller buildings, eat more, jump higher than anyone else; that our women are lovelier; our men are more honest; our children smarter; our history more dazzling than that of any people on the face of the globe. America needs to be reminded that we can lick our weight in wildcats ... that we build a bungalow or a school for every outhouse a dictator builds [NAM, 1940c, pp. 27–28].

Therefore, while its internal plans may have been more pragmatic about coalition-building, for public consumption NAM chose rhetoric that extolled the individual attaining new heights through the opportunities of the free market. It was a fateful decision. At this writing, this linking of American exceptionalist notions of individualism with free enterprise continues. However, since the days of NAM's tripod, the role of the state has become problematic in a different way — reflecting an unsettled bipolarity about what is considered a judicious role of the state relative to free enterprise and individuals.

On one hand, as the nation finds itself dealing with the turmoil of a difficult recession, government officials, accompanied by business leaders, pundits and even many economists, have called upon Americans to uphold a covenant with free enterprise. *Newsweek* columnist Fareed Zakaria exemplified this viewpoint, maintaining that the state, representing the people, could intervene in a "large and systemic manner" to restore free enterprise:

> Modern capitalism depends on credit, and credit depends on confidence. By the middle of last week, fear was pervasive and no one was ready to lend money to anyone for any purpose. It turned out that only government intervention could change this psychological paralysis. The lesson of the almost 100 (smaller) financial crises of the past three decades is that only government intervention can stabilize the system when it chokes.... [Next] should come the fixes needed to better structure America's massive and complex financial markets [2008, p. 22].

This covenantal thinking was dramatically apparent in the fall of 2008 as the Bush Administration successfully advocated the routing of $700 billion in taxpayer funds to distressed corporations on Wall Street. A *New York Times* piece on Treasury Secretary Henry Paulson's efforts to explain the funding revealed a continuing rhetoric of association between individualism and free enterprise:

> Resolving the financial problems is of paramount importance, not just for major corporations and investment banks but for people who have never set foot in the corridors of corporate and political power, Mr. Paulson said. "Their retirement savings, their home values, their ability to borrow for college" and their chance to find and keep good jobs depend on it, he said [Stout, 2008].

Thus, Americans were informed that huge infusions of tax funds into large capital enterprises were necessary, as the individual's fate was inexorably linked to the firm financial footing of Wall Street financial institutions.

Alternatively, as the federal government also seeks to assert itself into the realm of healthcare, it finds that, to many Americans, the state's efforts run counter to the covenant between free enterprise and individualism. Many citizens went to "town hall" meetings with congressional representatives and voiced concerns that the United States government intended to take over the health care industry and, therefore, break up this particular conjunction of individual choice and the private marketplace. Aside from the partisan hyperbole that often accompanies any major government initiative, the town hall skirmishes revealed lingering concerns about the proper place of government that reflect the legacy of NAM's jeremiad of American exceptionalism. That jeremiad not only held up the American idea of individualism exerting itself through free enterprise — it insisted that this form of living was so fundamental, and so negating of other alternatives, that it would be "difficult to imagine how else things could be" (Lewis, 1999, p. 258). Wilson (1998), however, has pointed out that many nations develop in similar ways, but at different rates. Since the end of World War II, most industrialized nations have seen their governments take an increasing role in health care as part of the development of the welfare state. Wilson likened those nations to a convoy that moves in the same direction. The United States, he said, is toward the rear of that convoy, but "the direction in which the American state heads is in the direction of the convoy's other members" (1998, p. 131).

Wilson's observations concerning this matter are prescient. Today, the American state does appear more active, whether it is attempting to subsidize stability in certain business sectors or advance legislative changes (like health care reform) that affect other profit-making enterprises. And the fundamental tension that Americans face for the foreseeable future is to grapple with the decades-long exceptionalist notion that free enterprise is linked inextricably with individuals and that each American

> is confident that with all his problems, his troubles, and his uncertainties, he is better off here than elsewhere, and that in such a free society a wider range of individual opportunity and a higher level of living are attainable than where arbitrary power controls the minds and work and destinies of men [NAM, 1941, p. 2].

The recent economic downturn in the United States has placed under renewed examination this notion of the individual advancing optimally through the agency of the free market. Ironically, it was not the "arbitrary power" of the government that brought this long strand of exceptionalism under revived scrutiny. Instead, it was the financial captains of free enterprise themselves — long acclimated to their own primacy in the United States — who, when faced with the loss of their economic moorings, acquiesced to financial interventions from the state. These interventions called into question the long-held, mythical notion that individuals and free enterprise, unhampered by a quiescent state, worked together to advance America. Essentially, NAM, during the New Deal, had trumpeted the idea of big individualism.

However, in 2008, when Wall Street accepted federal funds and associated mandates, the decades-long aversion to marked government penetration into the private sphere went into at least partial eclipse. So, too, have some of the American exceptionalist links between individualism and free enterprise — at least until the pair can be recontextualized again.

Notes

1. Ellul's concept of integration propaganda is similar to the bandwagon approach identified by Alfred and Elizabeth Lee (1939) in *The Fine Art of Propaganda*. However, there appear to be some subtle differences. The bandwagon tactic stresses that the individual pay attention to how peers are "on board" with a propagandist's message. Ellul's idea of integration propaganda addresses how the propagandist leverages the individual's unquestioning association of personal values to the wider culture. Therefore, the bandwagon approach may be more successful on an almost faddish or fleeting level. Conversely, integration propaganda strategies attempt to forge more deeply held associations between the individual's worldviews and the needs, wants and desires of the vested interest behind the propaganda.

References

Bercovitch, S. (1978). *The American Jeremiad*. Madison: University of Wisconsin Press.
Cunningham, S. (2002). *The Idea of Propaganda: A Reconstruction*. Westport, CT: Praeger.
"Curbs on Industry Found Unpopular; Survey for Manufacturers Shows Majority of Public has Faith in Business; Recovery Held its Task; 60 Percent of Those Questioned Say Government Should Take the Advice of Industrialists." (1939, December 8). *New York Times*, p. 18.
Ellis, R. (1993). *American Political Cultures*. New York: Oxford University Press.
Ellul, J. (1965). *Propaganda: The Formation of Men's Attitudes*. New York: Random House.
Ewen, S. (1996) *PR! A Social History of Spin*. New York: Basic.
Jones, J. M., and R. Rowland (2005). "A Covenant-Affirming Jeremiad: The Post-Presidential Ideological Appeals of Ronald Wilson Reagan." *Communication Studies, 56*, 157–174.
Jowett, G. S., and V. O'Donnell (1999) *Propaganda and Persuasion* (3d ed.). Thousand Oaks, CA: Sage.
Kammen, M. (1972). *People of Paradox: An Inquiry Concerning the Origins of American Civilization*. New York: Alfred A. Knopf
Lee, A., and E. Lee (1939). *The Fine Art of Propaganda: A Study of Father Coughlin's Speeches*. New York: Harcourt Brace.
Lewis, J. (1999). "Reproducing Political Hegemony." *Critical Studies in Mass Communication, 16*, 251–267.
Lipset, S. (1996). *American Exceptionalism: A Double-Edged Sword*. New York: W.W. Norton.
McNamee, S., and R. Miller (2009). *The Meritocracy Myth* (2d ed). Lanham, MD: Rowman and Littlefield.
Murphy, J. M. (1990). "A Time of Shame and Sorrow: Robert F. Kennedy and the American Jeremiad." *Quarterly Journal of Speech, 76*, 401–414.
NAM [National Association of Manufacturers]. (n.d.a.). *Industry Must Speak* [Pamphlet]. Acc. 1411, Box 843, Series I. NAM Archive, Hagley Museum, Wilmington, DE.
_____ (n.d.b.). *Industry and the Public* [Speaker's bureau speech]. Acc. 1411, Box 110, Series I. NAM Archive, Hagley Museum, Wilmington, DE.

_____ (n.d.c.). *Social Justice: What Is It?* [Pamphlet]. Acc. 1411, Box 114, Series I. NAM Archive, Hagley Museum, Wilmington, DE.
_____ (n.d.d.). *So This is America!* [Pamphlet]. Acc. 1411, Box 114, Series I. NAM Archive, Hagley Museum, Wilmington, DE.
_____ (n.d.e.). *Your City's Stake in Industry* [Speaker's bureau speech]. Acc. 1411, Box 115, Series I. NAM Archive, Hagley Museum, Wilmington, DE.
_____ (n.d.f.). *Let George Do It.* [Pamphlet]. Acc. 1411, Box 114, Series I. NAM Archive, Hagley Museum, Wilmington, DE.
_____ (n.d.g.). *Industryville: The Story of Your Town.* [Pamphlet]. Acc. 1411, Box 110, Series I. NAM Archive, Hagley Museum, Wilmington, DE.
_____ (n.d.h.). *Memo.* Acc. 1411, Box 113, Series I. NAM Archive, Hagley Museum, Wilmington, DE.
_____ (1936). *What Is Your American System All About?* [Pamphlet]. Acc. 1411, Box 114, Series I. NAM Archive, Hagley Museum, Wilmington, DE.
_____ (1937). *A Suggested Public Relations Program for Smithville* [Unpublished memorandum]. Acc. 1411, Box 111, Series I. NAM Archive, Hagley Museum, Wilmington, DE.
_____ (1939a). *Declaration of Principles Relating to the Conduct of American Industry* [Pamphlet]. Acc. 1411, Box 110, Series I. NAM Archive, Hagley Museum, Wilmington, DE .
_____ (1939b). *A Key to More Jobs* [Pamphlet]. Acc. 1411, Box 115, Series I. NAM Archive, Hagley Museum, Wilmington, DE.
_____ (1940a, March 15). *The Triangle of Freedom* [Transcript of unpublished speech delivered at joint regional meeting of NAM and the Associated Industries of Kentucky, Louisville]. Acc. 1411, Box 2, Series I. NAM Archive, Hagley Museum, Wilmington, DE.
_____ (1940b, April 9). *Freedom to Progress* [Transcript of unpublished speech delivered at regional meeting of the NAM and the Virginia Manufacturers Association, Richmond]. Acc. 1411, Box 2, Series I. NAM Archive, Hagley Museum, Wilmington, DE.
_____ (1940c, July). *NAM Speaker Bulletin.* Acc. 1411, Box 110, Series I. NAM Archive, Hagley Museum, Wilmington DE,
_____ (1941). *I'm Glad I'm an American* [Pamphlet]. Acc. 1411, Box 111, Series I. NAM Archive, Hagley Museum, Wilmington, DE.
Owen, A. (2002). "Memory, War, and American Identity: *Saving Private Ryan* as Cinematic Jeremiad." *Critical Studies in Media Communication, 19,* 249–282.
Rojecki, A. (2008). "Rhetorical Alchemy: American Exceptionalism and the War on Terror." *Political Communication, 25,* 67–88.
Sobel, R. (1998). *Coolidge: An American Enigma.* Washington, DC: Regnery.
Sproule, J. M. (1997). *Propaganda and Democracy: The American Experience of Media and Mass Persuasion.* New York: Cambridge University Press.
Stout, D. (2008). "Paulson Argues for Need to Buy Mortgages." *The New York Times.* Retrieved from http://www.nytimes.com/2008/09/20/business/economy/20paulson.html.
Tedlow, R. (1979). *Keeping the Corporate Image: Public Relations and Business, 1900–1950.* Greenwich, CT: JAI.
Wall, W. (2008). *Inventing the "American Way": The Politics of Consensus from the New Deal to the Civil Rights Movement.* New York: Oxford University Press.
Wilson, G. (1998). *Only in America? The Politics of the United States in Comparative Perspective.* Chatham, NJ: Chatham House.
Zakaria, F. (2008, September 29). "Big Government to the Rescue: Markets Can't Exist Without Regulation. *Newsweek,* 22.

CHAPTER 5

The Redeem Team Saves USA Basketball
An Analysis of the U.S.-China 2008 Olympic Games

KATHERINE L. LAVELLE

Dwayne Wade, one of the brightest stars in the National Basketball Association (NBA), described his experience playing for the U.S. national basketball team against China in the 2008 Beijing Olympics as "just over the top" (quoted in Spears, 2008, para. 5). Despite losses by the U.S. national team in the 2004 Olympics and in the 2002 and 2006 World Championships, the United States was still considered the home of the best basketball players on the planet. Given those prior losses, the 2008 Games were a turning point for the American team, marking the first time it had entered the Olympics as the underdog. Team USA's opening round opponent was China, a country that had invested heavily in improving its own international basketball team. The game was billed as a showdown between the most powerful nations on earth ("U.S. Set to Hand," 2008), and was expected to be the most watched basketball game in history, with an estimated one billion viewers (Spears, 2008).

While China is not a superpower in basketball, this particular game was significant because longstanding political and economic tensions between China and the United States. Seen in this context, the commentary from the August 10, 2008, game between the U.S. and China serves as an example of American exceptionalist discourse. In this chapter, I argue that the NBC broadcast of the U.S.-China game exemplified American exceptionalism as "an ensemble of traditional myths [evoking] the attitudes of national autonomy and superiority" (Ivie and Giner, 2009, p. 360), and I apply exceptionalist standpoint to the American team and its players. Specifically, I focus on the manner in which the national autonomy and superiority of the U.S. basketball squad — and by extension, the U.S. as a whole — was discussed by the NBC sportscasters during the game. As a result, this chapter defines and situates American exceptionalism within the contexts of sports and its media coverage.

American Exceptionalism

Many scholars have defined the phrase "American exceptionalism" including Lipset, (1996); Lockhart (2003), and Rodgers (2004). There is usually a "mythic" component to these various conceptions of American exceptionalism (Butterworth, 2008), often; it is even considered part of the "foundation of the nation" (Kaplan, 2009). Sometimes the prominence of capitalism is considered to be part of American exceptionalism (Kohut and Stokes, 2006). To other scholars, American exceptionalism is simply concerned with what makes America unique in the world, including its ethnic and racial diversity, its size, and its historical background lacking feudal ties (Markovits and Hellerman, 2001).

Exceptionalism has been around in various forms for centuries, ever present and always framing discussions about the United States. Edwards (2008) frames his interpretation of American exceptionalism using Tocqueville's nineteenth-century observation of the United States, stating that the nation "is a unique and superior nation that has a special role to play in human history" (p. 5). Madsen (1998) argues that exceptionalism "permeates every period of American history and is the single most powerful agent in a series of arguments that have been fought down the centuries concerning the identity of America and Americans" (p. 1); for Madsen, exceptionalism "is a form of interpretation with its own language and logic" (p. 2). As a result, certain terms and ways of framing issues help justify the ways that the United States operates in the world, whether unilaterally or in concert isolated actions and involvement with other nations; often, actions that might otherwise seem inappropriate function within an exceptionalist framework because they work to promote U.S. interests. American exceptionalist discourse often characterizes the United States as "exemplary" and "moral," as the nation that sets the example for the rest of the world (Rojecki, 2008).

Since American exceptionalism needs to operate within a specific context in order to have meaning, other global arenas, such as sports, can be spaces for its development. "Sports are our most explicit and mythologized public spectacles of competition, power, and domination" (Stempel, 2006, p. 82). At the same time, sports act as a form of international relations; athletes and teams can act as ambassadors of their home countries as their thoughts and actions are made in public (Hill, 2004; Tomlinson and Young, 2006). That is, unlike diplomatic actions, which might occur behind closed doors, sports are broadcast on an international stage with millions of eager fans watching complex, often political interactions. At times national controversies can spill out onto athletic playing fields through rivalries between different national teams. This is most visibly the case in football (American soccer), particularly in Europe, where centuries old rivalries between politically competitive nation-states are played out on the athletic field (O'Donnell, 1994). The 2006 World Cup final in Germany was the setting for a contretemps between France and Italy when Italian player Marco Materazzi allegedly insulted French player Zinedine Zidane by making rude comments about Zidane's mother and sister ("I'm Sorry But," 2006).[1]

Part of the reason that sports engender so many intense feelings and such complex interactions with political tensions is that they are part of a country's national identity (Cronin and Mayall, 1998; Hill, 2004; Riordan, 1999). As explained by Kassing et al., "Sport is a powerful cultural institution that acts as a highly significant site for identity construction and enactment (including resistance) across local, national, and global boundaries" (2004, pp. 380–381). Not only do sports promote national identity to a world outside of the sport itself, they are a means of expressing domination over other nations (Dyreson, 1998; Jarvie, 2003; MacClancy, 1996). In the case of the U.S., exceptionalist discourse is often promoted in sports.

American Exceptionalism and the 2008 Beijing Olympics

Discourse in sports can cover a wide variety of ostensibly unrelated issues, including gender (Goodman, Duke, and Sutherland, 2002; Hogan, 2003), race (Kassing et al., 2004), and nationality (Butterworth, 2007; Cronin and Mayall, 1998; Jarvie, 2003; O'Donnell, 1994). Indeed, one of the primary ways that national identity is promoted is through sports media discourse, including sports broadcasters' discussions (Halone, 2008; Hansen, 1999; Mean, 2010). A specific site of such identity promotion is the Olympic Games. The American media have been important promoters of the Olympics (Goodman, Duke, and Sutherland, 2002; Riggs, Eastman, and Golobic, 1993; White, Silk, and Andrews, 2008). As Dyreson explains,

Since 1896 Olympic sport has played an important role in American political culture. Through essays, polemics, and exposés about the experiences of "America's athletic missionaries," American thinkers generated a new national language that allowed communication between intellectual and popular culture [1998, p. 207].

The Olympics are also "key sites in the discursive construction of nation" (Hogan, 2003, p. 101). The way in which the national team's abilities are discussed provides critical insight into the understanding of how American exceptionalism is promoted in and through the Olympics.

While all sports can help promote American exceptionalism, the Olympics are a unique vehicle for promoting exceptionalist discourse, as they frequently serve as a forum for domination over other countries (Butterworth, 2007). For example, media coverage often highlights the "medal count" which displays how many first-, second-, and third-place finishes each competing country has won at any point during an Olympiad (Miller, 2003). At times, the Olympics have been a place for the expression of conflict over political issues, as evidenced by the United States the USSR-hosted 1980s Games and the subsequent Soviet boycott of the U.S.-hosted Games in 1984 (Miller, 2003).

In 2008, China had a great deal at stake in its basketball game against the United States. As Ono and Jia (2008, pp. 407–408) explain:

> China appears [to be] afflicted by an archaic authoritarian rule, unable to master rapid and comprehensive modernization, prone to seeking unfair advantage, dominating Tibet, a victim of an Earthquake, and inferior to U.S. and western culture. Underlying all of this is an unstated assumption that, because of the changed global position of the United States, overall, the United States must not push democracy too hard or disrespectfully challenges China on human rights, as its dependence on China grows.

China, still struggling to forge its identity as an international superpower, had already begun to assert itself as a global leader in terms of its population size and its economic investments in the United States. Additionally, the United States has been negotiating for some time with China on trade and international agreements (Schiller, 2008). Thus, the relationship between the two nations had been marked for years by an uncomfortable blend of competition and cooperation, providing much of the (extra) tension underlying the Olympic basketball match-up.

Hosting the Olympics allows a country to promote itself on the global stage; for that reason, host nations schedule elaborate events throughout the two-week competition period. Perhaps predictably, then, Beijing used the Olympics as a means to promote the nation by running an efficient and lavish tournament. In order to deflect the world's attention from its unpopular political positions, such as its treatment of Chinese prisoners and dissidents, as well as its diplomatic and economic ties to Sudan, China made a number of cosmetic improvements to its infrastructure, enhanced its air quality, and produced a spectacular opening ceremony to demonstrate its modern identity. Despite China's visible efforts, there were still some critics who questioned the nation's ability to host a modern Olympic Games. Other pundits, however, were convinced; as Donegan (2008, para. 6) noted, "The few remaining souls who still doubt China's willingness to embrace Western culture need worry no longer. They even do cheerleaders these days, not to mention hot dogs on sticks."

In addition to the integration of western ideas into sporting events, these games allowed China to showcase its own homegrown NBA superstar, six-time NBA All-Star Yao Ming. Yao came back early from an injury to try to help his country reach the medal round (Spears, 2008). The presence of Yao Ming on the Chinese team was not just a matter of national pride. Yao was also the centerpiece of several U.S.-based corporations' business strategies developed to take advantage of the huge Chinese market: the NBA, Nike, and other major marketers had cultivated a supportive fan base in China, with audiences of regular season NBA games often averaging 34 million Chinese viewers per week ("NBA China Games," 2007). For these and other reasons, the basketball game between the U.S. and China was eagerly awaited. "Basketball is No. 1 and getting more popular with each passing day. It can easily be argued that this match with the Americans is the most eagerly anticipated team athletic event in Chinese history" (Ryan, 2008, para. 6).

For the United States, this game had significance regardless of the opponent. It was the opening game for the "Redeem Team." In 2008, the U.S. National team was attempting to recapture the gold medal they had won for decades but had not won in 2002, 2004, or 2006. The 2008 U.S. team was designed to restore the nation's former international basketball glory and therefore truly needed to win at the Olympics in order to demonstrate that its squad was worthy of the acclaim often lavished on the team in earlier times. As Bond (2008) observed, "The Americans should be particularly anxious about a return to international play, giving their shoddy record in recent years, and a pre–Olympics guarantee of a gold medal from LeBron James" (para. 5). Moreover, the professional arm of the sport had a great deal riding on the Olympics match-up. As Ryan put it, "The NBA has a lot at stake here, doesn't it? The USA/NBA is 0 for 3 in the last three major international competitions. Players are starting to leave America to go overseas for lucrative contracts, not the other way around" (2008, para. 18). If the U.S. wanted to maintain the perception that it was not only a leader in international basketball but that it was truly exceptional, its national team had to win its 2008 match-up with China, a game described as "perhaps the most anticipated early event of the Olympics" (Whiteside, 2008, para. 3).

Although struggling to win international competitions, the U.S. team was actually far superior to the Chinese team. "In the grand basketball universe, the United States and China still roam in different stratospheres" (Thamel, 2008, para. 7). However, the ceremonial significance of the Olympic game was critical—so important, in fact, that the leaders of the two nations attended the match (Spears, 2008). President George W. Bush even participated in a pre-game pep talk then "put his arms in with the rest of the players and chanted '1-2-3, U-S-A!'" (Abramowitz, 2008, para. 2), an unusual show of support that only added to the international significance of the game.

American Exceptionalism in the Game

In order to conduct this analysis, I transcribed the NBC broadcast of the August 10, 2008, first-round basketball game between the United States and China. My 16,720-word transcript, produced from a DVD recording of the broadcast, includes the entire 40-minute game coverage, as well as the pre-game and half-time shows. Six television personalities participated in the NBC broadcast, many of them employees of other networks. Mike Breen, an ABC/ESPN basketball play-by-play commentator; Doug Collins, a Turner Network Television (TNT) basketball commentator, former NBA coach, and 1972 Olympian; Jim Lampley, a commentator for HBO sports; Craig Sagar, a sideline reporter for TNT basketball; Jimmy Roberts, a commentator for NBC Sports; and Eyee Hsu, a Chinese-American who works for the Chinese Central television station.

In order to examine American exceptionalist discourse in the broadcast of the game, I conducted a textual analysis of the transcript using Ivie and Giner's (2009) definition of American exceptionalism as "an ensemble of traditional myths [that] typically evokes attitudes of national autonomy and superiority" (p. 360). This definition is particularly well suited to the analysis of the context of a basketball game broadcast because there are many comparisons made between the two sides that go well beyond the superficial discussion of the athletes' game performance. Specifically, I analyzed five themes present in the transcript: the context of the game, the mission of the U.S. team, the U.S. team's domination, American superstars and role players, and Yao Ming.

Context of the Game

NBC's description of this game suggested a battle of great significance for both teams. The game's venue was described as "an 18,000-seat facility that now witnesses its finest hour" (para. 3). The match-up was referred to by the commentators several times as "a historic event." The presence of the presidents of the competing nations, George W. Bush of the United States and Hu Jinto of China, was mentioned. Bush's pre-game chant was mentioned. Craig Sagar shared a story about the second in command in China's support for his national team: "Wen-Jio Bo has been to every practice" (para. 21). The enthusiasm of the fans and their excitement for the game was discussed, and the game itself was called as an "electric experience" (para. 68). According to the commentators, the support of the crowd did not waver at any point in the game, even though the United States pulled away and maintained an early lead in the second quarter. As Mike Breen explained, "The Chinese fans [are] still applauding every positive play in the game from their team. Despite the fact that they are down by 29 points" (para. 258). To provide context for the significance of the game, the development of basketball in China as a professional sport was emphasized. Mike Breen described it as follows: "a culmination of many, many years of building relationships between these countries, with the development of the sport of basketball in China having grown to such proportions [that] it is now the most popular sport in this country" (para. 272). These conditions were framed almost as a consolation prize to the Chinese team: although they were not nearly as good as the U.S. team, they were allowed to be part of such an exciting match-up, which should be compensation enough for them.

Mission of the Team

Part of the reason that the United States–China game was significant was that it represented the first step on the U.S. team's path to recapture gold. The term "quest" was used to describe the U.S. team's trajectory over the previous three years (Ebersol, 2008), invoking the idea that the United States was apart from other nations, yet held together as one on their journey. The success of other countries did not seem to factor into the fortunes of the United States; rather it was exclusively their responsibility to find success at the Olympics and failure being attributable only to their own lack of abilities.

The American team had two separate missions that were identified in the transcript. First, they had a mission to win gold. The significance of this goal was discussed at several points in the broadcast. As Mike Breen explained,

"They have shown real dedication in the last couple of years, wanting to come back and reclaim gold for the United States. And tonight, it's a good first step" (para. 266). The term "reclaim" is interesting here because it suggests that the United States always possessed the gold and that only their recent inability to work well together prevented them from winning it in 2004. Also, there was specific tracking of the improvement of the team, and discussion about how its members had to work in order to maintain standards necessary to recapture gold. The commentators used the term "slippage" and stated that the team had to avoid "bad habits." These prescriptions for the U.S. squad suggested that they would lose only if they failed to work for their victory: it was irrelevant if other countries were improving or were becoming successful on the international stage. As long as the United States was making the necessary effort, the broadcasters suggested, they would win. Placing the responsibility for the success of the U.S. team solely on the squad, instead of also considering the United States' relationship to its opponents, emphasized the superiority that the broadcasters were using to frame the Americans. Absent from their commentary was any discussion about other successful national teams. Even though this team was designed to win, it had not won in the 2006 World Championships against many of its Olympic competitors.

In addition to winning the China game, the second goal identified for the U.S. team was to reclaim its status as the de facto home team in international competition, a status that had been lost, or at least tarnished, due to its own arrogance during the previous two Olympic Games. In the 2000 Sydney Games, Alonzo Mourning had proclaimed, "If we play five players the whole game, I couldn't see us losing. We might not win by a big margin, but I still can't see us losing" (quoted in Wise, 2000, para. 12). And when the U.S. team lost in Athens in 2004, its members blamed factors such as the international rule and the lack of superstar players like Kobe Bryant (Fitzpatrick, 2004; McCallum, 2004). These previous experiences were a far cry from the 1992 Olympics, where opposing players asked members of the American team for their autographs (Araton, 2005).

Working in the 2008 U.S. team's favor in basketball-knowledgeable China was the fact that the American squad's members were already popular with the crowd. Still, the American broadcasters were aware of lingering tensions. Mike Breen referenced the delicate balance that the United States had to strike in order to build goodwill with the Chinese fan base. "[They] felt that they way that they conducted themselves in this game against China, even if they really blew them out, it would set a tone for how the Chinese fans would go for them the rest of the games" (para. 236). Here, the U.S. commentators argued that the United States decided if the fans would support them or not, not the other way around. Doug Collins referred to this as "a little bit of a home court advantage" (para. 237). This comment suggested that the U.S. team was not only better, but also more likely than other teams to win international fans at the Olympics simply by dint of being American.

The U.S. Team's Domination

The U.S. team's ability to dominate its competitors was a persistent theme in the NBC commentary. One of the ways that this domination was explained was by presenting the United States and China as each other's foil. As Mike Breen explained, "The United States pressure is to win gold. They say, anything less, obviously, would be very disappointing. For China, big pressure, at least to get into the medal round. And here you see the pressure" (para. 24). Less was expected of China; for them, merely getting into the medal round would be seen as a great accomplishment. But if the U.S. team achieved anything less than a championship, they would be considered failures. Another way the United States was framed as superior team was in the discussion of the relative of the two squads' players. Doug Collins referred to the U.S. team's roster as "the deepest one here" (para. 31). The U.S. team was praised for having "the most talent" (para. 76), even considering the American failures at recent international competitions.

In contrast, the Chinese team was presented as inferior to the Americans. Mike Breen noted that "depth is not a strength of China" (para. 42). While the United States possessed "incredible speed and quickness, and their ability to get out on the open floor" (para. 132), the Chinese team could not keep up. "Now, you are going to see some fatigue. The energy, the adrenaline that you saw China running on in the beginning of this game; it's starting to wear off a little bit... The United States [is] starting to make a bit of a run" (para. 92). Even though it was acknowledged several times during the broadcast that the rest of the world was improving and had challenged the United States for basketball domination, the descriptions of China's team were condescending, the broadcasters suggesting that the Chinese were just fortunate to be on the same court as the United States. As Breen summarized what this game meant to the Chinese team, "This is a building block game for them too, and people might say, hey, wait a minute, they are behind by 27, but there are a lot of positives for them in this game. If they are ever going to reach their goal of making the medal round" (para. 260). It was assumed, in other words, that the U.S. team would medal, but based on their performance in this one game, China would have difficulty doing so. These comments contributed to and built upon the myth of the national autonomy and superiority of the U.S. team. China had had "a nice night here" (para. 273), while the United States was "a group of all-stars" (para. 129). These contrasting characterizations of the teams gave support to the belief that the U.S. team was exceptional in international sports. Instead of relying on the U.S. team's ability on the court, the broadcasters' negative comments about the Chinese helped frame the U.S. team as superior.

American Superstars and Role Players

These discourses of domination were omnipresent in the discussion of the players in the games. There were two groups of players profiled in the broadcast: superstars and role players. The superstars were the famous players, those who had had success in the NBA, and perhaps won a title or two. For the United States, the term "superstar" was linked with the highest level of NBA success. The United States seemed to have three clear superstars: LeBron James, Kobe Bryant, and Dwyane Wade. All three players were multiple All-Stars,[2] and often competed for league-wide scoring titles. By the summer of 2008, James had led his Cleveland Cavaliers to the NBA Finals once. Bryant was a three-time champion with the Los Angeles Lakers and the reigning league-wide MVP for the 2007–08 season. Wade was coming off an injury, but was a Finals MVP and winner of the 2006 NBA Championships with the Miami Heat. James and Wade had been members of the 2004 U.S. Olympic team. These players had substantial American and global name recognition due to their on-court success and their prolific product endorsements and were considered among the best in the NBA.

The game commentary supported the perception that James, Bryant, and Wade were the best players in the sport at the time. James was called "the real vocal leader of this team" (para. 8) and "unstoppable" (para. 33). Doug Collins opined that James "might be the best player in the open court in the NBA" (para. 126). Later, Collins remarked that James could have been a football running back because of his athletic abilities. In addition to James's on-court abilities, the commentators remarked on how popular James was in China.

Bryant, it was noted, was even more famous than James. There were several references to him getting "mobbed" by fans in China and comments about how difficult it was for him to maneuver through crowds there because so many people were so excited to get close to him. (The point was even supported by NBC showing—on two occasions—footage of Bryant attending the women's basketball game and being surrounded by eager fans.) Moreover, Mike Breen noted, "Bryant heard chants of 'MVP' at an exhibition game here in Shanghai last week. They love him here in China" (para. 109). Even though Wade was not a starter for Team USA, he too was praised for his versatility and myriad of on-court abilities. As commentator Mike Breen enthused, "Wade with the steal! And that's where the United States was so strong, and that's going to be trouble for China and their point guards, especially when their leader Liu Wei sits down" (para. 51). Wade was also praised for his "upper body strength" (para. 138). The combined discussion of all three players suggested on-court abilities beyond those of other nations' athletes.

This framing of the American players as superior to the Chinese players was visible also in the discussion of the role players from the respective countries. The American teams, even when losing, were always "all-star teams" (Hack, 2004), even if the definition of "all-star" meant different things for various NBA squads. For instance, a team with Michael Jordan and Magic Johnson would be seen as superior to one with Jason Kidd and Vince Carter because Johnson and Jordan had won NBA Championships and enjoyed broader worldwide name recognition. The American team was so good there weren't enough minutes in the game for all of the players to contribute substantially. For instance, Doug Collins shared a story about Carlos Boozer from an exhibition game against Australia. Collins quoted Coach Mike Krzyzewski as saying, "Carlos, I'm sorry; I can't even imagine the last time that you didn't get into a game as a player" (para. 219).

Usually, role players play when needed, and are not necessarily stars on their own teams. However, during the NBC broadcast, the U.S. role players were introduced with brief biographical information and followed up with positive descriptions. For example, Utah's Deron Williams, playing in his first Olympics, was described as "one of the premiere point guards in the NBA" (para. 262). Shooter Michael Redd, from the Milwaukee Bucks, was called, "so important" (para. 271). Even veteran Jason Kidd of the Dallas Mavericks, who won a gold medal on the 2000 team, was described as "an amazing point guard" (para. 130) at 35, an age considered old in professional basketball. All of these players are successful NBA players and the reinforcement of their success reminded the audience that the U.S. team comprised "a group of all-stars" (para. 129), further underscoring the notion that the U.S. team was superior.

These descriptions stood in clear contrast to the characterizations of the Chinese players. A few of the 2008 Chinese players had NBA experience. Yi Jianlian, a rookie during the 2007–08 season, was described as "struggling" in the NBA and in this game. Doug Collins said of Jianlian that "you see flashes of brilliance out of him ... a big part is that you've got to be consistent" (para. 173). Sun Yue was linked with Kobe Bryant since he had just signed a deal with the Los Angeles Lakers. Wang Zhizhi was described as "a familiar face" after commentator Mike Breen listed the three NBA teams where he briefly played in the early 21st century (para. 57). Liu Wei, the Chinese point guard, was described as Yao Ming's best friend, but also as having a short-lived NBA career. "There was some NBA interest for Liu Wei; he's played about 20 games for the Chinese national team" (para. 141). Chen Jianghua, who was making his Olympic debut, was described as "not showing any fear playing against the mighty United States" (para. 55). In isolation, these were positive comments about the Chinese team. However, in comparison to the comments made about the United States, they suggested that China was inferior to the United States, and certainly not anywhere near its levels and abilities. Even the American role players had had successful NBA careers. The Chinese team had not. Instead, they were framed as inferior to the U.S. team because they had not been successful in the NBA.

Yao Ming

In contrast to the United States' trio of superstars, China had but one, Yao Ming. By 2008, Yao was an established player in the NBA, appearing in every All-Star game for which he had been eligible, as well as helping his team, the Houston Rockets, make the NBA playoffs four times. Leading up to the Olympic Games, it was questionable if Yao would be able to play due to a broken foot suffered in February of 2008. His rehabilitation was frequently cited during the NBC broadcast. Doug Collins said that Yao was "more active and mobile than I expected him to be" (para. 195). But praise for Yao's abilities was undercut by awarding Patrick Ewing credit for Yao's success. Ewing, a former American NBA player, had worked with Yao on NBA techniques when he was an assistant in Houston. Ewing was a multiple All-Star player with a Hall of Fame caliber career. This framing seemed to suggest that any success Yao had on the court came from working with an American and former U.S. Dream Team member, not as a result of his own abilities. Most of the discussion of Yao's playing was contextualized by the idea that it would be difficult for Yao to make it through the entire Olympics with a healing foot. He was the superstar of the China team, yet framed by the NBC commentators as unable to carry his team in the game because of injuries.

Instead of focusing on Yao's superstar abilities in the NBA, the broadcasters played up unnecessary biographical information. The broadcast team was keen to introduce Yao, even though he was already familiar to U.S. audiences. By 2008, Yao had played in the NBA for six seasons. He had been in the league longer than LeBron James or Dwyane Wade, yet the commentators' focus regarding those two athletes was on their on-court abilities, while Yao was considered primarily in the context of his personal biography. The commentators discussed his contributions to the Sichuan earthquake relief effort, his fear of not getting a girlfriend because he was so tall, and his feelings about the importance of the Olympics. He was framed as a figurehead and as a character in a human-interest story, but not primarily as an elite basketball player. In addition, there was a segment during the halftime show in which Yao's impact was discussed. The story suggested that everyone in China knew who Yao was, but also implied that the Chinese fans related better to American players like Kobe Bryant and Allen Iverson who weren't over seven feet tall. Even in his own country, Yao was not characterized as a hero on the court; instead, he was framed as an ambassador of China in the NBA and therefore less imposing on the court than the American NBA players who were framed as superstars.

Implications for Future Study

There are two implications from the 2008 China and U.S. Olympic game commentary. Since this game took place in China, NBC's broadcast was the medium between the United States and the U.S. audience. The team was framed as superior in international basketball despite the various improvements on the abilities of other nations' teams. By 2008, the legitimacy of international teams and players was clear. International players were regular NBA All-Stars, integral to several NBA championship teams, and represented among the cadre of league-wide Most Valuable Players.[3] But these facts were not addressed in the NBC game commentary. Instead of conceding that international basketball was more competitive than before, the commentators focused on the superiority of the American players in relation to their global competitors. This emphasis was contradictory to the notion that the U.S. team had to work to be competitive in 2008. What was not clearly addressed in the commentary was whether the U.S. team had reset itself and was ready to be competitive on a consistent basis. In other words, has the U.S. learned its lesson from prior international competitions? Had the U.S. team recognized that they had to commit to actually building a team as opposed to merely throwing together an "All-Star" squad at the last minute? Either way, this framing of the U.S. team clearly cast the United States as exceptional in relation to other international teams.

Second, in this game's commentary, basketball was used to remind the audience of the United States' superiority to the rest of the world. Such framing on the part of the NBC broadcast raises the question: Are sports still the one place where the U.S. can clearly dominate other countries? This question touches on an increasingly sensitive subject: sports maybe are the one area where the United States has been consistently strong, while America's economic competitiveness and the global diplomatic power have been greatly variable, dependent largely on geopolitical events beyond American control. In the 2008 Olympic basketball game against China, U.S.-based sportscasters suggested that the United States is and was powerful and strong. However, outside the arena of sport, China competes with the United States for world domination. Did the NBC commentary support the posturing of the United States as superior to other countries?

As this analysis suggests, evaluating how the American basketball team is positioned in the Olympics is critical to understanding how American exceptionalism is promoted through sports. When the Olympics are presented as a shared American event, the role of U.S. professional athletes is critical because their presence provides a vehicle for American exceptionalist discourse. Nations' sports programs are directly compared during competition, and unlike traditional routes of diplomacy, they actually compete to determine who wins. Understanding this discourse works best through examining the commentary of American broadcasters, who have extensive knowledge of the players and their experiences in the world. Commentary is an effective vehicle because when the games are played outside of the United States, the commentary is often the only access the American audience has to the games. Due to the nature of play-by-play commentary, discussions of the event and team are common, so understanding how these comments work provides an access route for examining how American exceptionalism is promoted through the discourses of sports and its media coverage.

Notes

1. This incident was more than just a storyline from a soccer final: it was an international incident that sparked anger and discussion about Arab-French relationships in Europe. France had been engulfed with Arab demonstrations against Muslim discrimination in the Parisian suburbs that summer. While those incidents are newsworthy, the World Cup incident was something specific and memorable that embodied these tensions.

2. Each year, 12 players from the Eastern and Western conferences are selected to represent their conference in the All-Star game. The starters are chosen by the fans, the reserves by the coaches.

3. San Antonio had won three championships in five years, thanks in part to France's Tony Parker and Argentina's Manu Ginobli. Germany's Dirk Nowitzki (2007) and Canada's Steve Nash (2005, 2006) were league-wide MVPs (Brooks, 2007).

References

Abramowitz, M. (2008, August 11). "An Indifferent Tourist Becomes an Enthusiastic First Fan." *Washington Post*, p. A13.

Araton, H. (2005). *Crashing the Borders: How Basketball Won the World and Lost its Soul at Home.* New York: Free.

Bond, F. (2008, August 10). "The Clash of the Superpowers." *Daily News* (New York), p. 52.

Brooks, M. (2007, May 15). "Dirk Nowitzki Q & A." NBA.com. Retrieved from http://www.nba.com/features/Nowitzki_Q_A_070515.html.

Butterworth, M. L. (2007). "The Politics of the Pitch: Claiming and Contesting Democracy through the Iraqi National Soccer Team." *Communication and Critical/Cultural Studies, 4,* 184–203.

Butterworth, M. (2008). "Fox Sports, Super Bowl XLII, and the Affirmation of American Civil Religion." *Journal of Sport and Social Issues, 32,* 318–323.

Cronin, M., and D. Mayall (1998). "Sport and Ethnicity: Some Introductory Remarks." In M. Cronin and D. Mayall (Eds.), *Sporting Nationalisms: Identity, Ethnicity, Immigration, and Assimilation* (pp. 1–13). Portland, OR: Frank Cass.

Donegan, L. (2008, August 11). "Yao's Towering Presence Cannot Stop China Defeat." *The Guardian* (London), p. 9.

Dyreson, M. (1998). *Making the American Team: Sport, Culture, and the Olympic Experience.* Urbana: University of Illinois Press.

Ebersol, D. (Producer). (2008). *2008 Beijing Olympics on NBC: United States versus China* [Television broadcast]. New York: National Broadcasting Company.

Edwards, J. A. (2008). *Navigating the Post-Cold War World: President Clinton's Foreign Policy Rhetoric.* Lanham, MD: Lexington.

Goodman, J. R., L. L. Duke, and J. Sutherland (2002). "Olympic Athletes and Heroism in Advertising: Gendered Concepts of Valor?" *Journalism and Mass Communication Quarterly, 79,* 374–393.

Hack, D. (2004, August 17). "For the U.S. Stars, It's a Bad-Dream Team." *International Herald Tribune,* p. 20.

Hill, C. (2004). "Prologue." In R. Levermore and A. Budd (Eds.), *Sport and International Relations: An Emerging Relationship* (pp. 1–5). London: Routledge.

Hogan, J. (2003). "Staging the Nation: Gendered and Ethnicized Discourses of National Identity in Olympic Opening Ceremonies." *Journal of Sport and Social Issues, 27,* 100–123.

"I'm Sorry but No Regrets" (2006, July 12). BBC Sport. Retrieved from http://news.bbc.co.uk/sport2/hi/football/world_cup_2006/5169342.stm.

Ivie, R. L., and O. Giner (2009). "American Exceptionalism in a Democratic Idiom: Transacting the Mythos of Change in the 2008 Presidential Campaign." *Communication Studies, 60,* 359–375.

Jarvie, G. (2003). "Internationalism and Sport in the Making of Nations." *Identities: Global Studies in Culture and Power, 10,* 537–551.

Kaplan, A. (2009). "Imperial Melancholy in America." *Raritan, 28,* 13–31.

Kassing, J. W., A. C. Billings, R. S. Brown, K. K. Halone, K. Harrison, B. Krizek, L. J. Mean, and P. D. Turman (2004). "Communication in the Community of Sport: The Process of Enacting, (Re)producing, Consuming, and Organizing Sport." *Communication Yearbook, 28,* 373–409.

Kohut, A., and B. Stokes (2006). *America Against the World: How We Are Different and Why We Are Disliked.* New York: Times.

Lipset, S. M. (1996). *American Exceptionalism.* New York: W. W. Norton.

Lockhart, C. (2003). *The Roots of American Exceptionalism: Institutions, Culture, and Policies.* New York: Palgrave Macmillian.

MacClancy, J. (1996). "Sport, Identity, and Ethnicity." In J. MacClancy (Ed.), *Sport, Identity, and Ethnicity* (pp. 1–20). Herndon, VA: Berg.

Madsen, D. L. (1998). *American Exceptionalism*. Jackson: University of Mississippi Press.
Markovits, A. S., and S. L. Hellerman (2001). *Offside: Soccer and American Exceptionalism*. Princeton, NJ: Princeton University Press.
Miller, D. (2003). *The Official History of the Olympic Games and the IOC, 1894–2004*. Edinburgh: Mainstream.
"NBA China Games to Reach 209 Countries." (2007, October 16). NBA.com. Retrieved from http://www.nba.com/news/china_games_071016.html.
O'Donnell, H. (1994). "Mapping the Mythical: A Geopolitics of National Sporting Stereotypes." *Discourse and Society, 5,* 345–380.
Ono, K. A., and J. Y. Jia (2008). "China in the US Imaginary: Tibet, the Olympics, and the 2008 Earthquake." *Communication and Critical/Cultural Studies, 5,* 406–410.
Riggs, K. E., S. T. Eastman, and T. S. Golobic (1993). "Manufactured Conflict in the 1992 Olympics: The Discourse of Television." *Critical Studies in Mass Communication, 10,* 253–272.
Riordan, J. (1999). "The Impact of Communism on Sport." In J. Riordan and A. Kruger (Eds.), *The International Politics of Sport in the 20th Century* (pp. 48–66). New York: Routledge.
Rodgers, D. T. (2004). "American Exceptionalism Revisited." *Raritan, 24,* 21–47.
Rojecki, A. (2008). "Rhetorical Alchemy: American Exceptionalism and the War on Terror." *Political Communication, 25,* 67–88.
Ryan, B. (2008, August 10). "No Longer Gold Standard, U.S. Has Something to Prove." *The Boston Globe*, p. C1.
Schiller, D. (2008). "China in the United States." *Communication and Critical/Cultural Studies, 5,* 411–415.
Spears, M. J. (2008, August 11). "Slam-Bang Start. Men's Basketball Team Rolls Past China in Opener." *Boston Globe*, p. C1.
Stempel, C. (2006). "Televised Sports, Masculinist Moral Capital, and Support for the U.S. Invasion of Iraq." *Journal of Sport and Social Issues, 30,* 79–106.
Thamel, P. (2008, August 25). "For China, a 101–70 Loss, but Possibly a Net Gain." *International Herald Tribune*, p. 20.
Tomlinson, A., and C. Young (2006). "Culture, Politics, and Spectacle in the Global Sports Event — An Introduction." In A. Tomlinson and C. Young (Eds.), *National Identity and Global Sports Events: Culture, Politics, and Spectacle in the Olympics and the Football World Cup* (pp. 1–14). Albany: State University of New York Press.
"U.S. Set to Hand China a Lesson on the Pine." (2008, August 9). *Weekend Australian*, p. 52.
White, R. E., M. L. Silk, and D. L. Andrews (2008). "Revising the Networked Production of the 2003 Little League World Series: Narratives of American Innocence." *International Journal of Media and Cultural Politics, 4,* 183–202.
Whiteside, K. (2008, August 20). "Among Hoops Loving Chinese, It's a Slam Dunk: Kobe is King." *USA Today*. Retrieved from http://www.usatoday.com/sports/olympics/beijing/basketball/2008-08-20-kobe_N.htm/.
Whittell, I. (2007, February 10). "People's Game Captures the Imagination of the New Market." *The Times* (London), p. 99.
Wolff, A. (2008, August 8). "Everybody Knows the Redeem Team is Good — Now They Have to Prove It." SportsIllustrated.com. Retrieved from http://sportsillustrated.cnn.com/2008/olympics/2008/writers/alexander_wolff/08/08/us.mens.basketball/index.html.

PART II

Challengers to American Exceptionalism

Chapter 6

Mormonism and America as Promised Land in Joseph Smith's Letter from Liberty Jail

David Charles Gore

American exceptionalism epitomizes what is peculiar about America, unique to her and to no other country or people. America is exceptional in being the first country to protect its citizens from religious establishment and to secure the free exercise of religion. Flowing from this, America is exceptional because of the distinctively American religions that arose within the climate of religious liberty and the vast expanse of wilderness.[1] Exceptional even among these American religions is Mormonism because it goes further than any other sect in its creation of American Scripture and in its conjuring of the meaning of America in both pre–Columbian and contemporary times.[2] The vast majority of Mormon Scripture was published between 1830 and 1844, and falls into two different genres: (1) the divine translations of Scriptural works written by ancient prophets, the *Book of Mormon* and the *Pearl of Great Price*; and (2) revelations given to Joseph Smith, the Mormon founder, collected in the *Doctrine and Covenants*. In both genres, considerable sections address America as exceptional. Smith's letter from Missouri's Liberty Jail, written to the Latter-day Saints Church on March 20, 1839, is one of the writings canonized in the *Doctrine and Covenants*.[3] The epistle builds on the LDS theme of America as a land of liberty and equal rights while holding that notion of America in tension with the Mormon experience of persecution. Indeed, Smith's letter from Liberty Jail is a defense of religious liberty and Mormonism via an appeal to a unique vision of American exceptionalism that aims to discredit Mormonism's persecutors.

Written during Smith's longest imprisonment without conviction for any crime, the letter defends Mormonism by way of both a prophetic condemnation of America and a prophetic defense of American promise. Smith was incarcerated on the charge of treason by the Missouri militia during what has come to be known as the Missouri Mormon War of 1838 (see Baugh, 2000, and LeSueur, 1990). Written by Smith after six months in prison, and just weeks before he and his fellow captives were allowed to escape, the letter implies that the enemies of his church have failed to grasp what is exceptional about America, particularly America's commitment to religious liberty.

The present chapter is a rhetorical analysis of Smith's letter from Liberty Jail. It aims to contextualize the letter within the American exceptionalist rhetoric of Mormon Scripture, of which the letter became a canonized part in 1876 (see Jessee and Welch, 2000), as well as the pressing context of the Missouri Mormon conflict. Part of Smith's criticism of Missouri rests on his claim that the Missourians are denying Mormons basic rights, including property rights, voting rights, and religious rights. Part of his defense rests on his capacity to show that he has no treasonous intentions toward the United States or the state of Missouri. Simultaneously, then, his criticism of the failure to defend religious liberty is held in tension with his praise of American promise.

American Exceptionalism in Mormon Scripture

The *Book of Mormon*, first published in March 1830, contains numerous references to America as a "choice," "covenant," and "promised" land of "inheritance" and "liberty."[4] Beginning in Jerusalem with the story of a Jewish prophet named Lehi, a descendant of Joseph who was sold into Egypt, the *Book of Mormon* follows the trajectory of Lehi's descendants, the Nephites and Lamanites. A contemporary of Jeremiah and King Zedekiah around 600 B.C., Lehi warned the scattered Israelite inhabitants of the land of Judah to repent or they would, like earlier Assyrian captives, be carried away to Babylon. Shown in a dream that he must flee Jerusalem, Lehi departed into the wilderness with a few other families, all leaving their homes, wealth, and security behind. They journeyed southeastward through the Arabian Peninsula, setting sail over the Indian and Pacific Oceans, and ultimately landing on the west coast of Central America (Givens, 2002).

The *Book of Mormon* is unique in American Scripture because it argues that the exceptional status of America as a promised land originated in the ancient world.[5] Indeed, before the departure, Nephi, Lehi's son and successor as prophet, is given a conditional promise from the Lord that "inasmuch as ye shall keep my commandments, ye shall prosper, and shall be led to a land of promise; yea, even a land which I have prepared for you; yea, a land which is choice above all other lands" (1 Nephi 2:20). After their arrival in this new land, Lehi prophesies of a covenant binding upon the land:

> We have obtained a land of promise, a land which is choice above all other lands; a land which the Lord God hath covenanted with me should be a land for the inheritance of my seed. Yea, the Lord hath covenanted this land unto me, and to my children forever, and also all those who should be led out of other countries by the hand of the Lord... . And if it so be that they shall serve him according to the commandments which he hath given, it shall be a land of liberty unto them [2 Nephi 1:5–7].

This passage constitutes what might be called a Mormon Jeremiad, as it contains the three crucial elements of the Puritan Jeremiad — covenant, declension, and prophecy (Bercovitch, 1980; Miller, 1953) — but also something more. The Puritan Jeremiad was "a way of conceiving the inconceivable, or making intelligible order out of the transition from European to American Experience" (Miller, 1953, p. 31). As a literary type it repeats the themes of Isaiah and Jeremiah through an imagining of parallels, suggesting that as it was with ancient Israel so it may be with contemporary Puritans. The Mormon Jeremiad, by contrast, is not so much a literary type intended to accomplish a psychological purpose as much as it is, for believers in the *Book of Mormon*, a literal covenant about America, combining a warning, a promise, and a revelation of a distinct contract between God and a remnant of the House of Israel. As a result, unique ideas about America emerge. Believers in the *Book of Mormon*— particularly American believers — are revealed to be literal inheritors of an ancient promise. While the Pilgrims purified European Christianity in a new land, the Latter-day Saints invented a new, distinctly American Christianity that endowed America with divine status. For the Latter-day Saints, Christianity is restored, not introduced, to America. Thus, the very land of America is under a sacred and binding covenant: its inhabitants must serve Jesus Christ or be swept from the face of the land. America's unique position as a refuge for religious dissenters extends not only to the Native Americans, but even farther back, to the descendants of Joseph in Egypt. Indeed, the *Book of Mormon* records that "the Lord hath reserved their blessings, which they might have received in the land, for the Gentiles who shall possess the land" (Mormon 5:19), suggesting that Smith's American contemporaries are a fulfillment of ancient promise.

An important aspect of the extension of religious liberty into antiquity is that it predates the establishment of the American republic. Although the

Book of Mormon's status as a historical record is contested, and although the *Book of Mormon* was published more than 40 years after the founding of the American republic, Mormon believers understand that its text transforms historical time. The *Book of Mormon* "Christianized prophetic discourse, even in pre–Christian times" (Bushman, 2005, p. 134). Just as Mormon Scripture gave theological history a different shape, it likewise brought a different shape to political history, by extending the quest for religious and political liberty to the ancient inhabitants of the Americas. The problem for contemporary Americans, then, becomes one of holding on to liberty through righteousness rather than through a balance of political powers.

Although the emphasis of the *Book of Mormon* is not on politics, but on religion, and not solely on America, but on Israel and its covenants, it nevertheless has political consequences. As Bushman (1976) argues, "In the classic version of America's past, the first settlers flee the oppressions of Europe to establish themselves as free people in the new land" (p. 102). However, in the *Book of Mormon*, American history is interpreted in a different, albeit parallel, context. Bushman explains that, in one of Nephi's visions,

> Nephi sees the Spirit of God work upon a man (presumably but not indisputably Columbus) who "went forth upon the many waters, even unto the seed of my brethren who were in the promised land." The Spirit then works upon "other Gentiles; and they went forth out of captivity, upon the many waters." In time "their mother Gentiles were gathered together upon the waters, and upon the land also, to battle against them." In the ensuing struggle, presumably the American Revolution, the power of God delivers these Gentile migrants, and they go on to "prosper in the land." That was the story that Americans would recognize as their own. But the American story does not control the narrative [1976, p. 102].

The *Book of Mormon*'s narrative is also driven by biblical ideas, including Jeremiad-like promises regarding the ultimate destiny of the Americas and Americans (Bushman, 2005, p. 102–103). As Joseph Smith declared in a sermon on July 19, 1840, "the redemption of Zion is the redemption of all North and South America" (quoted in Jessee, 1979, p. 392). By mapping these biblical ideas to the American context, the *Book of Mormon* deepens the religious context in which American exceptionalism is understood and applied by Latter-day Saints.

Although the *Book of Mormon* takes a broad view of the Americas, the revelations of Joseph Smith touch on various religious and political topics unique to the United States. One such revelation, received at Kirtland, Ohio on August 6, 1833, after initial reports of Latter-day Saint persecution in Missouri arrived, spoke directly of the United States Constitution, declaring in the voice of the Lord that the Constitution must be defended:

> And that law of the land which is constitutional, supporting that principle of freedom in maintaining rights and privileges, belongs to all mankind and is justifiable before me. Therefore, I, the Lord, justify you, and your brethren of my church, in befriending that law which is the constitutional law of the land; And as pertaining to law of man, whatsoever is more or less than this, cometh of evil. I, the Lord God, make you free, therefore ye are free indeed; and the law also maketh you free [*Doctrine and Covenants* 98:5–10].

The revelation reiterates that God is the source of all freedom, including American freedom, and that he works through men to achieve his purposes. The Latter-day Saints are thus enjoined to "befriend" the constitutional law of the land and to find honest leaders.

A second revelation, occurring to Smith on December 16, 1833, echoes the first in recommending constitutional solutions to disagreements:

> And again I say unto you, those who have been scattered by their enemies, it is my will that they should continue to importune for redress, and redemption, by the hands of those who are placed as rulers and are in authority over you— According to the laws and constitution of the people, which I have suffered to be established, and should be maintained for the rights and protection of all flesh, according to just and holy principles; That every man may act in doctrine and principle pertaining to futurity, according to the moral agency which I have given unto him, that every man may be accountable for his own sins in the day of judgment. Therefore, it is not right that any man should be in bondage one to another. And for this purpose have I established the Constitution of this land, by the hands of wise men whom I raised up unto this very purpose, and redeemed the land by the shedding of blood [*Doctrine and Covenants* 101: 76–80].

Asserting that the Constitution of the United States was established by God through "wise men," presumably the American founders, this revelation emphasizes a spiritual purpose for the Constitution: "that every man may be accountable for his own sins in the day of judgment."

The revelations indicate the extent to which ideas of American exceptionalism, including its mission in representing freedom to the world, are a part of Latter-day Saint Scripture. Both revelations emphasize the universal nature of American liberty as belonging "to all mankind" and "for the rights and protection of all flesh." For Joseph Smith, this meant that liberty and freedom should be all-inclusive and extend over the whole world, while, at the same time, the United States uniquely serves to *originate* that religious liberty for the world. Because all rights are God-given, any attempt to disrupt or limit these rights becomes an offense not merely against those denied, but against God. The resulting posture of such beliefs characterized Smith's rhetoric throughout his life, and contributed, in part, to the drive to evangelize foreign countries.

The idea that religious liberty is God-given encouraged Mormons to believe in the Constitution, but also to believe beyond it, promoting the idea that a religious covenant is both prior to and superior to the structure and system of any earthly government. This also made it possible for Mormons to see the Constitutional government as potentially of short duration and as something that could fall into dissolution. Indeed, early Mormons imagined that they might be called upon to rescue the United States from its own folly because of their determined righteousness and/or America's wickedness (Jessee, 1979). To this day, Mormons often harbor anxieties, perhaps exaggerated, about the health and future of American liberty if the commandments of God are neglected, but there is no reason internal to Latter-day Saint doctrine for these anxieties to prevail.[6] Regardless, Mormonism's American Scriptures reinforce American exceptionalism, broaden it to include the Americas as a whole, and extend it into antiquity. And these unique Latter-day Saint ideas about American promise clashed profoundly with the experience of persecution in Missouri.

Missouri Mormon War of 1838

Nineteenth-century Missouri was at the crossroads of national issues such as western expansion, federalism, and slavery. Less than a year before the outbreak of the Missouri Mormon War, Elijah Lovejoy, a Presbyterian minister, journalist, and abolitionist, had been murdered in Illinois by an armed mob of Missourians. In late summer and fall of 1838, conflicts between Missourians and Mormons that had been simmering for years escalated into violence. On August 6, 1838, election day in Gallatin, Missouri, fiery speeches incited the people of Daviess County to stop the Mormons from voting, even though no Mormon candidates were on the ballot (Bushman, 2005). Fights with fists, clubs, and rocks broke out as the Mormons refused to be denied their voting rights. Rumors spread that two or three Mormons had been killed and that they were being driven from Daviess County. Once violence had broken out, no one seemed able to halt the spread of animosity or quell the flames of agitation.

The resulting "Missouri Mormon War" consisted of seven military episodes or campaigns ending in November 1838. The violence spread from Daviess County to nearby Ray County. The Missouri state militia was engaged in the fighting, although a number of Mormons were themselves legitimate members of that group; Mormons also constituted the leadership of the Caldwell County militia. The Battle of Crooked River, a skirmish between the

Latter-day Saint militia and the Missouri militia fought on October 25, 1838, left three Mormons and one Missouri militiaman dead. Tensions escalated further on October 27, when Governor Boggs issued his now infamous order that the Mormons must be treated as enemies and therefore either driven from the state or exterminated (Boggs, 1838). On October 29, some 250 men surrounded Haun's Mill, one of the earliest Mormon settlements in Caldwell County. The massacre that ensued left 18 Mormons dead, including a boy of nine who was shot through the head at close range (Arrington and Bitton, 1992).

The conflict arose over religious, political, and social differences. Many Missourians perceived Smith and his followers as threats to law and order as they represented a prophetic and organized religion that went beyond the Bible. Such Missourians "regarded the Mormons' beliefs as obnoxious [and] resented the Saints' claims to being God's chosen people," considering them fanatics and victims of Smith's prophetic schemes (LeSueur, 1990, p. 17). At the same time, Missourian motives and anxieties were exacerbated by resentment of Yankees, fears of racial and Indian unrest, and the sense that the Mormons posed an economic threat. Because the Mormons initially asked the Northern Missourians for permission to settle in what would become Caldwell County, many Missourians believed the Saints would confine themselves to that county. When an influx of Mormon immigrants overflowed into other counties, tensions reached a boiling point (LeSueur, 1990).

Among the Latter-day Saints was a reciprocal charge that the Missourians were forcibly denying them their basic rights as citizens regardless of religion. The Mormons brought a "volatile mixture of courage, intelligence, leadership, and chauvinism" to the process of pioneering, civilizing, and conquering the west (LeSueur, 1990, p. 23). Since Mormonism originated in upstate New York, many of its adherents had northern attitudes about race and slavery. For religious reasons, the Mormons evangelized to the American Indians. These facts led to rumors that the Mormons were race agitators, tampering with slaves and Indians, and in the process endangering the Missouri populace (Arrington and Bitton, 1992). Finally, the Mormons were an insular community, living on large tracts of land, voting as a bloc, trading primarily among themselves, and sharing a powerful religious vision (Arrington and Bitton, 1992). Still, none of this constituted a legal reason for expulsion from the state of Missouri.

On October 31, 1838, the Missouri militia drew up a mile and a half south of the town of Far West, with the Mormon defensive forces drawn opposite. As the leaders of both sides gathered for what Smith believed would be a discussion about the conflict, Samuel Lucas of the Jackson County Militia seized the Mormon leaders and charged them with crimes against the state. That very night Lucas held a court-martial that convicted the prisoners of treason and sentenced them to be executed the next morning. Smith was not himself a militia member and thus not subject to military law, thus making the court-martial illegal (Bushman, 2005). Nevertheless, the prisoners were eventually brought to the Fifth Circuit Court in Richmond for a hearing before Judge Austin King. The one-sided inquiry completed, the prisoners were sent to Liberty Jail to await trial for nearly six months.

American Exceptionalism in the Letter from Liberty Jail

On March 19, 1839, the post arrived at Liberty Jail containing letters from Joseph Smith's wife, Emma; his brothers Don Carlos and William; and Bishop Edward Partridge. Incarcerated at Liberty Jail with five others, including his brother Hyrum, Joseph Smith was desperate for news from family and friends.[7] Emma's letter contained news about the family and the tender concern and longing of a wife. Don Carlos and William assured their brothers Joseph and Hyrum that their families were being cared for and reported a rumor that Missouri Governor Boggs was going to set them free. Bishop Partridge's letter concerned business of the church, discussion of a land deal, and reassurance about Joseph and Hyrum's families. This correspondence seems to have provoked Smith's feelings. On March 20, Smith wrote a letter in which he poured out his heart and soul to his people, defending them through an appeal to American religious liberty, and relying on the Constitution to wage a rhetorical battle against American provincialism, bigotry, and religious persecution.

Smith's earlier letters, written during his incarceration at Richmond and in the initial days of his imprisonment at Liberty, had reflected anger at those who betrayed him to the Missouri militia, but at the same time had proclaimed his own innocence (Bushman, 2005). However, in his March 20 letter, written after being imprisoned for nearly six months, Smith directs his wrath at the Missouri Governor and the prison guards. He blames the persecution of the Mormons on Missouri's desire for war and identified his persecutors as demons, criticizing their drunken, blasphemous, hypocritical behavior. Mormon rights are being denied by a corrupt and bigoted state government, Smith maintains, and at the heart of his protest is a defense of religious liberty.

Smith compares Mormonism to the flow of the nearby Missouri River. He compares the Governor of Missouri, Lilburn W. Boggs, to wimbling willows on the shore that catch the flood wood. In a defiant and radically prophetic tone, Smith argues that persecution of his people will only make them stronger. The cause of the Latter-day Saints is not lost

> because renegades, liars, priests, thieves, and murderers who are all alike tenacious of their crafts and creeds have poured down from their spiritual wickedness in high places and from their strong holds ... a flood of dirt and mire and filthiness and vomit upon our heads [Smith, 2002, p. 438].

Mormonism is more powerful, Smith asserts, than hell, burning volcanic lava, or "the most terrible of the burning mountains," Vesuvius and Etna. By harnessing the awesome power of nature, the letter exemplifies at times what Matthew Arnold (1869/2001) referred to as the "fire and strength" of the Hebrew prophets.

The energy of the letter captures a growing sense that from now on Smith intends to play offense in public affairs. From the very beginning of their church's founding, the Latter-day Saints were urged to keep historical records.[8] But now, as Smith points out in his March 20, 1839, letter, such records are to capture not merely internal, ecclesiastical matters, but also the injuries, slander, and damages leveled against the Latter-day Saints, as well as the documentation of their treatment in the popular media. Smith urges the Saints to gather up the facts of their suffering, the abuse, the loss of property, and personal injuries, as well as the names of those who oppressed them:

> And perhaps a committee can be appointed to find out these things and to take statements and affidavits and also to gather up the libelous publications that are afloat and all that are in the magazines and encyclopedias and all the libelous histories that are published and that are written and by whom and present the whole concatenation of diabolical rascality and nefarious and murderous impositions that have been practiced upon this people. That we may not only publish to all the world, but present them to the heads of the government in all their dark and hellish hue as the last effort which is enjoined on us by our Heavenly Father before we can fully and completely claim that promise which shall call him forth from his hiding place and also that the whole nation may be left without excuse [Smith, 2002, p. 443].

By alluding to the rights of the press and petition, Smith indicates familiarity with the First Amendment. Smith's "fire and strength" are also plainly evident. Although imprisoned for five months, Smith's attitude remains one of self-defense and energy. He calls for a public affairs campaign to utilize the freedom of the press for self-defense. This campaign is not merely to redeem himself or his people, however. Its ultimate aim is to publish to the world the opposition against the Mormons so "that the whole nation may be left without excuse." The publication of abuses will hasten the judgments of God against the United States for failing to live up to their ideals by abridging the rights of an obscure sect.

In warning his people against bigotry and prejudice, Smith presents a model of sectarian cooperation and mutual recognition of rights while refusing a turn toward a purely secular society where religion is obliged to remain private. If members of the Latter-day Saint Church cannot learn to act with respect and tolerance toward those of other faiths, they cannot expect the same in return. Of course, Smith acknowledges, members of one sect or another will inevitably have stronger feelings for those of their own faith, but the political community depends on interactions between people of different faiths, inevitably bringing the subject of religion into the public sphere.

> Our religion is between us and our God, their religion is between them and their God.... There is a principle also which we are bound to be exercised with that is in common with all men such as governments and laws and regulations in the civil concerns of life. This principle guarantees to all parties, sects, and denominations, and classes of religion, equal, coherent, and indefeasible rights. They are rights that pertain to this life. Therefore, all are alike interested. They make our responsibilities one toward another in matters of corruptible things. While the former [religious] principles do not destroy the latter [political principles], but bind us stronger and make our responsibilities not only to one another but unto God [Smith, 2002, p. 445].

Religious principles, for Smith, are based in agreements made between an individual or community and God. Political principles are often informed by religious principles, but they are to maintain rights. A system of good government would promote cooperation between religious sects, but it would not allow one sect to hold sway over another in purely political matters. Smith imagined a world where people of different faiths fulfilled their obligations toward one another responsibly, but maintained a distinction between religious and civil concerns. The U.S. Constitution, in Smith's mind, defends the right of conscience, but is likewise a means for moderating intergroup relations.

In Smith's letter, the Constitution is treated as an instrument of sectarian cooperation and a means for securing the rights of worship for all the peoples of the earth.[9] His rhetoric suggests that the Constitution was inspired by God to secure for all on Earth, not merely the citizens of the United States, the right of living one's religion. Specifically, in his Liberty Jail letter, Smith refers to the Constitution by an analogy to the protective power of nature:

> Hence we say that the Constitution of the United States is a glorious standard. It is founded in the wisdom of God. It is a heavenly banner. It is to all those who are privileged with the sweets of its liberty like the cooling shades and refreshing waters of a great rock in a thirsty and weary land. It is like a great tree under whose branches men from every clime can be shielded from the burning rays of an inclement sun [Smith, 2002, p. 445].

To Smith, the primary function of the Constitution is defensive and comforting: the Constitution shields and protects as well as shades and refreshes.

The words "standard" and "banner" evoke militaristic images, but Smith never strays far from nature, especially as presented through biblical narrative. The parallels to the story of Moses giving drink to the Israelites in the desert (Exodus 17:6) are obvious, and the image of refreshing waters flowing out of the great rock is intended to quench the thirst of American Mormons for religious liberty. Even more broadly, the American Constitution represents a promise of religious liberty to those "from every clime," constituting a global invitation to the peoples of the earth to live freely and worship freely.

Smith's claim that the Constitution is "founded in the wisdom of God" evokes a sense of the sacred at the center of public life. In a system that protects religious liberty, no sect can claim a monopoly on sacredness, but it does not follow that human society can exist without some idea of the sacred at its core. If the Constitution protects the dominant Protestant sects then it must also find a way to protect the Latter-day Saints.

> We ... are deprived of the protection of this glorious principle by the cruelty of the cruel, by those who only look for the time being for pasturage like the beasts of the field only to fill themselves, and forget that the Mormons as well as the Presbyterians and those of every other class and description have equal rights to partake of the fruit of the great tree of our national liberty. Notwithstanding ... that fruit is no less precious and delicious to our taste. We cannot be weaned from the milk, neither can we be drawn from the breast, neither will we deny our religion because of the hand of oppression, but we will hold on until death. We say that God is true, that the Constitution of the United States is true, that the Bible is true, that the Book of Mormon is true, that the book of covenants is true, that Christ is true, that the ministering angels sent forth from God are true, and that we know that we have a house not made with hands, eternal in the heavens, whose builder and maker is God — a consolation which our oppressors cannot feel when fortune or fate shall lay its iron hand on them as it has on us [Smith, 2002, pp. 445–446].

The truth of the United States Constitution is on par with the truth of the Bible and the *Book of Mormon* because its guarantees are universal. They do not apply merely to Mormons or Presbyterians, but to every class and description, and, according to earlier revelations, to all flesh. By elevating constitutional claims to a cosmic, universal level, Smith's constitutional theory is broad in outlook, reflecting his conviction that freedom of conscience is necessary to be accountable before God. In his 1839 Liberty Jail letter (and in an in-person meeting later that year in Washington, DC, with President Martin Van Buren), Smith implies that the Constitution gives the federal government the power and obligation to intervene in controversies concerning the denial of rights to certain classes or groups — a claim that was by no means a settled matter of constitutional law at the time.

In the letter from Liberty Jail, Smith's feelings of oppression and urgency are palpable even in the midst of his rights claims. Notwithstanding his hope that American liberty will extend to all, Smith likens his church to a baby ripped from the breast of its mother. Smith and his followers cannot be weaned from American liberty or the Constitution's promises, even in the midst of persecution and unjust imprisonment. The promise of American liberty is too sweet to be forgotten, even when denied. The only hope for the Saints may be life after death or the possibility that "fortune or fate" will reverse the roles of oppressor and oppressed. If the government fails to rise to its ideals, the only consolation may be God's biblical promise that He is building a heavenly mansion for his saints to dwell in for eternity. Although it has been noted that the Constitution itself does not mention God (Kramnick and Moore, 1997), Smith's religion includes the rights of the Constitution. This inclusion and internalization of American rights, together with Smith's revelations regarding heavenly inspiration for the American founders, allows him to speak of Constitutional rights in a religious vein. To Smith, constitutional truths are as valid as scriptural promises about the after-life, and thus the country can reach its potential only if it realizes how precious these truths are.

From start to finish, Smith's letter highlights the wrongs against his people as he understands them. Smith seeks to frame these wrongs as wrongs against the country. Initially held for treason, Smith reverses the charge by implicating the Missourian willingness to deny the Mormons the rights to vote and to practice their religion as crimes against the United States Constitution. Although Smith is locked in prison, roughly handled, and ill-fed, his letter speaks instead of the wrongs against his people as proof of wrongs against the American ideals held high in the God-inspired United States Constitution. The Constitution holds the best hope of defending the persecuted from the persecutor. The Constitution is the best protection from the whims of elected officials and loosely organized frontier militias. Just as the best defense is a good offense, Smith recommends that his church keep a close and careful record of the abuses against them and publish to the world the justice of their claims. Simultaneously, Smith uses the letter as an opportunity to highlight the weakness of human political power in the face of God and His promises of deliverance. One way or another, either by securing their rights through political means or military might, or by building them a house in heaven, God's promises to his Saints are as good as gold — whether they come through the Latter-day Mormon scripture revealed to the prophet or through the latter-day Constitutional scripture that sprang from the pens of the American founders.

The defining characteristic of the Missouri conflict, as Smith sees it, is the Missourian (and, thus, American) failure to uphold the rights of the First Amendment. The conflict is presented as one between a religious sect and a corrupt government. It is not merely the failure of the state of Missouri, however, but also that of the popular press that must be curtailed if the Saints are to have any hope of being rewarded their rights. By the epistle's final pages, the United States Constitution is presented as the only sure defense against mobs, renegades, liars, priests, and thieves. Without the promise of the Bill of Rights as a standard and banner, the Latter-day Saints have no claim. The heart of Smith's protest is thus grounded in the uniquely American invention of religious freedom, together with the rights of the press, petition, property, assembly, and speech. Given that Smith's conflict with the Missouri government takes place during the antebellum period, the determination that the Federal government is to protect minority rights, and peculiar minorities at that, is by no means yet a settled aspect of constitutional theory or practice. Still, this does not stop Smith from arguing that the truth of the Constitution is as universal as the truths of Holy Scripture, and that the rights of the Latter-day Saints are as precious to God as they ought to be to every citizen of the United States because the Constitution regulates all citizens in the common affairs of life.

The act of calling the nation to account, although perceived by non–Mormon neighbors as hostile rhetoric, is certainly radical and prophetic.[10] The implication is that the nation must answer and account for its failure to defend the Mormons from persecution. Indeed, Smith's time in Liberty Jail marks a major turning point in his approach to political and public affairs. After his escape, Smith was no longer content with being carried downstream by political forces. He was now going to make political decisions and political realities for himself in an effort to defend his people. In the roughly five years following his escape from Liberty Jail to the time of his death, Smith would found the city of Nauvoo, Illinois, where he would serve as mayor and Lieutenant-General of the local militia; travel to Washington, DC, to petition President Van Buren for redress; be arrested on three additional occasions on Missouri charges, but have those charges quashed by Nauvoo judges; join a Freemasonry lodge in Nauvoo; and launch a campaign for President of the United States. The days of passively waiting for the United States to deliver him were now over, even though the hope and expectation that religious liberty would be made absolute would endure.

Conclusion

This chapter situates Joseph Smith's 1839 letter from Liberty Jail within the context of Latter-day Saint ideas about American liberty that reach back to pre–Columbian times. Smith's letter is a rhetorical act of profound social protest that ties notions of American religious liberty to those of American destiny. The epistle discredits religious persecution and bigotry by an appeal to the American Constitution and an implicit civil religion. Smith's claims point to three conclusions about American exceptionalist rhetoric.

First, it is time to speak of American exceptionalisms. The Latter-day Saint perspective presents unique ideas about the history of liberty on the North and South American continents and about the development and meaning of the United States Constitution. This perspective suggests that there may be innumerable ways to think about and see America. To state that American exceptionalism has long been associated with American religion is obvious, but how the various American religions imagine and speak of America is a pressing question. The Latter-day Saints had broad ideas about the magnitude and expansive nature of religious freedom, and when these ideas came into conflict with the wider society, the Saints looked for creative ways to defend their claims. This creativity was not widely respected in the 1830s, but, as often happens, ideas of and about America that are not accepted at one point in time are often supported later as social attitudes and practices evolve.

Second, it is important to recognize, as Seymour Lipset (1996) has done, that American exceptionalism is a double-edged sword. The unique elements of religious freedom were tools that Joseph Smith used to highlight deficiencies in the American system. A government that purported to defend religious liberty but did not do so in practice was a sham. Although Smith was charged with acts of treason, he implicitly returned a charge of treason against his persecutors by an elaboration of the meaning of the American Constitution and its power to secure, defend, and protect civil liberties. This defense was unique in its time, but its implications go much deeper. Indeed, Smith's rhetoric manages to simultaneously defend and attack America, inviting it to become a better version of itself. This double-edged nature of American civil rights rhetoric represented by Smith's epistle deserves greater attention in studies of 19th-century American rhetorical artifacts. It is also a theme that recurs repeatedly in civil rights rhetoric in the 20th century, including perhaps most famously in Martin Luther King, Jr.'s, April 16, 1963, "Letter from Birmingham Jail."

Finally, the broad historical sense of Mormon ideas about American promise are worthy of greater attention. That the Latter-day Saints have a unique view of history should be obvious. What is interesting is how this view of history connects with popular and political ideas about America and American uniqueness. Latter-day Saint ideas about American uniqueness suggest that it may be time for our theorizing of American exceptionalism to move beyond the United States itself, both chronologically and geographically. Latter-day Saint scripture, at least, interprets the continents of North and South America to be part of an ancient covenant and reasons that the continents have long been a refuge for those seeking religious liberty. Regardless of whether one subscribes to the possibilities of such covenants or ancient seekers, that ideas regarding them held powerful sway in nineteenth-century religious discourse is surely significant. Perhaps the lesson of greatest importance to be found in Smith's American exceptionalist rhetoric is his inability to restrict his imaginative scope concerning the meaning and promise of America.

Notes

1. For a good overview of the process of Americanizing and democratizing Christianity, see Hatch (1989). For a critical examination of American religion, including Mormonism, see Bloom (1992).

2. The phrase "American Scripture" is used to refer to texts written in America that are treated by a community as spiritually authoritative, as distinguished from scriptural texts that are imported, like the Bible. "American Scripture" is sometimes used by scholars of American civil religion to refer to sacred political texts such as the Declaration of Independence, and although this is not my intended meaning, as the argument unfolds it is shown that the distinction between these two kinds of American Scripture in the Latter-day Saint mind is untenable. See Givens (2002) and Maier (1998) for more detailed explanations.

3. All quotations from Smith's 1839 Liberty Jail Letter are taken from Jessee's (2002) edited collection, *Personal Writings of Joseph Smith*. I have not reproduced typographical indications that a word or phrase was inserted or struck words and phrases, and I have modernized spelling, capitalization, punctuation, and abbreviation in all quotations from this source. For canonized selections from the letter, see sections 121, 122, and 123 of *Doctrine and Covenants*.

4. There are numerous passages in the *Book of Mormon* about the special status of the Americas. Among them are 1 Nephi 2:20; 4:14; 7:1, 13; 13:12, 30; 14:2; 17:13–14; 18: 8, 22–23; 2 Nephi 1:3, 5, 10, 19, 24; Mosiah 10:15; Ether 6:5, 8, 12, 16; 7:27.

5. The scholarly treatment of the *Book of Mormon* is voluminous. For the best general study, see Givens (2002). For treatment of the *Book of Mormon* as American Scripture, see Bloom (1992); Bushman (1976, 1984, 2005); Hatch (1989); and Wood (1980). For general but important treatment, see O'Dea (1957) and Shipps (1985).

6. For an interesting popular introduction to how these Mormon anxieties inspired anti-communism and Glenn Beck's 9/12 Project, see Zaitchik, 2009. For an alternative Mormon perspective on Beck's sources, see Midgley, 1971.

7. The five moved to Liberty Jail with Joseph Smith were Sidney Rigdon, Smith's counselor in the First Presidency of the Church; Lyman Wight; Hyrum Smith, Joseph's brother; Alexander McRae, a 31-year-old captain of the Missouri Militia who had been active in the defense of the saints; and Caleb Baldwin, a veteran of the War of 1812, who at 47 was the oldest of the prisoners. See Arrington (1973) for additional information.

8. On April 6, 1830, the day Smith organized the church, he received a revelation that began, "Behold, there shall be a record kept among you." See *Doctrine and Covenants* 21:1.

9. As Smith later put it in his later Wentworth letter, the Latter-day Saints "claim the privilege of worshipping Almighty God according to the dictates of our own conscience, and allow all men the same privilege, let them worship how, where, or what they may" (Smith, 1842/1980, p. 535).

10. In this respect, Smith's rhetoric fits well in the American tradition of radical prophetic rhetoric. For more on that tradition, see Darsey (1997).

References

Arnold, M. (2001). *Culture and Anarchy: An Essay in Political and Social Criticism*. Cambridge: Cambridge University Press. (Original work published 1869.)

Arrington, L. J. (1973). "Church Leaders in Liberty Jail." *BYU Studies, 13*, 1–5.

_____, and D. Bitton (1992). *The Mormon Experience: A History of the Latter-Day Saints* (2d ed.). Urbana: University of Illinois Press.

Baugh, A. L. (2000). *A Call to Arms: The 1838 Mormon Defense of Northern Missouri*. Provo: BYU Studies.

Bercovitch, S. (1980). *The American Jeremiad*. Madison: University of Wisconsin Press.

Bloom, H. (1992). *The American Religion*. New York: Chu Hartley.

Boggs, L. W. (1838). "Governor Boggs' Extermination Order." Missouri State Archives, Missouri Mormon War Collection. Retrieved from http://www.sos.mo.gov/archives/resources/findingaids/miscMormonRecords.asp?rec=eo.

Book of Mormon. (1981). Salt Lake City: Church of Jesus Christ of Latter-day Saints.

Bushman, R. L. (1976). "The Book of Mormon and the American Revolution." *BYU Studies, 17*, 1–17.

_____ (1984). *Joseph Smith and the Beginnings of Mormonism*. Urbana: University of Illinois Press.

_____ (2005). *Joseph Smith: Rough Stone Rolling*. New York: Alfred A. Knopf.

Darsey, J. (1997). *The Prophetic Tradition and Radical Rhetoric in America*. New York: New York University Press.

Doctrine and Covenants. (1981). Salt Lake City: Church of Jesus Christ of Latter-day Saints.

Givens, T. L. (2002). *By the Hand of Mormon: The American Scripture That Launched a New World Religion*. Oxford: Oxford University Press.

Hatch, N. O. (1989). *The Democratization of American Christianity*. New Haven: Yale University Press.

Jessee, D. C. (1979). "Joseph Smith's 19 July 1840 Discourse." *BYU Studies, 19*, 390–394.

_____ (Ed.) (2002). *Personal Writings of Joseph Smith*. Provo: Brigham Young University Press.

_____, and J. W. Welch (2000). "Revelations in Context: Joseph Smith's Letter from Liberty Jail, March 20, 1839." *BYU Studies, 39*, 125–145.

King, M. L., Jr. (1963, April 16). "Letter from Birmingham Jail." *The Papers of Martin Luther King, Jr*. Retrieved from http://www.stanford.edu/group/King/frequentdocs/birmingham.pdf.

Kramnick, I., and R. L. Moore (1997). *The Godless Constitution: The Case Against Religious Correctness*. New York: W.W. Norton.

LeSueur, S.C. (1990). *The 1838 Mormon War in Missouri*. Columbia: University of Missouri Press.

Lipset, S. M. (1996). *American Exceptionalism: A Double-Edged Sword*. New York: W.W. Norton.

Maier, P. (1998). *American Scripture: Making the Declaration of Independence*. New York: Random House.

Miller, P. (1953). *The New England Mind: From Colony to Province*. Cambridge, MA: Harvard University Press.
Midgley, L.C. (1971). "The Cult of Conspiracy." *Dialogue: A Journal of Mormon Thought*, 6, 100–108.
O'Dea, T .F. (1957). *The Mormons*. Chicago: University of Chicago Press.
Shipps, J. (1985). *Mormonism: The Story of a New Religious Tradition*. Urbana: University of Illinois Press.
Smith, J. (1980). "Wentworth letter, 1 March 1842." In B. H. Roberts (Ed.), *History of the Church* (Vol. 4, pp. 535–541). Salt Lake City: Deseret. (Original work published 1842.)
_____ (2002). "To the Church at Quincy, Illinois, 20 March 1839." In D. C. Jessee (Ed.), *Personal Writings of Joseph Smith* (pp. 429–446). Provo: Brigham Young University Press. (Original work published 1839.)
Wood, G. S. (1980). "Evangelical America and Early Mormonism." *New York History, 61*, 359–386.
Zaitchik, A. (2009, September 16). "Meet the Man who Changed Glenn Beck's Life: Cleon Skousen Was a Right Wing Crank Whom Even Conservatives Despised." Salon.com. Retrieved from http://www.salon.com/news/feature/2009/09/16/beck_skousen/index.html.

CHAPTER 7

Henry Cabot Lodge and the Rhetorical Trajectory

MICHAEL J. HOSTETLER

Donald W. Meinig (1986) argues that history has "geographical character" which is not "the determination of history by the fundament of nature," but rather "the human creation of places and of networks of relationships among them." Geography becomes therefore a "special way of looking at the world" (p. xv). Similarly, critical theorists have explored space and place as important factors of constructed reality. Doreen Massey, John Allen, and Phil Sarre (1999, p. 17) claim the "geographical imagination" is a critical component of "that 'real world' which we socially construct, and has immense influence on the ways in which people act within it." According to Massey and her colleagues, the "politicized imaginings of geopolitics" are one component of this geographical imagination. The expression of geographical character or imagination may occur in music or visual or performing arts, but its most obvious practical and political expression occurs rhetorically. The interaction of physical surroundings and the rhetorical construction of those surroundings is deep and complex. At the very least, it is seen in common spatial orientation metaphors which are ubiquitous in all forms of communication from interpersonal exchanges to geopolitical discourse. More specifically, in American national discourse, distance imagery in particular has been a salient force. As I have discussed elsewhere, the size of the North American continent struck European settlers as huge beyond belief (Hostetler, 2002, 2006). As Jean Baudrillard once observed, "As soon as you set foot in America, you feel the presence of an entire continent — space there is the very form of thought" (1988, p. 16).

The sheer size of North America has had an obvious influence on American development from the quest for a constitutional structure that would unite a huge republic to debates over internal improvements — the roads, bridges and canals — that could make transportation and commerce over great distances possible. A more overlooked influence of geographical size on the national psyche, however, is its impact on American exceptionalism, the belief that somehow the United States' political culture, capitalist energy, and moral example are destined by Providence to be the example and the hope of the world (McCrisken, 2003). Jason A. Edwards (2008) has pointed out three ideas that have informed this belief: "the United States is a special nation with a special destiny; the United States is qualitatively different from Europe; and the United States can escape the trappings of history" (p. 6). To this list we may add a fourth factor: size. Not only is America exceptional because of its *qualitative* difference from Europe, but also due to its *quantitative* difference. The contrast is stark. In terms of area, North America, at 24,256,000 square kilometers, is just about two and a half times bigger than Europe (9,938,000 sq. km.). France, for example, is smaller than Colorado and New Mexico combined. It is a truism that, "while Europe has had too much history and not enough geography, America has relatively little history and plenty of geography" (Kaplan, 1998, pp. 113–114).

Somehow the Europeans landing in America were obliged to come to grips with the enormous dimensions of their new home. Frequently, this task was described with a rhetoric of "overcoming" or "conquering" space and distance. For those who saw the New World as a verdant garden, the task was to prune and tend it. For those who found a howling wilderness, the challenge was to subdue it (Marx, 1964). In either case, space needed to be conquered.[1] The movement inherent in the idea of conquering space was naturally and inevitably westward. The mythical American frontier always lay just beyond the western horizon. The geographical reality of western movement was reinforced by the rhetoric of expansion which in turn created and conditioned the impetus for further westward movement.[2] This ongoing interaction of westward settlement and the rhetoric of western destiny is a variation on "rhetorical trajectory," a construct discussed by critic Leland M. Griffin. Following on the work of Kenneth Burke, Griffin (1984) argued that

> rhetoric, indeed, "maketh a ready man," that we are moved by our rhetoric as our rhetoric is designed to move others, and that by the tracing of the terminological trajectories in the rhetoric of an individual or a collectivity we may gain understanding as to how a particular state of readiness is achieved [p. 127].

For most of the nineteenth century Americans conceived of their special role and destiny in the world to be intimately connected to westward geographical movement.³ As a result, the rhetoric of American exceptionalism, conditioned by physical geography, had a particular rhetorical trajectory that was directional, creating a language and a logic of geographical movement from east to west.

Toward the end of the nineteenth century, however, new geographical and political realities challenged the continued saliency of the directional rhetoric of exceptionalism. First, the limit of geographical expansion in North America was reached. In his celebrated paper of 1893, Frederick Jackson Turner famously announced the closing of the American frontier. At the same time, American victories in two wars ushered the United States onto the world stage as a potential colonial power. Victory in the war with Spain ignited a vigorous debate over the disposition of seized territories, some of which, like the Philippine Islands, were half a world away from North America. Twenty years later, in the wake of the First World War, another major foreign policy debate commenced over the role of the United States in the proposed League of Nations and what many saw as the far-flung obligations that participation in the League would entail. These new historical conditions called into question the customary rhetoric of American exceptionalism and expansion. Could the rhetoric of America's exceptional destiny with its implied directional quality be adjusted to the new realities of the closing of the North American frontier and the emergence of the United States as a potential colonial power? At least a partial answer to this question can be discovered in the rhetoric of one of the most important American foreign policy makers at the turn of the twentieth century, Senator Henry Cabot Lodge.

Lodge played a pivotal role in postwar debates over Philippine annexation and the League of Nations. His rhetoric in these debates reveals both the resiliency and the malleability of the directional aspect of the rhetoric of American exceptionalism. Two of Lodge's speeches in particular illustrate that even after the perceived "closing" of the frontier, the rhetoric of westward movement could still be invoked to preserve and enhance America's special calling in the world. In fact, this rhetoric was quite flexible. Depending on the situation, it could be invoked by the same speaker in different ways in pursuit of seemingly disparate rhetorical ends. Lodge employed directional logic in arguing for both the *extension* and the *curtailment* of American involvement overseas. In 1900, he argued that the United States should extend its power and influence westward into the Pacific by annexing the Philippine Islands. Nineteen years later, however, he argued against American entry into the League of Nations as established in the Treaty of Versailles.

How Lodge could champion American imperial engagement in the one case and isolationist disengagement in the other shows how the directional nature of exceptionalism could be used both as a warrant to expand and restrict American influence. In the Philippine annexation debate Lodge used the inevitable western movement of American civilization to refute objections that the Philippines were too far away to be governed. Later, in the League of Nations debate, he argued that turning America's attention to a League based in Europe was a move in the wrong direction, an unimaginable reversal of America's westward movement. A careful reading of two of Lodge's speeches on these issues illustrates the enduring relevance and flexibility of the directional, exceptionalist rhetoric of American destiny and at the same time casts light on what seem to be contradictions in Lodge's thinking.

Henry Cabot Lodge: Supreme Tactician

Henry Cabot Lodge was an upper class Bostonian who, in 1876, received one of the first three doctoral degrees ever conferred by Harvard University. Henry Adams was his mentor and Theodore Roosevelt his closest friend. Lodge was elected to the Massachusetts Assembly and the U.S. House of Representatives before serving in the United States Senate from 1893 until his death in 1924. As the influential chairman of the Foreign Relations Committee, Lodge developed a reputation for his hard work, notorious partisanship and acerbic personality (Garraty, 1965). Warren Zimmermann characterizes him as a "tenacious" partisan, "the supreme political tactician of his time" (1998, p. 54). Similarly, Herbert F. Margulies (1989, p. 11) says of Lodge, "There was 'pepper' in his makeup, but much caution and resourcefulness too."

Lodge was no ideologue. His positions on issues were invariably worked out in the crucible of politics, a fact that seems inevitably to open politicians to criticism. David Fromkin (1996) charges that Lodge's foreign policy positions were ambiguous because Lodge was both an expansionist and an isolationist. However, Fromkin's claim that these seemingly disparate views can be chalked up to political considerations, that in order to win elections, it became "second nature" for Lodge "to hide, deny, or misrepresent his opinions" (p. 76), is not only ungenerous, but naïve. David Zarefsky has rightly pointed out that political and social beliefs seldom "derive systematically from philosophy and ideology" (1996, p. 3). On the contrary, they are worked out rhetorically in light of the opportunities and restraints inherent in practical political situations. This was certainly true of Henry Cabot Lodge. His positions were often skillfully crafted mosaics of various factors, including the interests of the New England fishing industry, the partisan considerations of the Republican Party, and the conservative influences of his class. As a result,

Lodge was neither a reformer nor a reactionary in domestic policy (Garraty, 1965). In foreign affairs, especially in the aftermath of the Spanish War in 1900, he was an expansionist, but not an imperialist. During the League of Nations debate in 1919, he was a nationalist, but no isolationist. "Lodge's isolationism was never more than occasional.... Lodge's imperialism was but a gloss on his conception of the nature of international relations and of how foreign policy ought to be conducted" (Widenor, 1980, p. 67).

Lodge was not a "great orator" in the nineteenth century mold, but he was a careful and able communicator. Garraty claims that he "set an exacting standard of intelligence and responsibility in his public utterances. Nearly all his speeches were logical arguments, sticking closely to the points at issue, and free of oratorical bombast, appeals to prejudice, and personalities" (1965, p. 125). Lodge was so meticulous in his speech preparation that "he always verified even the most familiar of the literary allusions he loved to use, and his habit of so thoroughly digesting his remarks as to be able to speak fluently for hours on end with only a few scribbled notes in his hand" showed his penchant for detail and organization (Garraty, 1965, p. 229). Margulies observes, "With his thumbs adjusted in his armpits and with a copy of Shakespeare in his pocket, he spoke, in rasping tones, words that were brilliant but often bitter" (1989, p. 11). Lodge was conscious of the fact that he occupied the Senate seat of Daniel Webster and Charles Sumner and he undoubtedly saw himself as responsible for continuing a long and storied tradition of Senate oratory. Scott E. Atkins (1998, para. 2) points out that Lodge's speech, "The Pilgrims of Plymouth," delivered in 1920, "explicitly sets itself up as a parallel to Webster's 1820 'Plymouth Oration.'" It is not surprising, therefore, that Lodge chose March 7, 1900, to deliver a major speech on Philippine annexation. It was the fiftieth anniversary, to the day, of Webster's celebrated speech, "The Constitution and the Union."

Lodge and the Philippines: The Inevitability of Westward Movement as "Our Great Mission in the World"

The Treaty of Paris, ending the war with Spain, was signed in December of 1898 and submitted for Senate confirmation in the following month. Richard E. Welch, Jr., (1971) claims that the ensuing debate "was one of the more intelligent, reasoned, and significant debates in American history" (p. 221). Constitutional and moral issues dominated the discussion, which Welch sees as a classic confrontation of the American ideals of Manifest Destiny and Mission. However, other more mundane concerns, such as the remoteness of seized Spanish holdings, were not absent from the debate. Theodore Draper observes, "In the pre-war period, the Philippines were so far away and little known that they might have existed on a different planet" (1999, pp. 43–44).

After the war, opponents of annexation made an issue of distance. For example, in August 1898, Andrew Carnegie railed against annexation in an article entitled "Distant Possessions: The Parting of the Ways." He argued that due to its distance from the United States, the Philippines would be too hard to defend and that instead of incurring vast costs trying to govern a far-flung dependency, a more pressing need was "to improve our internal waterways" in order to transcend the still daunting distances of North America. "All these enterprises [various canal projects] would be as nothing in cost in comparison with the sums required for the experiment of possessing the Philippine Islands, seven thousand miles from our shores" (p. 246). When the annexation debate reached the Senate in early 1899, Lodge's fellow Republican and Massachusetts colleague, George Frisbie Hoar, argued against acquiring the Philippines, at least in part due to the problem of distance—both geographical and cultural. He describes the Filipinos as "a distant people, dwelling in the Tropics, aliens in blood, most of them Moslem in faith, incapable to speak or comprehend our language, or to read and write any language, to whom the traditions and doctrines of civil liberty are unknown" (p. 494).[4]

The argument based on the geographical remoteness of the Philippines was not lost on the Democrats. In his speech to the party's National Convention in the summer of 1900, William Jennings Bryan (1900) compared the distance of the United States from Puerto Rico and from the Philippines:

> If the Puerto Ricans, who welcomed annexation, are to be denied the guarantees of our Constitution, what is to be the lot of the Filipinos, who resisted our authority? If secret influences could compel a disregard of our plain duty toward friendly people living near our shores, what treatment will those same influences provide for unfriendly people 7000 miles away? [pp. 205–207].

Although the Treaty of Paris was confirmed on February 6, 1899, the debate over Philippine policy continued. When, in early 1900, the discussion turned to the presidential powers needed to govern the islands,[5] Lodge delivered what Welch terms "the most detailed brief imperialism was ever to receive in America" (1971, p. 261). The three-hour speech consisted of a careful refutation of the various and oft-repeated objections to American expansion (Lodge, 1900). No explicit reference is made to geographical distance as a factor in Philippine annexation until the speech's peroration where Lodge deals with the issue indirectly. Essentially, Lodge sees the distances that might stand in the way of American empire as being mitigated by an inexorable geo-political movement based on natural law. He argues that American history can be understood in geographical terms as an inevitable movement from east to west. The claim is made in grand terms:

> This mighty movement westward, building up a nation and conquering a continent as it swept along, has not been the work of chance or accident. It was neither chance nor accident which brought us to the Pacific and which has now carried us across the great ocean even to the shores of Asia, to the very edge of the cradle of the Aryans, whence our far distant ancestors started on the march which has since girdled the world [1900, p. 2629].

Lodge's argument regarding the inevitability of American westward expansion is based on a belief in historical determinism which, in turn, grows out of the concept of "natural law" that was popular at the turn of the century. He claims that what Americans "have done was inevitable because it was in accordance with the laws of our being as a nation" (1900, p. 2630). Although he "should be the last to deny the doctrine of free will" (1900, p. 2630), nevertheless, he holds to an idea of natural law that decrees, "that when certain conditions are given, certain results are sure to come" (1900, p. 2630). In the following telling passage, Lodge creates an image of American expansion beyond the Pacific Ocean that at first magnifies distance by drawing an analogy to astronomy and then collapses that distance by invoking natural law:

> We stand like children on the seashore, knowing only the shells and the pebbles where we tread, understanding only the ripple of the waves breaking at our feet, while far away before us stretches the great ocean of knowledge, whose confines we can not see, and whose possessions we can only dimly guess. We catalogued the visible stars and then photographed the heavens, only to find far beyond the bodies which the most powerful telescopes can disclose myriads of stars and systems glimmering away into infinite space. What they are, what other worlds than ours there may be we do not know, but we have learned that they move in obedience to law [1900, p. 2630].

For Lodge, the laws of nature apply equally to history and politics. The "children on the seashore" peering into the "ocean of knowledge" may just as easily be seen as Americans standing on the western shores of North America scanning the Pacific. The perceived distances are indeed intimidating, but they are brought to heel by natural law. As in astronomy, law mitigates distance because it applies equally, near or far. Therefore, distance is no longer an obstacle to empire because it is mitigated by inevitable movement which is the manifestation of universal natural law.

Lodge's natural law argument for expansionism provides only a partial answer to anti-imperialism critics like Bryan. The Democrats and anti-imperialist Republicans such as Hoar, claimed that imperialism was immoral. Early in the speech, Lodge argues the opposite:

> I believe that to abandon the islands, or to leave them now, would be a wrong to humanity, a dereliction of duty, a base betrayal of the Filipinos who have supported us, led by the best men of Luzon, and in the highest degree contrary to sound morals [1900, p. 2618].

To defend this assertion, he spends a good deal of time in the speech's first section dealing with moral objections that had been raised against Administration policy.[6] As he concludes the speech, however, his natural law argument, outlined above, gives expansionism a rational or "scientific" warrant, but not a moral one. Lodge moves to rectify this shortcoming and to provide a fitting conclusion to his earlier claims by reaching for further moral justification for expansion. He does this by vaguely connecting natural law to God in the following *a fortiori* argument:

> If we say with reverence, as the greatest of poets said, that we are in the care of Him "who doth the ravens feed; yea, providently caters for the sparrow," are we to suppose that nations alone are not subject to law? [1900, p. 2630].

Lodge was not a religious person, but this reference to God, however weak, provides the necessary link between natural law and morality. If God's law applies to lesser things, then, obviously it must apply to greater. He goes on to say that America "has a great mission in the world—a mission of good, a mission of freedom" (1900, p. 2630). The logic is inescapable: if American expansion is the result of natural law which is an expression of the will of God, how can it be anything other than good? For Lodge, the westward direction of American destiny was supported by both natural law and moral warrant.

For Lodge, American exceptionalism needed little ontological justification—it was natural and, therefore, moral. The question Lodge addressed was one of policy. What direction should America's destiny take? The vast expanse of the North American continent had always beckoned Europeans westward. Even when the land ran out, the logic of westward movement endured. Nothing could be more natural than for America to find its destiny beyond the western shores of California in the Pacific Rim. This vision of Pacific destiny may be seen as a critical factor in sowing the seeds of an eventual military confrontation with Japan.

Lodge and the League of Nations: The Impossibility of Eastward Movement Fulfilling "The Best Hopes of Mankind"

When George Frisbie Hoar gave his anti-imperialism speech in the Senate in early 1899, Senator Orville H. Platt of Connecticut responded by saying, "We have spread [our] civilization across the continent until it stood at the Pacific Ocean looking ever westward" (1899, p. 503). He then quoted a line from a poem by Bishop George Berkeley: *Westward the course of empire takes its way.*

Two decades later, the question confronting the United States was quite different. Could the American empire find a way eastward, back across the Atlantic, into the affairs of Europe? For Henry Cabot Lodge, the answer was clearly no. Lodge's position, of course, ran counter to that of President Wilson and his idea of a League of Nations which was perceived to commit the United States to a greater diplomatic role, particularly in relation to Europe. For Wilson, the Covenant of the League was the centerpiece of the Versailles Treaty and he would have no treaty rather than abandon the League. In the Senate debate on the Treaty and the Covenant, Lodge employed the same westward rhetorical trajectory as a warrant for disengagement from Europe that he invoked to support expansion into Asia in 1900. Just as he had done in the earlier debate, Lodge capitalized on the potential for movement inherent in geographical distance imagery, but that movement could only be in one direction. A careful reading of the speech, entitled "Treaty of Peace with Germany" (Lodge, 1925), shows how the Senator invoked the imagery of geographical movement for his rhetorical ends.

Lodge gave his major Senate address opposing the Covenant on August 12, 1919. At the very beginning of the speech, he engages the idea of movement by posing a contrast between repetitive and progressive motion. He discounts the "popular fallacy" that "history repeats itself," claiming that "history never exactly repeats itself" (1925, p. 380). He says the fallacy of seeing history as repetitive "springs from the undoubted truth that mankind from generation to generation is constantly repeating itself" (1925, p. 380). The distinction Lodge draws between the alleged repetitive movement of history and the actual repetitiveness of human behavior is no quibble. Indeed, the argument of his speech depends on the distinction. For Lodge, history is a natural force that moves progressively and inexorably forward even if human beings are caught in the foolish repetitions of past behavior. This forward, "progressive" movement of history is, of course, part and parcel of Lodge's natural law philosophy and his vision of American destiny.

While the locus of westward movement was in the conclusion of his Philippine Annexation speech, Lodge's invocation of the same imagery occurs primarily in the overall structure and movement of this speech. In the first part of the speech, he focuses on Europe, drawing an analogy between the end of the Napoleonic Wars and World War I to prove his point about foolish, repetitious human behavior. In the second section, he draws attention away from Europe to the Covenant itself as he outlines a host of objections to several of its specific Articles. Finally, Lodge moves to a discussion of more domestic concerns: refuting his opponents' accusations that he and his allies are selfish isolationists, lamenting the possible effect of European involvement on immigrants in America, and invoking patriotic sentiment. In sum, the speech itself enacts what Lodge believed to be the movement of history — or, at least, America's exceptional place in that history — by moving the audience's attention from east to west, starting with Europe and then moving away from it, towards America and beyond.

Lodge begins his oration with a long, involved historical narrative portraying Europe as complicated and treacherous. The narrative focuses on the development of the Holy Alliance, beginning with the Peace of Utrecht and the Treaty of Paris in 1815. Lodge claims that noble sentiments of European peace and cooperation, discussed in the eighteenth century, were invoked in the formulation of the Treaty of Paris in the wake of Napoleon's defeat. The analogy between the European political situation in 1815 and that of 1919 is clearly implied. By showing that an attempt to assure "the peace of the world by a combination of the nations is no new idea" (1925, p. 380), Lodge proves his point that people, but not history, repeat themselves. According to Lodge, the treaty, in spite of its lofty language, did nothing more than establish a new evil alliance, a fact quickly ascertained by the British, who broke away from the agreement by 1822. The Holy Alliance, "so hostile and dangerous to human freedom," constitutes "a lesson for us at the present moment, showing as it does what may come from general propositions and declarations of purposes in which all the world agrees" (1925, p. 385).

By beginning with a narrative of Europe's historical failures, Lodge creates a starting point for the movement of his speech. The focus of the second section of the address is not on Europe, but on several articles in the League of Nations Covenant as they relate to American interests. Lodge finds the wording in the Covenant to be grandiose yet ill-defined. The Covenant's vague and sweeping stipulations would, according to Lodge, undercut national sovereignty and lead the United States into all manner of unwanted foreign involvement. He develops several undesirable scenarios for United States foreign policy based on possible implications of the Covenant's wording. As he does so, he shifts the attention of the audience from Europe's past to America's possible future, rhetorically enacting his view that (American) history moves geographically westward.

Movement from east to west is more specifically invoked in the last section of the speech where Lodge refutes charges that Republican opposition to the League grew out of selfishness and isolationism. He dismisses the accusation of isolationism by referring to Philippine annexation which he championed twenty years previously.

> I think the Spanish War marked the entrance of the United States into world affairs to a degree which had never obtained before. It was both an inevitable and an irrevocable step, and our entrance into the war with Germany certainly showed once and for all the United States was not unmindful of its world responsibilities [1925, pp. 404–405].

Interestingly, Lodge's deterministic view of history made expansion into Asia "inevitable," but it does not have the same effect on the projection of American interests into the postwar affairs of Europe. In fact, he goes on to cite "our geographical situation" (1925, p. 405) as a positive factor in shielding the United States "from the broils of Europe" (1925, p. 405). In terms of the Philippines, Lodge was suggesting, geographical distance was an obstacle to be overcome by the march of history, but when it comes to involvement in a European-sponsored League of Nations, our geographical situation is a protective barrier against unwanted foreign entanglements. The factor that enables Lodge to use distance imagery in these two differing ways is the image's implication of movement which, for Lodge, is always from east to west. This is brought out again two paragraphs later where he argues that involvement in the affairs of Europe will undercut efforts to assimilate immigrants. "We cannot Americanize them if we are continually thrusting them back into the quarrels and difficulties of the countries from which they came to us" (1925, p. 406). Immigrants are like history, they move west, not east.

The trajectory of Lodge's address reflects his view of the inevitable movement of history — westward, away from Europe. By the time he arrives at the speech's conclusion, Lodge has left Europe behind. The malicious old world is replaced with a shining vision of American nationalism:

> You may call me selfish if you will, conservative or reactionary, or use any other harsh adjective you see fit to apply, but an American I was born, and an American I have remained all my life. I can never be anything else but an American, and I must think of the United States first, and when I think of the United States first in an arrangement like this I am thinking what is best for the world, for if the United States fails the best hopes of mankind fail with it [1925, pp. 408–409].

Not only does the rhetorical movement of the "Treaty of Peace with Germany" speech enact Lodge's view of history, it also clarifies his opening assertion that "history never exactly repeats itself." People repeat mistakes, but according to Lodge, history moves on. The whole idea of Wilson's League of Nations is fundamentally flawed because it moves against the grain, against history itself. The United States is exceptional among the nations of the world not only because of its location and huge size, but because it stands in the vanguard of western movement. By this reckoning, unlike any other nation, the destiny of the United States becomes *world* destiny. Accordingly, Lodge claims that what's good for America is good for the world, and if America fails, mankind fails with it. This exceptional status could only be undermined by getting enmeshed in a "combination of the nations" (1925, p. 380), with unrealistic goals. Only by resisting the backward pull of European involvement could the United States move westward, not only to its own destiny but to the destiny of history itself.

Conclusion

Lewis Mumford argues that "the influence of the land" is even more important to civilized societies than it is to primitive ones. "As a matter of fact," Mumford writes, "the importance of the land increases with civilization" (1931, p. 59). Civilized people order—or exploit—the earth to their own needs. "The continued culture of the land, and the culture of the mind through the land, is the mark of a high civilization" (Mumford, 1931, p. 60). One way the land has exerted influence on the culture of the American mind is through a rhetoric of geographical movement as a critical part of America's destiny. Cultural expressions of this rhetoric abound. For example, the façade of the U.S. Custom House at Bowling Green in Manhattan depicts the continents of the world in the form of four female figures. Designed by Daniel Chester French around 1907, the regal figure of Europe sits stationary, surrounded by ancient symbols of tradition and power. In contrast, the figure representing the Americas sits among symbols of liberty and prosperity. The most noticeable characteristic of the American figure, however, is that she is clearly *moving*. The wind is in her hair. French was careful to clearly portray the dynamism Americans believed to be integral to their national culture.

The speeches of Henry Cabot Lodge also depict dynamic movement. Lodge's generation could see that the prodigious distances that threatened to overwhelm the first settlers in North America had significantly receded with the advent of the railroad, telephone, and the still embryonic developments of the automobile and airplane. Lodge's discourse shows that even as the American frontier closed, the rhetoric of western movement could still exert a powerful influence on political debate. It was a rhetorical trajectory that endured beyond its accompanying physical possibilities. For Lodge, America's destiny still lay in westward movement, but the movement was primarily logical. The idea of a directional destiny—from east to west—was naturally connected to prevailing philosophies of natural progress and historical determinism. By using these ideas to keep destiny in motion, Lodge was able to craft a policy trajectory that transcended the Pacific Ocean even as it separated America from Europe. This was one part of the strategy that enabled him to articulate American exceptionalism in terms of expansionism and nationalism without being either an imperialist or isolationist.

Notes

1. People as utterly different as John C. Calhoun and Frederick employed the same language of "conquering space." In the climactic speech of his career in the House of Representatives in 1817, Calhoun (1817/1959) argued for the public works of the Bonus Bill by declaring, "Let us conquer space!" Douglass (1852/1979) invoked a similar vision of a shrinking world in the peroration of his notable "July Fifth Oration" in 1852, when he declared, "space is comparatively annihilated."

2. Gerald P. Mohrmann (1987, p. 146) observed that "spatial images are very far from being static. They may suggest a security anchored in our sense of physical stability, but at the same time, they are often freighted with ramifications connected with the potential for movement."

3. Interestingly, Richard Weaver (1985) described nineteenth century rhetoric as "spacious" based on its intellectual characteristics. This intellectual spaciousness was surely conditioned by the physical spaciousness of the country and its mythical frontier. Toward the end of the nineteenth century the spacious old rhetoric began to wane at the same time the frontier closed. Arguments over American imperialism may have been the last great public debate conducted in the spacious "old" rhetoric.

4. Hoar refers again to the Filipinos as "distant peoples" (p. 495) and to "distant Oriental seas" (p. 496).

5. The debate was on S. 2355, a bill that gave the president the power to appoint governors of the islands as soon as the Philippine insurrection was put down.

6. Lodge argues early in the speech that far from dishonoring the American ideal of government by the "consent of the governed," Philippine annexation is moral because it extends the ideal to an area where it was unknown and, therefore, without American tutelage, impossible. Further, since the Filipinos are ignorant of self-government, to give it to them at once, "is to dower them with a curse instead of a blessing" (1900, p. 2620). In other words, the principles of moral government, taken for granted by Americans, are just not applicable to the Philippines. To try to apply them there is a disservice to the Filipinos, and therefore immoral.

References

Atkins, S. E. (1998). "Excursus: Henry Cabot Lodge and the Plymouth Tercentenary." *The Capitol Project: The Puritan Tradition and American Memory*. American Studies Group, University of Virginia, Richmond. Retrieved from http://xroads.virginia.edu/~cap/puritan/purtrad.html#lodge.

Baudrillard, J. (1988). *America* (Trans. C. Turner). London: Verso.

Bryan, W. J. (1900, July 4–6). "The Paralyzing Influence of Imperialism." *Official Proceedings of the Democratic National Convention* (pp. 205–207). Kansas City, MO.

Calhoun, J. C. (1959). "Speech on Internal Improvements." In R. L. Meriwether (Ed.), *The Papers of John C. Calhoun* (pp. 389–409). Columbia: University of South Carolina Press. (Original work published 1817.)

Carnegie, A. (1898, August). "Distant Possessions: The Parting of the Ways." *North American Review*, 239–249.

Douglass, F. (1979). "What to the Slave is the Fourth of July?" In J. W. Blassingame (Ed.), *The Frederick Douglass Papers. Series One: Speeches, Debates, and Interviews. Vol. II*

(pp. 1847–1854). New Haven: Yale University Press. (Original work published 1852.)
Draper, T. (1999, March 18). "The Four-Sided War." *New York Review of Books,* 43–44.
Edwards, J. A. (2008). *Navigating the Post–Cold War World: President Clinton's Foreign Policy Rhetoric.* Lanham, MD: Lexington.
Fromkin, D. (1996). "Rival Internationalisms: Lodge, Wilson, and the Two Roosevelts." *World Policy Journal, 13,* 75–80.
Garraty, J. A. (1965). *Henry Cabot Lodge: A Biography.* New York: Alfred A. Knopf.
Griffin, L. M. (1984). "When Dreams Collide: Rhetorical Trajectories in the Assassination of President Kennedy." *Quarterly Journal of Speech, 70,* 111–131.
Hoar, G. F. (1899). "Senate Speech of January 9, 1899." *Congressional Record, 55th Congress, 3d Session,* pp. 493–503.
Hostetler, M. J. (2002). "Washington's Farewell Address: Distance as Bane and Blessing." *Rhetoric and Public Affairs, 5,* 393–407.
_____. (2006). "David Ramsay and Louisiana: Time and Space in the Adolescent Rhetoric of America." *Western Journal of Communication, 70,* 134–146.
Kaplan, R. D. (1998). *An Empire Wilderness.* New York: Vantage.
Lodge, H. C. (1900). "The Philippine Islands." *U.S. Congressional Record-Senate, 56th Congress, Session I, 1899–1900* (vol. 33, pp. 2616–2630).
_____ (1925). *The Senate and the League of Nations.* New York: Charles Scribner's Sons.
Margulies, H. F. (1989). *The Mild Reservationists and the League of Nations Controversy in the Senate.* Columbia: University of Missouri Press.
Marx, L. (1964). *The Machine in the Garden: Technology and the Pastoral Ideal in America.* London: Oxford University Press.
Massey, D., J. Allen, and P. Sarre (1999). *Human Geography Today.* Cambridge, UK: Polity.
McCrisken, T. B. (2003). *American Exceptionalism and the Legacy of Vietnam: U.S. Foreign Policy Since 1974.* New York: Palgrave Macmillan.
Meinig, D. W. (1986). *The Shaping of America: A Geographical Perspective on 500 Years of History.* New Haven: Yale University Press.
Mohrmann, G. P. (1987). "Place and Space: Calhoun's Fatal Security." *Western Journal of Speech Communication, 51,* 143–158.
Mumford, L. (1931). *The Brown Decades.* New York: Dover.
Platt, O. H. (1899). "Senate Speech of January 9, 1899." *Congressional Record, 55th Congress, 3d Session,* p. 503.
Weaver, R. M. (1985). *The Ethics of Rhetoric.* Davis, CA: Hermagoras.
Welch, R. E., Jr. (1971). *George Frisbie Hoar and the Half-Breed Republicans.* Cambridge, MA: Harvard University Press.
Widenor, W. C. (1980). *Henry Cabot Lodge and the Search for an American Foreign Policy.* Berkeley: University of California Press.
Zarefsky, D. (1996, March 12). *The Rhetorical Evolution of Lincoln's Anti-Slavery Position.* Lecture delivered at Wabash College, Crawfordsville, IN.
Zimmermann, W. (1998). "Jingoes, Goo-Goos, and the Rise of America's Empire." *Wilson Quarterly, 22,* 42–65.

CHAPTER 8

Discursive Characterization as Embodiment and Critique
The Divergent Rhetorical Trajectories of Pat Tillman as an American Hero

ARTHUR W. HERBIG

On May 3, 2004, Navy SEAL Stephen White delivered a eulogy that became the first official account of former NFL star Pat Tillman's death in the "War on Terror." White told the heroic story of a soldier who charged into an enemy ambush and sacrificed his life in defense of his brothers in arms. Less than a month later, that story was impugned by Army Lieutenant General Philip R. Kensinger's announcement that friendly fire was a "probable" cause of Tillman's death. Further complicating Lt. Gen. Kensinger's statement, author Jon Krakauer's (2009) investigation into Tillman's death produced proof that not only was the Army aware that Tillman's death was a result of friendly fire on the day Kensinger announced it, but also that the military had deliberately deceived White and then attempted to further cover it up by holding the press conference on a Saturday, when it would normally receive less attention from the press. As details continue to be uncovered about how the story of Pat Tillman's death has been shaped, changed, and even distorted, a wide variety of theories have emerged as to how Tillman really died and why information was concealed. Beginning with White's eulogy at the memorial, explanations of the how and why have ranged from a mythic tale of heroic sacrifice to a conspiratorial assassination plot of the Army's most famous soldier. Given that Tillman's death occurred at a time when President George W. Bush was experiencing falling approval ratings largely due to an unpopular war, some have even named the former president as a co-conspirator. Yet throughout the many variations on the tale, what remains constant is the recognition of the political and ideological significance the life of Pat Tillman.

Pat Tillman lives on as a contested character in U.S. political discourse even after his death. Tillman's willingness to forgo a multi-million dollar contract and a successful career in the National Football League (NFL) to join the Army drew a great deal of attention, as captured in headlines such as "Sacrificing Riches for Country" (Boeck, 2002) and "Tillman Is Army of One" (Olsen, 2002). He became a recognizable name and face at a time when soldiers were more often nameless images in television news reports or faceless casualty statistics. Following his death, descriptions of Tillman's sacrifice included sentiments like "an authentic American hero" (Towle, 2004, p. xvii) and "Pat's story, Pat's life, his journey — that's the real American Dream" (California Governor Arnold Schwarzenegger, quoted in Associated Press, 2004). As more information about how Tillman died became available, accusations became more prominent that the story of his death was deliberately manipulated in order to serve a political agenda. Those suspicions were confirmed by an investigation conducted by the U.S. House of Representatives Committee on Oversight and Government Reform, but the extent of the cover-up remained a mystery because "on the key issue of what senior officials knew, the investigation was frustrated by a near universal lack of recall" (2008, p. 1). Rumors that the military, or even President Bush, had Tillman murdered surfaced as an undercurrent in discussions of Tillman's sacrifice (Associated Press, 2007; Baldwin, 2006; Coll, 2004a, 2004b; Dickinson, 2007). The relationship between celebrations of Tillman's life and the exploitation of his death have allowed divergent trajectories to develop in how Pat Tillman was characterized as a representation of American values.

Indeed, this chapter has very little to do with the person Pat Tillman; it is instead an investigation into the rhetorical characterization of *Pat Tillman*. While the person Pat Tillman lived a life that ended on a hill in Afghanistan, the characterizations of *Pat Tillman* have become a means for discussing contemporary American values. Although Tillman was predominantly celebrated as a hero for his actions in life, the handling of his death made his name also synonymous with scandal and conspiracy. The military's cover-up of how he died shifted some of the focus from the story itself to the manner of its manipulation. In his testimony before Congress, Pat Tillman's brother Kevin claimed that

> in the days leading up to Pat's memorial service, media accounts, based on information provided by the Army and the White House, were wreathed in a patriotic glow and became more dramatic in tone. A terrible tragedy that might have

further undermined support for the war in Iraq was transformed into an inspirational message that served instead to support the nation's foreign policy wars in Iraq and Afghanistan [quoted in United States House of Representatives Committee on Oversight and Government Reform, 2008, p. 8].

Critics like David Zirin argued that "death rendered Tillman helplessly compliant — and far more useful to the masters of war than he had been in life" (2005, p. 131). Sociologist David Altheide examined how stories of Pat Tillman were "used to promote patriotism and the politics of fear" (2006, p. 185). The distinction that these critics draw regarding the differences between the actions of Pat Tillman and how those actions were employed by others who sought to capitalize on Tillman's memory engages the ways in which characterizations of *Pat Tillman* functioned as more than just a reference to the life of a person.

While the veneration of the life of Pat Tillman was rarely challenged, the fact that the story of his death had been manipulated has been a subject of great scrutiny. Stories such as those about Tillman's early struggles to garner the attention of college football scouts and his willingness to risk his life have become the building blocks for those who wish to create a heroic example of the best America has to offer (Rand, 2004; Towle, 2004), while questions about how and why Tillman died opened the door to insinuations such as the one voiced by author and *New York Times* columnist Frank Rich:

> Tillman's death followed the worst month of bad news for the country and, more pertinently, for the Bush-Cheney reelection campaign, since the start of the Iraq war. Against this backdrop, it would not do to have it known that the most famous volunteer of the war might have been a victim of gross negligence or homicide [2006, p. 129].

The name *Pat Tillman* has come to represent more than just a person who lived and died. It is simultaneously a symbol of heroic sacrifice and a context for an investigation into government misconduct. Despite the fact that these various and sometimes conflicting characterizations of *Pat Tillman* were voiced by people from different political perspectives and different backgrounds, interwoven into both these trajectories was the idea that America is, or is supposed to be, exceptional.

In this chapter, I examine how rhetorical characterizations of *Pat Tillman* as an embodiment of American values and a subject of critique that were both underscored by a belief in American exceptionalism. On one hand, characterizations of Tillman's life were articulated as exemplifications of American values and a dedication to principles that distinguish America from other countries. On the other hand, criticisms of how Tillman's death was handled by the military and the government were grounded in a belief that Americans can hold their representatives and officials to a higher standard that promotes a belief (useful especially in times of war) that America is an ideology that can be employed as a basis for critique. In order to explore the connections between these seemingly divergent rhetorical trajectories, I have chosen to examine perspectives voiced by U. S. Senator John McCain (R.-Ariz.) and MSNBC television host Keith Olbermann.

Both McCain and Olbermann frequently employed characterizations of *Pat Tillman* in their rhetoric, but to differing ends. McCain held press conferences, was called on to do interviews, and even included a biographical chapter about Tillman as an example of "Citizenship" in his book *Character is Destiny* (McCain and Salter, 2005) which retold the lives of people as embodiments of particular values. For McCain, Tillman's "uncommon choice of duty to his country over the profession he loved and the riches and other comforts of celebrity and his humility that made Pat Tillman's life such a welcome lesson in the true meaning of courage and honor" (McCain and Salter, 2005, p. 60). In contrast, Olbermann frequently cited the handling of Tillman's death as an example of the worst aspects of the Bush Administration. In his quest to understand how and why people were misled about the events that led to Tillman's demise, Olbermann spurred a growing conversation about actions taken by the White House and even speculated that Tillman "was indeed murdered" (2007). Despite the fact that he was accusing the president of the United States of murder, Olbermann's accusations were not a critique of America. They were a critique of a person. By exploring the divergent perspectives that were voiced by McCain and Olbermann, I provide insight into how both of these contrasting characterizations of *Pat Tillman* relied on the belief in American exceptionalism. The discourse about Pat Tillman provides a unique opportunity to understand the different ways in which American exceptionalism underscores both the embodiment of values and the criticism of institutions in U.S. political culture.

Investigating American Exceptionalism through Rhetorical Characterization

Historian Richard Hofstadter once wrote that it is the fate of America "not to have ideologies, but to be one" (1955, p. 7). Building on that idea, Hodgson (2009) has argued that the belief that America is distinct from other nations because of its commitment to certain principles has exaggerated the role of "differentness" and "uniqueness" in discussions of national values (p.

xv). Hodgson discusses American exceptionalism as a form of self-aggrandizement that has motivated some positive social progress, but also perpetuated a belief in empire that has been used to justify U.S. actions throughout the world. By Hodgson's estimation, the belief that America is distinguishable from both its predecessors and its contemporaries ignores how the principles and values that are associated with America have been practiced throughout the world. According to Kazin and McCartin (2006), American exceptionalism (which they refer to as "Americanism") has been enacted as two separate rhetorics: The first is a recognition of "what is distinctive about the United States" and the second is "loyalty to that nation, rooted in a defense of its political ideals" (p. 1). These two rhetorics of American exceptionalism come to represent two different frameworks: embodiment and criticism. The former is a descriptive rhetoric that employs people and events as representations of the values that are unique to American life. The articulation of this rhetoric uses examples like "the founding fathers" or "the Revolutionary War" to support nationalistic positions that place America above other nations. The latter employs principles and ideals, which are often taken for granted within those characterizations, as evaluative standards. This brand of exceptionalism can be seen in State of the Union addresses which focus on the relationship between U.S. policy and American values and in the speeches of civil rights leaders who question whether America has lived up to the promise that all men (and women) are created equal. Both of these rhetorics perpetuate the perception of America as exceptional, but they employ that exceptionalism to differing ends.

These two rhetorics of American exceptionalism perpetuate the uniqueness of America by promoting the belief that America is synonymous with principles like freedom and liberty. Stories such as those of famous figures like Abraham Lincoln and Frederick Douglass become characterizations of American values through how they are historicized. Their names become synonymous with a belief that America is on a constant journey toward what the Constitution describes as a "more perfect union." While embodiments are easy to identify as celebrations of American values, this becomes more complicated when examining criticism. Much of the criticism of governmental institutions is framed as a commentary on how particular laws or politicians failing to live up to the principles that are framed as American. These criticisms avoid a critical perspective on the connection between America and ideology and focus instead on how particular laws and politicians undermine the belief that America is exceptional. This type of public criticism takes American exceptionalism for granted, but employs it as a means for critique. The difference between embodiment and criticism can be seen in how a particular person employs the belief that America is a nation based on a unique sense of values and principles.

One of the best ways to investigate how those values and principles are enacted is through rhetorical characterizations. Parry-Giles (1996) claims that "the characterological nature of the U.S. Constitution leads to a politics in America where ideological definition and understanding are fused with and embodied by particular individuals/characters who dominate public life" (p. 365). Using the questions and testimony from Supreme Court Justice Thurgood Marshall's confirmation hearings, Parry-Giles argues that the Justice became an ideological embodiment of "Civil Rights" that "is instructive of not only the ideological meaning of 'civil rights' in the American political language, but also of how this community's ideology is constructed in the public texts that express it" (1996, p. 376). According to Parry-Giles, "Ideological embodiment and cultural fragmentation work together to democratize government and to reveal the weakness, the fissures, in the ideological foundations of the community" (1996, p. 377). Thus, understanding the ways in which individuals such as Justice Marshall embody ideas like "civil rights" provides insight into the rhetorical formation of public values and principles. Analogous to the characterization of Thurgood Marshall that was produced during his confirmation hearings, the discourse produced about Pat Tillman created an ideological embodiment that promoted the belief that America is exceptional.

How then might a critic engage the relationship between "ideological embodiment and cultural fragmentation?" The answer to that question can be found in the critical approach to textual representations as "fragments" that was developed by McGee (1990). McGee argued that critics must see texts themselves as "simultaneously structures of fragments, finished texts, and fragments themselves to be accounted for in subsequent discourse" (1990, p. 279). According to McGee, "Rhetors *make* discourses from scraps and pieces of evidence" (1990, p. 279; emphasis in original) and it is the responsibility of the critic to examine how elements of a text interact with and comment on existing ideological and cultural perspectives. Like texts, characterizations represent fragmented associations between texts, ideologies, and contexts. It is the job of the critic to investigate how the stories and actions of a person's life are articulated with ideological, cultural, and personal associations that provide a framework for their understanding, while also acknowledging that critics themselves are producers of critical rhetoric that perpetuates the discourses they critique.

When looking at how two separate rhetorical approaches can be formed using similar bases of information, it is helpful to examine their development over time. Griffin (1984) employed the metaphor of a "rhetorical trajectory" as a means of examining the interrelationship of a series of fragments and a way of understanding the ideological journeys of particular characters. According to Griffin, the assassination of President John F. Kennedy by Lee Harvey Oswald was not simply a physical act of aggression — it was a moment of revolution that represented the collision of two separate rhetorical trajectories. Griffin argued that Kennedy was killed "because of the ideological (i.e., rhetorical) movement that he symbolized" (1984, p. 113). Griffin's synonymous use of rhetorical and ideological in this essay reinforced the notion that characters are ideological embodiments represent the interweaving of lived actions and interpretation. In this way, he explained the events put into motion on that fateful day in Dallas as rhetorical movements.

The distinction between Griffin's approach and my own is that Griffin chose to examine events rhetorically while I will be looking at the rhetoric of particular events. The story of Pat Tillman has been told in books (Krakauer, 2009; Rand, 2004; Towle, 2004), on television (Emerson, 2006), on film (Thompson et al., 2009), and in news reports too numerous to count. Each of these retellings is a fragment of the discourse that helped to perpetuate the existence of *Pat Tillman*. Each version interacts with new information that has been discovered about Tillman's death or revelations about his life. In the case of the distinctions that are made between the symbolic significance of Tillman's life and that of his death, examining the rhetorical trajectories taken in composition of the character *Pat Tillman* provides an opportunity to also examine the articulation of American exceptionalism.

In my analysis, instead of examining how a particular orator articulated a vision of *Pat Tillman*, I seek to understand how characterizations of Tillman's life were connected to American exceptionalism. Particularly in the time following Tillman's death, two distinct rhetorical trajectories in discussions of the life and sacrifice of Pat Tillman emerged. The positions taken by John McCain and Keith Olbermann are representative of those trajectories and provide an opportunity to examine their implications. My approach hinges on three important critical terms: *character, fragment,* and *rhetorical trajectory* as they were defined by Griffin (1984), McGee (1978, 1990), and Parry-Giles (1996). By applying their perspectives to my own analysis I can examine the ways in which *Pat Tillman* became a contested representation of American exceptionalism. Given that my analysis explores the interconnection of *Pat Tillman* with rhetorics of American exceptionalism, I will focus on how McCain's and Olbermann's characterizations represented rhetorics of embodiment and critique, respectively.

John McCain and Keith Olbermann: Two Distinct Rhetorical Trajectories in the Characterization of Pat Tillman

On April 23, 2004, the day news of Tillman's death became public, John McCain appeared on Keith Olbermann's MSNBC program *Countdown*. In that interview both McCain and Olbermann expressed the beginnings of the divergent trajectories they would take in characterizing the role of *Pat Tillman* in U.S. political discourse. John McCain spoke of Tillman as an embodiment of American values. In McCain's words, Tillman's example was something that puts "a certain pride in us, that we have young Americans like Pat Tillman." McCain claimed that Tillman's life and sacrifice serve as a reminder that "this nation produces young Americans who are willing to serve and sacrifice for somebody else's freedom, and there's nothing nobler." In contrast to the characterization offered by McCain, Olbermann asked questions about how Tillman's death might be related to the political and ideological realities of the wars in Iraq and Afghanistan. Olbermann investigated the role that Tillman could play as a symbol of war with questions like "Do you think that his loss, in Afghanistan, has just brought the real meaning of these conflicts in Afghanistan, in Iraq, to a sizable portion of the public with whom it had not previously registered?" and "Has Pat Tillman just become the American face of these conflicts in Iraq and Afghanistan?" In the wake of Tillman's battlefield demise, this encounter became the point of departure for divergent trajectories, each towing a distinct rhetoric of American exceptionalism: for McCain, embodiment; for Olbermann, criticism.

John McCain: Characterizing *Pat Tillman* as an Embodiment of American Values

In the period of time following Tillman's death, John McCain was a powerful political figure in the Republican Party, eventually earning the nomination for the presidency. During McCain's ascension to presidential candidate, Tillman served him as a symbol of a devotion to American values that he hoped to promote on the campaign trail and in the White House. Even before Tillman's death, McCain was quoted as saying "I don't think there will be any doubts about his capabilities as a soldier, but also as a recruiting tool. He'll motivate other young Americans to serve as well" (quoted in Campbell, 2002, p. 7). In a 2004 interview with National Public Radio's Juan Williams, McCain discussed Tillman's decision to serve his nation as an example of the type of American that motivated his book *Why Courage Matters: The Way to a Braver Life*:

> One of my favorite examples, although he's not in the book, is one Pat Tillman. He gave up over a million dollars a year as a safety for the Arizona Cardinals to enlist in the Army as a ranger after 9/11 and fought in Iraq. And it wasn't a moment of crisis and strife that motivated Pat Tillman. It was the recognition that the United States was under attack and he volunteered to defend it [McCain and Salter, 2004].

McCain had expressed interest in Tillman's story from as early as the time of his enlistment — and, despite having never met Tillman, the senator became one of the primary public figures asked to speak about his death. McCain's status as both a former prisoner of war as well as a senator from Tillman's adoptive state of Arizona gave him the *ethos* to comment on the meaning of Tillman's sacrifice. Despite the fact that Tillman himself had never explained his motivations for enlisting, McCain ascribed motives to Tillman's actions. He characterized *Pat Tillman* as a soldier who exemplified American values by being willing to quietly defend the nation that had become an ideology.

McCain's characterization was only amplified by Tillman's death. On April 23, 2004, the day news of Tillman's death became public, McCain held a press conference during which he stated, "I am heartbroken today by the news of Pat Tillman's death. The tragic loss of this extraordinary young man will seem a heavy blow to our nation's morale, as it is surely a grievous injury to his loved ones" (McCain, 2004a, para. 1). Versions of this quote appeared in the *Boston Globe* (Cafardo, 2004), the *Washington Post* (Wise and White, 2004), and circulated internationally via the French news service Agence France Presse (Rambourg, 2004). McCain's discussion of the connection between the greatness of the nation and his characterization of *Pat Tillman* was evident in that first press conference:

> But there is in Pat Tillman's example, in his unexpected choice of duty to his country over the riches and other comforts of celebrity, and in his humility, such an inspiration to all of us to reclaim the essential public-spiritedness of Americans that many of us, in low moments, had worried was no longer our common distinguishing trait [2004a, para. 1].

McCain's description of Tillman's sacrifice as an example of America's "common distinguishing trait" as "public-spiritedness," connected Tillman's actions with national service. His characterization framed Tillman's decision to join the army as an exemplification of devotion to the nation itself.

McCain subsequently extended his characterization, connecting his vision of Tillman's death as a symbol of sacrifice with the idea that success in America is measured by how it functions in service to the nation. Just over a week after Tillman's death, McCain delivered a eulogy at Tillman's public memorial which again focused on Pat Tillman as an embodiment of the values of the nation. While many of the eulogies delivered that day echoed the sentiment that the type of heroism embodied by Pat Tillman called into question the use of the word "hero" to describe athletes and celebrities, McCain's description focused on how service to the nation created a clear delineation between true heroism and empty cliché:

> We're not as familiar with courage as we once were. We ascribe the virtue to all manner of endeavors that only really require skill, fortitude, and a little daring, the qualities Pat Tillman showed on the football field. Pat's best service to his country was to remind us all what courage really looks like, and that the purpose of all good courage is love. He loved his country, and the values that make us exceptional among nations, and good. And he worried after the terrible blow we were struck on September 11th, 2001, that he had "never done a damn thing" to serve her. Love and honor oblige us. We are obliged to value our blessings, and to pay our debts to those who sacrificed to secure them for us [2004b, para. 3–4].

In the tradition of what Abraham Lincoln called "the last full measure of devotion," John McCain's eulogy cast *Pat Tillman* as a servant of his nation and, for McCain, that service defined Tillman as a hero:

> Our country's security doesn't depend on the heroism of every citizen. Nor does our individual happiness depend upon proving ourselves heroic. But we have to be worthy of the sacrifices made on our behalf. We have to love our freedom, not just for the ease or material benefits it provides, not just for the autonomy it guarantees us, but for the goodness it makes possible. We have to love it so much we won't let it be constrained by fear or selfishness. We have to love it as much, even if not as heroically, as Pat Tillman loved it [2004b, para. 6].

As is true of many eulogists (Campbell and Jamieson, 1978), McCain sought to inscribe the loss of an individual with a symbolic meaning for the community as a whole. In this eulogy, McCain used Tillman's willingness to forgo his career in the NFL, as well as the fame and wealth that accompanied it, as evidence that America and the values that it represents are worthy of such a sacrifice. He described Tillman's "love" as a devotion to the nation that McCain discussed as synonymous with freedom and goodness. He very clearly stated that Tillman "loved his country and the values that make us exceptional among nations and good." McCain defined Tillman's desire to serve through how it could be seen as an affirmation of the belief that America is exceptional.

During the early stages of McCain's presidential campaign, his characterization of Tillman's motivations to join the military allowed him to craft a version of *Pat Tillman* that simultaneously heralded the service of all soldiers and the spread of American values throughout the world. Nowhere was this tendency more evident than in McCain's biography of Tillman in his book,

Character is Destiny: Inspiring Stories Every Young Person Should Know and Every Adult Should Remember (McCain and Salter, 2005). In a book in which the story of Martin Luther King is used to represent "Fairness" and the life of Gandhi is emblematic of "Respect," Pat Tillman's life is crafted as a representation of "Citizenship." The central component of this characterization of *Pat Tillman* was his silence after his enlistment:

> They [Pat Tillman and his brother Kevin, who also enlisted] intentionally refused to talk about their decision. They shunned all publicity. They refused all requests for interviews... They didn't think they were better than any other soldier. And they were right. They were special, but no more special than the Americans they served with. But their modesty, as much as their sacrifice, taught us the first lesson in patriotism... Patriotism is the recognition that each of us is just one small part of a cause that is greater than ourselves, one small part, but a part we are honor bound to play [2005, p. 58].

McCain's biography of Tillman furthered the connection he sought to create between the perpetuation of values and conformity to the nation itself. McCain also used the biography to discuss his own position on the values that Pat Tillman's sacrifice upheld: "America is dedicated to the proposition that all men are created equal, and have equal right to freedom and justice. That is our cause: to prove the truth of that proposition. And that cause is far more important than the ambitions of any individual" (2005, pp. 58–59). As an example of citizenship, "Pat Tillman died as he had lived, bravely, in the service of his country" (McCain, 2005, p. 60).

McCain's characterization of *Pat Tillman* was representative of the type of rhetorical trajectory that framed the motivations behind Tillman's actions as an embodiment of American exceptionalism. However, that characterization was subsequently complicated by new fragments which conflicted with the notion that Tillman was simply a silent and loyal servant of America. In a September 25, 2005, interview with *San Francisco Chronicle* reporter Robert Collier, Tillman's mother, Mary, revealed her son's private political views and offered a competing version of his thoughts and motivations. While McCain was described in the article as an ally, the senator's claims about Pat Tillman's feelings and actions were contradicted by Mary Tillman's own assertions that her son was opposed to the war and considered the nation's actions illegal. Revelations that Tillman was critical of America's presence in Iraq and resisted being used as a political prop were antithetical to the characterization of *Pat Tillman* offered by a politician who had exhorted all Americans to follow the path of Tillman's service.

When it was revealed (White, 2005) that the details of Pat Tillman's death had been misreported and covered up, John McCain became one of the driving forces behind the inquiries into how and why this had happened. However, as Tillman's private feelings about the decisions that were being made by his government began to surface, McCain began to distance himself from the implications of those revelations. Just over a month after Tillman's private opinions became public, McCain confronted the tensions that had developed between his own characterization of *Pat Tillman* and the competing versions that had begun to emerge. When McCain was asked by Fox News Channel host Bill O'Reilly in November 2005 about how "the antiwar people… exploited" Tillman's positions, McCain's dismay over the divergent rhetorical trajectory that was beginning to take shape shone through:

> I don't think that's right. I think that Pat Tillman's case, an American hero, should be left out of the debate as to whether we should have gone to war in Iraq or not. It's not fitting. It's not fitting for his memory, because he's an example to young people all over America.

The distinction McCain made between the discussion of Pat Tillman as "an example to young people" and the use of Pat Tillman in discussions of the wars in Iraq and Afghanistan revealed the conflict that had emerged between the characterizations of *Pat Tillman* as the embodiment of American values and *Pat Tillman* as a subject of critique. McCain's characterization relied on the fact that Tillman's decision to serve in the Armed Forces was an affirmation of American values. However, the use of *Pat Tillman* as a means to critique America's actions called into question whether those values were aligned with McCain's political perspectives. McCain called the lies constructed about Tillman's death a "cover-up" and a "travesty," but as his candidacy for president advanced, he shied away from the later controversies associated with the incident and its connections the political failures and manipulations of the presidency of his fellow Republican, George W. Bush.[1]

Keith Olbermann: The Characterization of *Pat Tillman* as a Means for Critique of U.S. Political Institutions

In a 2008 profile in *The New Yorker*, Peter J. Boyer described Keith Olbermann as "a political polemicist … [who assumes] that the labored pretense of neutrality in the news business in a fruitless exercise" (p. 4). From his pointed attacks on his Fox News counterpart Bill O'Reilly (or "Bill-O the Clown," as Olbermann regularly refers to him) to his rants in which he once ordered President George W. Bush to "shut the hell up," Olbermann has gained greater and greater notoriety for his often brash voice as a liberal commentator. Beginning with his April 2004 tribute to Tillman and interview with McCain, Olbermann memorialized, hypothesized, and criticized, all in the name of Pat Tillman. In his characterization of *Pat Tillman*, Olbermann never denied that Tillman was a hero. In fact, Olbermann's criticisms relied heavily on the characterization of Tillman as an embodiment of American exceptionalism — but did so in order to articulate a contrast between Tillman's actions and those of the Bush Administration. Despite the issues that Olbermann was confronting in his criticisms and the fact that Pat Tillman was revealed to be openly critical of America's presence in Iraq, Olbermann focused his discussion on how the manipulation of Tillman's death was a reflection of the Bush Administration. By acknowledging that Tillman "was a hero enough as it was. Nobody had to embellish it. It didn't detract from it in the slightest," Olbermann embraced the characterization of *Pat Tillman* as an embodiment of American exceptionalism and used his service to his nation as a counterpoint to those who manipulated his death.

Olbermann's use of *Pat Tillman* as the public face of the costs of the wars in Iraq and Afghanistan took root in his first report on Tillman's death, and became a recurring feature of the *Countdown* series as more information was revealed about the military cover-up. In April 2004, just three days after Tillman's death was announced, Olbermann hypothesized that the story was already being politicized: "In war it is a fine line between honoring and exploiting. One or both [is] now happening to the late Pat Tillman." When Lt. Gen. Kensinger reported just over a month after Tillman's death that Tillman had been killed by friendly fire, Olbermann included that report in his Memorial Day broadcast, stating that "the U.S. military now says Tillman ... probably fell in Afghanistan when another U.S. Ranger mistakenly fired on a friendly Afghan fighter." As more lies about Tillman's death slowly surfaced, Olbermann led the charge to find out why those untruths had been propagated in the first place. As he proclaimed after the December 2004 *Washington Post* exposé (Coll, 2004a, 2004b) of the events that led to Tillman's death, "It turns out there was much more to tell, and there are now questions as to why it wasn't told."

In May 2005, after the Pentagon acknowledged that the military had misrepresented the events that led to Tillman's death, Olbermann began to hypothesize about why the story continued to change. Since Tillman's death, the stories had evolved from a heroic rescue of his brothers in arms to a case of probable friendly fire and now to a deliberate cover-up engaged by the very soldiers that he was said to be saving. On the May 4, 2005, episode of *Countdown*, Olbermann reported that there were "new details tonight about the death of Pat Tillman and they raise the question of whether good publicity might have been placed ahead of telling his family the truth about how he died." He described how military personnel involved "were told to keep the information secret even from Tillman's family, presumably to shield the unit from embarrassment." Olbermann discussed the social and political ramifications of those secrets in a May 23, 2005, interview with Josh White, the *Washington Post* reporter who had broken many of the details of the cover-up. In that interview, Olbermann and White speculated about whether the manipulations of Tillman's story represented more than just cover-up of a friendly-fire accident:

> OLBERMANN: Josh, his father, believes also, obviously, that this was a deliberate attempt to keep the truth silent, that it was to counter-effect the Abu Ghraib scandal, which was just breaking at the time, and then the start of the recruiting problems that we've seen since. Is there any evidence to suggest that those comments are more than just a father's anger and grief? Is there anything to suggest — to support the idea that this was deliberately done by the military?
> WHITE: Well, something was deliberately done at some level. It's clear from the evidence in the investigative reports that the truth was kept from people in the United States, specifically, the family, specifically, Pat's brother, and that as higher-ups found out, their suspicions — or at least that it was probably a friendly fire incident, that that information was not passed on.

Olbermann's use of the word "deliberate" was a reference to a May 2005 *Washington Post* editorial written by Tillman's father that claimed that "with respect to the Army's reference to 'mistakes in reporting the circumstances of [my son's] death': those 'mistakes' were deliberate, calculated, ordered (repeatedly) and disgraceful — conduct well beneath the standard to which every soldier in the field is held" (Tillman, 2005, p. A24). Both Tillman's and Olbermann's remarks reflected a new theme: contrasting the motivations of those who manipulated *Pat Tillman* against the motivations of Tillman himself.

In the May 23, 2005, *Countdown* interview, Olbermann's suggestion that the Abu Ghraib scandal could have served as a "motive" left the word "this" in the phrase "this was deliberately done by the military" open to speculation. Was he referring to a cover-up or the death itself? Clearly Olbermann believed that a crime had taken place, but the extent of that crime was left ambiguous. Almost a year later, on March 6, 2006, Olbermann interviewed Josh White again and continued to speculate about what was deliberately done by the military:

> And, Josh, to be clear, when we hear criminal negligence, the first thought I think that probably jumps into a lot of people's minds is somebody shot him on purpose. That's not what we're talking about here; it's about a cover-up, right? — and an embellishment perhaps to try to sell the death of Pat Tillman as a heroic self-sacrifice when it was a horrible accident. Is that the worst-case scenario, or is there something worse in here?

In March of 2006, approval ratings for President Bush and the war sunk to a new low ("Iraq Drives," 2006; Murray, 2006). At the same time, reports continued to trickle out about Tillman's death — and Olbermann continued to insinuate that what was being concealed by the military was more than just a cover-up of mistakes.

Almost three years after Tillman died, Olbermann was still pursuing answers and placing blame for what had happened on the President. In the introduction to a March 26, 2007, interview with Jon Soltz of votevets.org, Olbermann stated that "when he died in the spring of 2004, Pat Tillman was an all American hero... That spring, the spring of Abu Ghraib... the Pentagon and the president needed a hero. They could use one, and they did use one." During the interview, Olbermann made these comments:

> The thing I really don't understand is if there's a crime here, whether it's literally a crime or just figuratively one. If there was a cover-up, why was it undertaken? It seems it was unnecessary, pointless, panicky, stupid. I mean, Pat Tillman volunteered from obviously the purest motives of patriotism, gave up as much as anybody could. He died from friendly fire, accidental, happens in every war, good or bad, justified or not. Why would the fact that he died of — from that, of that as the cause, why would that, in the slightest, diminish what he did?

Olbermann relied on characterizations of *Pat Tillman* as an embodiment of American values — like those that were articulated by John McCain — which he contrasted to the actions of people who exploited Tillman's sacrifice for their own gain. Olbermann even went as far as to use the fact that Tillman's heroism can be taken for granted as evidence for his theory of a military cover-up: "He was a hero enough as it was. Nobody had to embellish it." Through the acknowledgment of Tillman's actions as heroic, Olbermann was able to create a story that had both heroes and villains. In this interview with Soltz, Olbermann employed his characterization of Tillman in order to question the integrity of Donald Rumsfeld and of the officers who were at Tillman's memorial, as well as the veracity of an investigation that was completed by those in the Army who had engaged in the original cover-up.

On March 27, 2007, Olbermann conducted an interview with Tillman's mother Mary and sportscaster Dan Patrick, walking both his guests through the story as it was then understood. He asked questions about the Bush Administration's use of *Pat Tillman* as a sales tool for the war and about the military conspiracy that prevented full knowledge about his death from coming out. The exchange then turned to what Mary Tillman believed about what happened to her son. Her response was "I don't know. I think there's three scenarios possibly, and I'd rather not get into them, but I really don't know what happened, because we have been told so many different things. I can't say that I really do know ultimately what happened to him." Olbermann responded by asking Tillman's mother point blank, "But you have included among those three things the possibility that someone deliberately shot him?" Her response was simply "I'm not excluding that."

On July 26, 2007, Olbermann took the story as far as it could go. In an interview with MSNBC political analyst Richard Wolffe and retired General Wesley Clark, Olbermann asked:

> Does it not begin to look more and more like we're going in the wrong direction in this? That they were not trying to protect something slightly negative from coming out, but in fact protecting the accusation that his mother has made and has not gotten a lot of attention that perhaps he was indeed murdered? Were we actually underestimating what was being covered up here?

Wolffe responded to Olbermann's question with "It's very possible" and added another voice to the accusation that the Bush Administration murdered Pat Tillman. The next day, in another interview with veterans' advocate Jon Soltz, Olbermann continued this line of investigation against the backdrop of a photograph of Pat Tillman beneath the caption "Motive for Murder?":

> Corporal Tillman held a number of personal views that were unpopular within the context of the Bush administration, perhaps also within the Army. He reportedly favored John Kerry in that election that year. We know he opposed the invasion of Iraq. He thought it illegal. He had plans to meet with Noam Chomsky. The Associated Press told us in a report last night that during the firefight a fellow soldier was hugging the ground, crying out to God and Tillman said, let me quote this directly, "Would you shut your [EXPLETIVE DELETED] mouth, God is not going to help you. You need to do something for yourself. You sniveling —." And that's all the quote was. Apparently at the last moment of his life. Explain how all of those details intensify the need for openness here that we are not getting now?

Olbermann's insinuation that Pat Tillman was deliberately killed to suit a political agenda added fuel to conspiracy speculations that had emerged on the Internet. *DailyKos* blogger Dburn (2007) cited General Wesley Clark's appearance on *Countdown* and claimed that "the orders came from the very top as Tillman was a political symbol. It was well known he was against the war in Iraq. No indication if orders were to murder him, but at the least to cover it up (Burned clothes — lost evidence etc.)." Also referencing Olbermann, Paul Joseph Watson (2007) of *InfoWars* wondered "how can any sane and rational individual weigh this evidence and not come to the conclusion that Tillman was deliberately gunned down in cold blood?"

Olbermann employed the controversy that had surrounded Tillman's death as a means to critique a government that was not living up to the American values that were symbolized by *Pat Tillman*. His characterization subsumed the life and death of the actual person Pat Tillman into the rhetorical characterization that he used as an evaluative standard. On March 27, 2007, the same day on which McCain avoided discussing investigations into the death of Pat Tillman with CNN's Wolf Blitzer, Olbermann began a five-month period in which he discussed *Pat Tillman* as a political issue at least twice a month. Instead of focusing on Tillman's life, Olbermann discussed Tillman as a "subject touching ... on the president and the war" and, in doing so, critiqued "the almost unbelievable" instance in which the president invoked executive privilege. Three years after Tillman's death, the topic of *Pat Tillman* was as relevant as it had ever been for Olbermann because it provided him with a context for commentary. On *Countdown*, Keith Olbermann relied on *Pat Tillman* as way of discussing how the people that had been chosen as the nation's representatives and decision-makers were undermining the belief in American exceptionalism.

The Discursive Implications of a Political Character

Through the rhetorical characterization of *Pat Tillman*, the story of a character with an unflinching and unquestioned devotion to the ideals of his country was coupled with the revelation of corruption and deception in that country's political and military institutions. Altheide observed that "on the one hand, he was honored, given medals, and celebrated.... On the other hand, the meaning of his death was given different interpretations and sparked rancor and reprisals against those who 'misused' his symbolic meaning" (2006, p. 186). Notre Dame athletic director Kevin White regarded Pat Tillman as an embodiment of values who was "without question the biggest hero of my lifetime" (quoted in Smith, 2004, p. 46). Others, such as Kevin Tillman, sought to critique how "terrible tragedy that might have further undermined support for the war in Iraq was transformed into an inspirational message" (quoted in United States House of Representatives Committee on Oversight and Government Reform, 2008, p. 1). The seemingly contrasting rhetorics of embodiment and criticism in these characterizations of *Pat Tillman* are interconnected through a shared belief in America as an ideology. By conflating the existence of a nation with a belief in principles like liberty, the life of that nation can be embodied by the best of its citizens and divorced from the worst. The ideology itself is distinct from the lives of people and becomes the means by which the actions of particular citizens are evaluated. With the addition of each successive fragment to the characterizations, *Pat Tillman* came to represent a devotion to that ideology that functioned as both an embodiment of ideals and as a standard for a critique of the actions of others.

The use of Tillman's story — not only by Olbermann, but also by other pundits — as a critique of the military and even the presidency did not invalidate the values that were central to characterizations of Tillman as a hero; if anything, those values were reaffirmed through the reporting and investigation of the story. On ABC's *Good Morning America* show in 2002, for example, then host Diane Sawyer called Tillman's decision to join the military "a story that's really about a question of values and it is something that happened this week and it has had us all talking and deliberating." Then after his death came laments like "In a perfect world, men like Pat Tillman would never die. They would live forever as symbols of sacrifice and profiles in courage" (Boteach, 2004, para. 1) and "Tillman isn't a hero for dying, but for living. For putting his morals where his mouth was and not just enlisting, but doing it in the most humble and honorable way" (Wetzel, 2004, para. 11). However, the manipulation of his death made *Pat Tillman* a part of a post–9/11 rhetorical trajectory that had shifted away from the celebration of shared values and instead toward rhetorics of critique. Just as David Talbot (2001, para. 3) documented "the calls to herd-like conformity" that undermined dissent in the wake of a flood of national pride following the 9/11 attacks, Gary Smith argued that the manipulation of Pat Tillman's death reminded him that the need for myths that make us feel better is so strong "that we'll even take the guy who came right out and said that myths are a load of crap and hoist him on our shoulders to make *another* myth" (2006, p. 100; emphasis in original). Yet the critiques that were made in the name of *Pat Tillman* were buoyed by the belief that Tillman's actions represented an ideological commitment to America. In 2009, cultural critic Jon Krakauer provided a detailed examination of the myths that were perpetuated about Pat Tillman and how those myths provided insight into America's war in Iraq and Afghanistan, concluding that "archetypically American, [Tillman] was confident that right would usually prevail over wrong" (p. 343). As a fragment of the discourse about those wars, Pat Tillman's death had become another reason (alongside the failed hunt for weapons of mass destruction and the Abu Ghraib prison scandal) to distrust the people who were directing the U.S. military. That distrust was coupled with a belief that a commitment to the ideological principles so closely tied to America would prevail.

Through their different characterizations, John McCain and Keith Olbermann articulated divergent perspectives on the role of Pat Tillman's memory that were intertwined by a belief in American exceptionalism. As bearers of competing political philosophies, the conservative McCain and the liberal Olbermann brought opposing ideological viewpoints to their perspectives on the meaning of Tillman's sacrifice — yet both relied on the underlying premise that America is exceptional. Through a series of ascriptions of Tillman's motives, McCain articulated a characterization of *Pat Tillman* premised on the idea that someone who acted based on a devotion to America affirms the values of the nation. In contrast, Keith Olbermann articulated a characterization of *Pat Tillman* premised on the idea that investigation and criticism are the means to identify, uphold, and thereby enact the nation's exceptional values. Both of these perspectives employ America as more than simply a land marked by borders; they frame the nation itself as an ideology that is put into practice by the actions of its people.

Notes

1. This included a March 2007 CNN interview with Wolf Blitzer that directly followed a story about the need for greater scrutiny into the events surrounding Tillman's death. Despite the fact that he had been one of Tillman's most vocal proponents, McCain never reacted to or discussed Tillman in that interview.

References

Altheide, D. L. (2006). *Terrorism and the Politics of Fear*. Lanham, MD: Altamira.
Associated Press. (2004, May 4). "Thousands Attend Memorial for Fallen Soldier." ESPN.com. Retrieved from http://sports.espn.go.com/nfl/news/story?id=1794644.
_____ (2007, July 26). "Was Tillman Murdered? AP Gets New Documents." *Editor and Publisher*. Retrieved from http://www.editorandpublisher.com/eandp/news/article_display.jsp?vnu_content_id=1003617692.
Baldwin, T. (2006, March 2). "Hero's Death Turns Into a Murder Investigation." Times Online. Retrieved from http://www.timesonline.co.uk/tol/news/world/us_and_americas/article737887.ece.
Boeck, G. (2002, June 3). "Sacrificing Riches for Country." *USA Today*, p. 9C.
Boteach, S. (2004, July 18). "A Man for a More Perfect World: Pat Tillman." The My Hero Project. Retrieved from http://www.myhero.com/myhero/hero.asp?hero=tillman.
Boyer, P. J. (2008, June 23). "One Angry Man: Is Keith Olbermann Changing TV News?" *The New Yorker*. Retrieved from http://www.newyorker.com/reporting/2008/06/23/080623fa_fact_boyer?currentPage=all.
Cafardo, N. (2004, April 24). "NFL Player Dies in Afghan Firefight." *Boston Globe*, p. A1.
Campbell, D. (2002, July 9). "The Man Who Wants to Tackle Terrorism." *The Guardian*, p. 7.
Campbell, K. K., and K. H. Jamieson (1978). "Form and Genre in Rhetorical Criticism: An Introduction." In K. K. Campbell and K. H. Jamieson (Eds.), *Form and Genre: Shaping Rhetorical Action* (pp. 9–32). Falls Church, VA: Speech Communication Association.
Coll, S. (2004a, December 5). "Barrage of Bullets Drowned Out Cries of Comrades." *The Washington Post*, p. A1, A14.
_____ (2004b, December 6). "Army Spun Tale Around Ill-Fated Mission." *The Washington Post*, p. A1, A14.
Collier, R. (2005, September 25). "Family Demands Truth: New Inquiry May Expose Events that Led to Pat Tillman's death." *San Francisco Chronicle*, p. A1.
Dburn. (2007, July 26). "Tillman, Three Headshots, 10 Yards Est, Source AP." Daily Kos. Retrieved from http://www.dailykos.com/storyonly/2007/7/26/212449/970.

Dickinson, T. (2007, July 27). "Propaganda, Wrapped in Lies, Covering Up Murder?" *Rolling Stone.* Retrieved from http://www.rollingstone.com/nationalaffairs/index. php/2007/07/27/propaganda-wrapped-in-lies-covering-up-murder/.
Emerson, M. (Director). (2006). "Pat Tillman" [Television series episode]. In S. Reda and L. Reda (Executive Producers), *Bio Presents.* Newark, NJ: A&E Television Networks.
Griffin, L. (1984). "When Dreams Collide: Rhetorical Trajectories in the Assassination of President Kennedy." *Quarterly Journal of Speech, 70,* 111–131.
Hodgson, G. (2009). *The Myth of American Exceptionalism.* New Haven: Yale University Press.
Hofstadter, R. (1955, February 27). "Without Feudalism." *New York Times,* pp. 7, 34.
"Iraq Drives Bush's Rating to New Low." (2006, March 14). CNN.com.
Kazin, M., and J. A. McCartin (2006). "Introduction." In M. Kazin and J. A. McCartin (Eds.), *Americanism: New Perspectives on the History of an Ideal* (pp. 1–21). Chapel Hill: University of North Carolina Press.
Krakauer, J. (2009). *Where Men Win Glory: The Odyssey of Pat Tillman.* New York: Doubleday.
McCain, J. (2004a, April 23). *Statement on the Death of Pat Tillman* [Transcript]. Retrieved from http://mccain.senate.gov/public/index.cfm?FuseAction=PressOffice.PressRe leases&ContentRecord_id=a8c30e42-4068-4594-8883-36053d04de27&Region_ id=&Issue_id=9a9181ea-b7c5-4e6a-845f-5824c7b23939.
_____ (2004b, May 3). *Senator McCain delivers eulogy for Pat Tillman* [Transcript]. Retrieved from http://mccain.senate.gov/public/index.cfm?FuseAction=PressOffice. Speeches&ContentRecord_id=E22E2498-35EB-4F44-9667-5CB5D44DA271.
_____, and M. Salter (2004). *Why Courage Matters: The Way to a Braver Life.* New York: Random House.
_____, and _____ (2005). *Character is Destiny: Inspiring Stories Every Young Person Should Know and Every Adult Should Remember.* New York: Random House.
McGee, M. C. (1978). "'Not Men, but measures'": The Origins and Import of an Ideological Principle." *Quarterly Journal of Speech, 64,* 141–154.
_____ (1990). "Text, Context, and the Fragmentation of Contemporary Culture." *Western Journal of Speech Communication, 54,* 274–289.
Murray, M. (2006, March 16). "Bush Ratings Continue to Drop to New Lows." MSNBC.com. Retrieved from http://www.msnbc.msn.com/id/11843383/from/%5 Benter%20URL%5D.
Olsen, L. (2002, September 15). "Tillman is Army of One." *Daily News,* p. 73.
Parry-Giles, T. (1996). "Character, the Constitution, and the Ideological Embodiment of 'Civil Rights' in the 1967 Nomination of Thurgood Marshall to the Supreme Court." *Quarterly Journal of Speech, 82,* 364–382.
Rambourg, G. (2004, April 24). "NFL Star Who Joined Army Killed in Afghanistan." *Agence France Presse.* Retrieved from www.lexisnexis.com.
Rand, J. (2004). *Fields of Honor: The Pat Tillman Story.* New York: Express.
Rich, F. (2006). *The Greatest Story Ever Sold: The Decline and Fall of Truth from 9/11 to Katrina.* New York: Penguin.
Smith, G. (2004, May 3). "Code of Honor: Pat Tillman, 1976–2004." *Sports Illustrated,* pp. 40–46.
_____ (2006, September 11). "Remember his Name." *Sports Illustrated,* pp. 86–101.
Talbot, D. (2001, September 29). "Democracy Held Hostage: We Are Fighting for Freedom — Including the Right to Vigorously Debate. But the War Fever Crowd Wants Us All to March in Step." *Salon.* Retrieved from http://dir.salon.com/story/news/feature/2001/09/29/democracy/index.html.
Thompson, M., R. DeBitetto, R. Sharenow, M. Davies and A. Ruheman (Executive Pro-

ducers), M. Monroe (Writer), and A. Bar-Lev (Director). (2009). *The Tillman Story* [Motion picture]. Los Angeles: Passion Pictures.

Tillman, P., Sr. (2005, May 28). "Failures and Blame in Pat Tillman's Death." *Washington Post*, p. A24.

Towle, M. (2004). *I've Got Things to Do with My Life: Pat Tillman and the Making of an American Hero*. Chicago: Triumph.

United States House of Representatives Committee on Oversight and Government Reform (2008, July 17). *Misleading Information from the Battlefield: The Tillman and Lynch Episodes*. Retrieved from http://oversight.house.gov/documents/20080714111050.pdf.

Watson, P. J. (2007, July 27). "New Evidence Clearly Indicates Pat Tillman Was Executed." Infowars.com. Retrieved from http://www.infowars.com/articles/military/tillman_new_evidence_indicates_tillman_executed.htm.

Wetzel, D. (2004, April 23). "A True American Hero." Yahoo! Sports. Retrieved from http://sports.yahoo.com/nfl/news?slug=dw-tillman.

White, J. (2005, May 4). "Army Investigator Withheld Details About Tillman's Death: Investigator Quickly Learned "Friendly Fire" Killed Athlete." *Washington Post*, p. A3.

Wise, M., and J. White (2004, April 24). "Ex-NFL Player Killed in Combat: Army Ranger Turned Down Millions to Serve." *Washington Post*, p. A1.

Zirin, D. (2005). *What's My Name, Fool? Sports and Resistance in the United States*. Chicago: Haymarket.

CHAPTER 9

The Sand Creek Massacre National Historic Site
Challenge to and Reification of American Exceptionalism

LINDSAY R. CALHOUN

On a freezing November morning in 1864, members of Civil War hero Colonel Chivington's 1st and 3rd Infantry Divisions attacked a sparse campsite on the dry frozen plains of Eastern Colorado. The people they attacked were a mixture of Cheyenne and Arapaho elderly, women, and children. The majority of the tribes' young adult men were not in the camp that day. They had turned over most of their arms to Fort Lyon earlier that fall in an effort to try to arrange a peace agreement between the Cheyenne and Arapaho peoples and the territorial authorities in Denver. When the first shots were fired on the camp, killing Chief White Antelope as he ran out to greet the attackers, the peace effort was officially finished. The causes and events that led up to the devastating massacre at Sand Creek are complex and controversial. In Sand Creek's aftermath, the response to the attack by the Denver media reflected both relief and pride. In Washington, DC, the response would eventually be one of condemnation. However, despite the federal government's public repudiation of the actions taken at Sand Creek, no one was ever prosecuted for the crimes committed that cold morning.

Sand Creek quickly faded into the memory of the majority of the American public but lived forever in the hearts and minds of the Cheyenne and Arapaho people, as they spent the next century and a half trying to survive and define their identity in the midst of American nation-building. As they continued to struggle to find their place in American society, they realized that the wrongs of the past would haunt them forever if they did not begin to find the means to reconcile themselves with what had happened at Sand Creek.

Over the last 140 years, the exact location of the massacre site was disputed between archaeologists, historians, and members of the four first nations involved in the attack: the Northern Cheyenne of Montana, Northern Arapaho of Wyoming, and the Cheyenne and Arapaho tribes of Oklahoma. While most people agreed on a general 12-to-20 square mile area suggested by historical accounts, the precise location of the campsite was still in debate. In the mid–1990s, the National Park Service in consultation with the tribes began using oral histories and other historical materials to locate and identify the Sand Creek Massacre site. The National Park Service and the tribes together began to seek public support for their efforts, including that of landowners living in the area many people believed was the location of the attack. This effort gained the attention of the media and of political leaders, including then U.S. Senator Ben Nighthorse Campbell, a member of the Northern Cheyenne people descended from those who were present at the Sand Creek attack, and the National Park Service. Additionally, they garnered the support of one of the primary landholders on the Sand Creek site who began allowing Cheyenne and Arapaho people onto his property to perform ceremonies honoring the victims of the massacre and providing spiritual healing for tribal members.

After many years of research and study, the location was verified, Congress officially designated it "The Sand Creek Massacre National Historic Site," and plans were drawn up to develop the site into a small but powerfully moving national monument. While the park was officially opened to visitors in April of 2007, very little has actually been decided regarding its interpretation and development. Moreover, several competing economic and political interests are implicated in the park's development and a variety of sensitive cultural issues still remain to be addressed.

The reemergence of Sand Creek as an issue for public policy and public discourse presents a challenge to conventionally understood notions of American exceptionalism, but it also serves a paradoxical purpose of unifying American people through redemption. This redemptive quality reifies American exceptionalism as well.

American exceptionalism begins with the idea that "that the United States was created differently, developed differently, and thus has to be *understood* differently — essentially on its own terms and within its own context" (Shafer, 1991). Bell (1991) and Shafer (1991) argue that while all ethnic groups claim a unique identity, it is the idea of American exceptionalism as a historical theme that gives the concept its weight. Bell in particular notes that America has embarked upon a unique historical path that is embedded in a redemptive framework, a saving grace, that is meaningful not only to Americans but to a global audience who are witnesses to America's special destiny.

The two most relevant threads of that literature concern treatments of the United States as "unique" and/or "different" and those framing America as "superior" or "transcendent." In his *Democracy in America*, Alexis de Tocqueville (1830/1948) defined U.S. exceptionalism in terms of its uniqueness, noting that America was "qualitatively different from all other countries" (Tocqueville, 1830/1948, pp. 36–37). Lipset (1996) maintained a similar argument, claiming that what made the United States unique was its people's adherence to a common ideology. He also asserted that America combined traits that other nations do not share. Liberty is defined specifically in terms of unique ideas about patriotism and egalitarianism, a curious combination of extreme individualism and populism, and laissez-faire attitudes about government. Additionally, the United States is unique for its absence of feudal structures, monarchies, and formal aristocracies, as well as its penchant to couch things in various religious terms.

Others characterize the United States as not only unique, arguing that American exceptionalism is based in the idea that Americans are fundamentally superior and even that America is a nation with a divine purpose. In his survey of the history of American exceptionalism, Daniel Bell (1991) asserted that America has embarked upon a unique historical path that is embedded in a redemptive framework that makes the United States an exemplar for other nations. Specifically, Bell noted that the idea of exceptionalism in America that has been used to describe American history and institutions

> assumes not only that the United States has been unlike other nations, but that it is exceptional in the sense of being exemplary ("a city upon a hill"), or a beacon among nations; immune from the social ills and decadence that have beset all other republics in the past; or that it is exempt from the historical course of "social laws" of development which all nations eventually follow [pp. 50–51].

Embedded within this quotation is the idea that what makes the U.S. truly exceptional is our superiority to other states. Many proponents of American exceptionalism (including every American president; see Campbell and Jamieson, 2008) hold that the United States is a beneficiary of divine providence and therefore is endowed with certain characteristics that make it better than others. The United States's greatness will never end because it is always striving to create a "more perfect union." In the pursuit of that "more perfect union" there is a constant sense of rebirth and renewal that other nation-states do not possess. Ultimately, the mission of Americans is to take those characteristics and pursue a special destiny, to fulfill our exceptionalist ethos through various means (Edwards, 2008; McCrisken, 2003; McDougall, 1997).

One specific fulfillment of that exceptionalist ethos pertinent to this analysis is America's migration westward. The so-called "frontier narrative" has been a staple of American political discourse since the founding (see Carpenter, 1990; Dorsey, 1995). The famous historian Frederick Jackson Turner (1961) first described the frontier narrative in his essay "The Significance of the Frontier in American History," writing that

> American social development has been continually beginning over and over again on the frontier. This perennial rebirth, this fluidity of American life, this expansion westward with its new opportunities, its continuous touch with the simplicity of primitive society, furnish the forces dominating American character. The true point of view in the history of this nation is not the Atlantic coast, it is the Great West.... In this advance, the frontier is the outer edge of the wave — the meeting point between savagery and civilization [p. 38].

Turner's quotation describes the cyclical nature of American history and identity. The "frontier" notion breathes new life into the understanding of a nation founded on the concept of breaking away from the traditions and shackles of older civilizations. This "rebirth" into "new life" was a metaphor for progress that grounded American identity. This thinking also led to the notion that America could become a new model of how to develop and progress for other nations. Heitala (2003) noted that with the frontier thesis,

> Americans speculated about the significance of their westward expansion upon their institutions and character as well as about its effects upon the world at large. In their own minds, Americans believed that their progress provided a beacon light to a world in darkness [p. 257].

For Americans, the way to demonstrate our uniqueness and our superiority was the push westward. Through territorial expansion, or "manifest destiny," the United States formed a rebirth and renewal. Proponents of manifest destiny believed that the United States was destined, perhaps even divinely ordained, to expand from the Atlantic coast to the Pacific Ocean (Stephenson, 1995). This expansion required rugged pioneers who could go into the wilderness, making the surrounding environment habitable for those who would arrive later by tilling the soil, using the land's vast mineral resources, and conquering and "civilizing" the "other" (the Native American). Native Americans were depicted as savages who lacked a centralized order, behaved like children, or epitomized evil. In order for the United States to fulfill its exceptionalist ethos, these savages needed to be "civilized" so they could not threaten America's "progress" westward. This meant assimilating them into dominant white culture, putting them on reservations, or fighting and exterminating them

(Rogin, 1987). Taming the land and "civilizing" Native Americans demonstrated the United States' divinely inspired progress as a nation, thus allowing the United States to argue that it was a "beacon of light" or a "city upon a hill" for the world to emulate. Thus, American exceptionalism was reified through not only the conquest and civilization of the frontier but also through the civilization of the savage.

In the modern era, however, manifest destiny was challenged, recast as an ideology of colonization and subjugation. America, the former colonial underdog, became associated with colonial empire building through its abuses to the indigenous peoples of North America, its manifest destiny grounded more in economic, political, and cultural exploitation than in progress and civilization. When America, once a colony, became the colonizer, the experience of America's growth as a world power did not look so exceptional or so moral, but rather like that of all too many empire nations of the past, whose armies, political systems, religious and cultural forces, and economic policies ran roughshod over various ethnic groups the world over. One event that cuts deep into the narrative of American exceptionalism is that of the Sand Creek Massacre, a tragic Civil War-era attack by the U.S. cavalry on a peaceful group of native peoples. This attack, while not unique in terms of U.S.-Indian relations at the time, was a major catalyst for the Indian Wars of the late 1880s.

In this chapter, I examine the contradictions of American exceptionalism by pursuing two major arguments. First, American exceptionalism itself is a paradox because in order to be exceptional, America must maintain its unique identity in the world, exhibiting qualities embodied by risk taking and the constant pursuit of the frontier. However, in pursuing the frontier, and in unifying different groups under the umbrella of a common national identity, America must always be pursuing the "other" in an attempt to absorb its essential differences while still maintaining its identity as internally diverse. It is my argument that the current memorialization of the Sand Creek Massacre National Historic Site embodies this essential paradox of American exceptionalism. Second, the qualities of moral transcendence inherent in the discursive formulation of American exceptionalism are based in Christian concepts of redemption and mortification. That is, as a nation with many Christian founders, America could be understood to be a nation of born sinners on the path to redemption. Only through our sins can we achieve our divine destiny. The "sin" of Sand Creek is recast in the American exceptionalist framework as a reification of divine transcendence through mortification, sacrifice, and suffering. Therefore, American exceptionalism itself is both reified and challenged through Sand Creek.

Sand Creek encapsulates the dilemma that the American Indian has always presented for American national identity, the ultimately unabsorbable other that, paradoxically, also defines the American historical experience. Philip Deloria explains that the figure of "the Indian" in our historical imagination contributes to the indeterminacy of American national identity because "Americans want to feel a natural affinity with the continent, and it was Indians who could teach them such aboriginal closeness. Yet, in order to control the landscape they had to destroy the original inhabitants" (1998, p. 5). Thus, the critical tension between the American Indian and American national identity is that of extermination versus inclusion, a tension that has never been resolved. Yet both options suggest control and objectification of the American Indian regardless of which one prevails. Thus the question for dominant American national identity has always been how to absorb the American Indian into the national historical imagination.

Moreover, American exceptionalism is rooted in a Christian redemption ethos that grounds American national identity in a perpetual cycle of sin and salvation. At the same time, American exceptionalism is predicated on the frontier narrative of exploration and colonization. These two predicates create a system of values and practices that ensure that occupation and colonization of exotic others, a practice that necessarily requires "getting your hands dirty" (i.e., "sin") is a necessary rite of passage on the path to exceptional global standing.

At Sand Creek, sacrifice and sin and redemption are dealt with in ceremonies that involve performances of long distance running by tribal members as well as purification rituals involving prayer, song, the drum, and the use of sweetgrass as a cleansing agent. The long distance running is witnessed by Indian and non–Indian participants and the prayer and song ceremonies are participated in by both Indians and non–Indians, both at the Sand Creek massacre site as well as at other relevant sites in the state of Colorado, such as the state Capitol Building. As a result, at Sand Creek, exceptionalism, the significance of the pursuit of the "other" on the American frontier, and the possibility of Christian-like redemption are inextricably intertwined as an integrated performance. So while the National Park Service and the popular and regional media sources seek to define Sand Creek in terms of a redemptive narrative that reifies American exceptionalism in terms of manifest destiny and sinners on the way to salvation, there are still many unabsorbable qualities with regard to Sand Creek that exist and, perhaps will persist in the face of what may ultimately be a predominantly European American interpretation of the site. Additionally, the Cheyenne and Arapaho people, who have had to sacrifice and compromise in order to preserve Sand Creek still utilize performance and reappropriate signs and symbols frequently used by Anglo-Europeans to celebrate American exceptionalism, like the American flag, as a form of resistance to rather than reification of American national identity. It is the practices and performances of the repertoire of Sand Creek, rather than the documentation, media coverage, and monuments of the archive of Sand Creek that remain unabsorbable. The one question that remains for the future of Sand Creek's development is whether those unabsorbable aspects of American Exceptionalism at Sand Creek will have enough room to be meaningfully understood and shared by any and all participants who visit Sand Creek. This chapter will pursue these arguments and questions by examining the contemporary narratives and performances that define Sand Creek and its memorialization in terms of redemption, manifest destiny and American exceptionalism.

Sand Creek: An Exceptional Frontier Narrative

In 2002, I began investigating the Sand Creek Massacre Site and observing how it was remembered by various communities, Indian and non–Indian alike. I made several trips to the site between 2002 and 2007, recording field notes of my observations. From those observations, I concluded that Sand Creek is a place where American exceptionalism and notions of the frontier are intertwined through a variety of commemorative performances.

The Frontier Scene

Sand Creek still resembles the wild and somewhat inhospitable frontier it was the day of the attack. Its landscape is a wide-open space where imagination and memory co-mingle to enable re-experiencing and re-traumatization of the frontier experience. Sand Creek looks and feels remote. It is not easily accessible by car and it has not changed significantly since the 1864 massacre. Thus, it currently has the potential to give people a sense of "frontier space" as a meeting point between freedom and its historical aftermath, colonization. Sand Creek is open to interpretation. The presence of tour guides, markers, and panels is limited.

Visitors are left with their own impressions when they visit Sand Creek, in stark contrast to other monuments to American Indian history, such as the site commemorating the Battle of the Little Bighorn. While the battle site is preserved, its surrounding landscape is a constant reminder of the ultimate end of the frontier. When I stood upon the high point of the ridge of Little Bighorn looking out over the battlefield, I could see cars whizzing by on Interstate 90, a modern visitors' center, and a large casino and gift shop with blinking signs. I could not escape the visible signs of Western economic infrastructure circumscribing the space, reminding me that while we may remember the frontier and preserve its memory, it no longer exists as an unbounded physical location.

At Sand Creek, the signs of economic infrastructure and the imposition of the dominant culture are not nearly as foregrounded as at Little Bighorn. One can almost imagine that the dirt roads have Indians and wagons on them instead of cars; that if you hold your thumb up to your eye you could just smudge out the little farmhouses that occasionally dot parts of the landscape, as if in a chalk painting. The signs of Western dominance at Sand Creek, while visible, are much more subtle. Sand Creek more nearly embodies the frontier aesthetic, giving the visitor the opportunity to "experience" the frontier, to feel a part of it, and to collapse the distance between past and present. Simply put, Sand Creek is a meeting point between savagery and civilization.

Exceptionalism, the significance of the frontier, and the possibility of Christian-like redemption are inextricably intertwined as an integrated performance in Sand Creek's remembrances. Moreover, as both Turner (1961) and Deloria (1998) argue, the frontier is also a meeting point, one that involves exchange and mutual influence. Indeed, colonization is never a one-way street. At the Sand Creek site, non–Indian Americans "play" Indian in various limited respects. Visitors are invited to partake in Sand Creek blessings, wear face paint, eat Thanksgiving brunch alongside Cheyenne and Arapaho people, participate as runners in Spiritual Healing Runs; and dance and sing in powwows. While this is happening, Cheyenne and Arapaho are present and mediating play and performance by non–Indian others, offering redemptive and community bonding opportunities. In doing so, non–Indians are absorbed as symbolic objects within the frontier notions of American identity.

Indigenous people have long survived by transforming their own religious practices, ideologies, symbols, and practices, seemingly submitting to the powerful forces of colonization (Taylor, 2005). But one can never really be completely certain about the authorship, meaning, or ownership of these practices from context to context, particularly as they are performed for diverse audiences. This is why I believe that performing for non–Indians at Sand Creek rituals and anniversaries is not really an act of submission. It is simultaneously an act of both accommodation and resistance.

Reenacting the Frontier: The Spiritual Healing Run

The Spiritual Healing Run and its corresponding blessing ceremony honor and symbolize the physical and cultural experience of the frontier, operating as a cross-cultural participatory event premised on both "savagery" and "civilization." The physical act of running symbolizes the physical challenge that the frontier imposed on its inhabitants and the way that the frontier transforms the body and owns it as much as the human attempts to transform and own the frontier. It also symbolizes and embodies the fear, trauma, and pain that the victims of the massacre experienced as they attempted to escape their pursuers' acts of savagery and violence

Before the Spiritual Healing Run, all the participants take part in a purification ceremony performed by a male tribal elder. Several other Cheyenne and Arapaho males play drums and sing traditional songs, including one White Antelope sang about the earth and the mountains on the morning he was killed in the 1864 attack. The tribal elder marks with red paint the foreheads of the runners and anyone else present who wishes to be blessed and spiritually cleanses them by waving burning sweet grass over their bodies, murmuring a prayer or blessing while doing so. Participants will then run from Sand Creek to the town of Eads for a Thanksgiving brunch.

Ceremonies the following day occur in Denver. They often start at Riverside Cemetery, one of the city's oldest. The prayers, songs, and flag raising begin at the gravesite of Silas Soule, a captain who refused to fire on the Indians at Sand Creek, ordered the soldiers under his command to stand down, and subsequently wrote letters to his commanding officer protesting the attack. After the American flag is raised near Soule's grave, the tribal leaders sing again and purify the runners and observers using the same ceremony they did the day before at the actual Sand Creek Massacre site. The runners then leave Soule's gravesite and head toward the city center, where, accompanied by visitors, they gather on the steps of the Capitol or at another government building to hear poems and speeches about Sand Creek. Occasionally, whites, members of other first nations, and people of other ethnicities will join in the run.

Taylor (2005) writes that the act of witnessing the performance of suffering is necessary to understanding the relationship between trauma, narrative, and collective memory. She states,

> Even studies that emphasize the link between trauma and narrative make evident in the analysis itself that the transmission of traumatic memory from victim to witness involves the shared and participatory act of telling and listening associated with live performance. Bearing witness is a live process, a doing, an event that takes place in real time, in the presence of a listener who comes to be a participant and a co-owner of the traumatic event [p. 167].

In the run, the suffering of the runners implicates the non–Indian participant witnesses in the suffering that occurred on the morning of the Sand

Creek attack. In that moment, "savagery" and "civilization" clashed violently and collapsed into one another, begging the question of who symbolized "savagery" and who symbolized "civilization." The justifications for the attack then and the characterization of the attack as a massacre today reverse the roles between the savage and the civilized. The Spiritual Healing Run indicates that the only way out of this embattled landscape is through spiritual purification and redemption performed through running and witnessing.

As I emphasized earlier, the qualities of moral transcendence inherent in the discursive formulation of American exceptionalism are based in Christian concepts of redemption and mortification. As a Christian nation, America could be understood to be a nation of sinners on the path to redemption. Only through our sins can we achieve our divine destiny. The "sin" of Sand Creek is recast in the American exceptionalist framework as a reification of divine transcendence through mortification, sacrifice, and suffering. The Run works to simultaneously emphasize suffering and mortification through witnessing and participating. It unifies participants in the memorial at Sand Creek precisely because it allows Cheyenne and Arapaho people and non–Indian American citizens to experience redemption and mortification together, momentarily uniting them under the umbrella of American exceptionalism.

The Spiritual Healing Run also invokes the savage experience of the frontier. Running, as a physical activity is one of the oldest and most basic forms of human exercise as well as one of the most brutal in its physical impact. Yet running has the power to really strip away the trappings of material society from the body. One does not need special training or equipment to run. A runner does not need other people or relationships. One does not have to be "civil" while running. Even in violent sports like hockey or football, there are still rules that govern a player's behavior towards an opponent. But in running, there are not many rules, even at the highest levels of the sport. And one can run without participating in the organized sport of running, whereas it is difficult to play hockey or football by oneself. What you need to run is pure will; will to power, in a Nietzschean sense. In that way, it is a true symbol of pure freedom and the suffering freedom brings.

In the Spiritual Healing Run, the runners reenact the experience of those who ran through the bitter cold the morning of November 29, 1864. In that instance, many of the Cheyenne and Arapaho people did what that people do when up against a force much greater than themselves yet choose to survive. They ran, as far and as fast as they could away from the danger. Today, the participants in the ceremonies at Sand Creek use their own running as a symbol of both freedom and resistance. The suffering of the runners becomes a physical demonstration of their history and identity, reifying the narrative that they spent many generations on the run both because of and against their will. Running was a conscious choice to survive on the morning of the Sand Creek attack. Because that was the case, the Spiritual Healing Run today challenges the absorbent tendencies of American exceptionalism while reifying them through the redemption and freedom running can symbolize. As a symbol of freedom, suffering, purification and survival, the spiritual running is offered in the runners' terms, not those of the people witnessing the run. They are no longer being chased out of their land. They are returning to it. This is a defiant act against the attack on Sand Creek, while also symbolizing the very best qualities of the American spirit: determination, hard work, and freedom. The running is not defined by the parameters of a race or competitive requirements of time and rules. It is not an undertaking that invites the public to participate as other traditional running events often do. At the same time the spiritual running does invite self-reflection and allows for witnessing and support on the part of the viewers of the run. It is simultaneously inclusive and exclusive, a symbol of freedom and a symbol of subjugation and suffering. It is a reminder of the pain of that day as well as a reminder of the survival of the Cheyenne and Arapaho people today. Through this Sand Creek spiritual healing run, the paradoxical qualities of American exceptionalism are both reified and challenged.

Resistance and Reification in the Use of Flags

One of the enduring symbols of Sand Creek is the American flag with 38 stars flying alongside the white flag of surrender. The Cheyenne and Arapaho use this flag in several Sand Creek anniversary ceremonies every year. For the Cheyenne and Arapaho, the American flag is a floating signifier with multiple, slippery, and conflicting meanings.

Of course, the American flag is a complex symbol for all Americans. Zelinsky (1984) argues that compared to other countries, the American flag tends to occupy a much stronger place in its citizens' national consciousness, noting that the flag's sacred quality and its ubiquitous aspects are frequently manifested in folk art and other aspects of national cultural and civic life. The flag is central to American exceptionalism in that, as a symbol, it articulates the dialectical principles of unity and diversity while also representing the possibility of transcendence central to American national identity. Similarly, Michael Angrosino (2002) argues that in a country as religiously and culturally diverse as the United States of America, national totemic symbols such as the American flag take on a sacred significance that transcends deep cultural and religious differences and thus unites the nation. For Angrosino (2002), the flag is part of a "civil religion" that transcends cultural and religious diversity within the United States and unites the country in a common spiritual commitment to a national culture.

The American flag is also central to the memory of the Sand Creek massacre. However, the flag's function at Sand Creek is not simply to reify American exceptionalism and pride in American ideals, nor is it solely a redemptive and transcendent symbol. The emphasis on the flag by the Cheyenne and Arapaho must be seen in part as an important axiom of resistance to transcendence. That the flag flew on the day of the massacre, and that that fact is retold and reemphasized over and over again, seeks to remind Americans of non–Indian descent that a sinner can never overcome his sinful nature; he can only be redeemed from it through forgiveness and sacrifice. Therefore, transcendence over human rights failures for America is perhaps impossible, but redemption is not. The unique qualities of the flag in American consciousness, and in particular its ability to unite the secular with the religious, speak to its role in constituting American exceptionalism as a sacred moral mandate that transcends differences. The flag functions as an effective symbol for balancing difference with unity, a symbolic function necessary for maintaining the paradox of American exceptionalism.

For Plains Indians such as the Cheyenne and Arapaho, the ritual and symbolic use of the American flag in cultural and civic life is not unusual. Schmittou and Logan (2002) explain that the use of the flag motif is prevalent in Plains Indians' art. In asking why oppressed peoples would adopt the preeminent symbol of their oppressors and employ it in their decorative arts, Schmittou and Logan (2002) explain that the flag as both symbol and material object is wrapped up in Plains Indians' spiritual reverence for and understanding of sacred symbols and objects as part of their complex relationship with the U.S. government and military. However, flag imagery in Plains Indian art did not emerge until the beginning of the reservation era (Pohrt, 1975). Further, according to Schmittou and Logan, the use of the flag in Native art was a result of the ongoing ethnic conflict which pressured the Plains groups to utilize the American flag in their crafts as part of a larger strategy for survival.

By establishing parallel use of the flag motif in Plains Indian artwork and crafts, the flag could serve the people economically as a symbol that had meaning both for the tribes and for potential buyers of their products. Also, the flag could be portrayed simultaneously in terms of both reverence and protest. Historically, flags were given to American Indian chiefs when explorers and leaders visited the tribes as a gift, both for protection of the tribe and to engender loyalty and allegiance from the tribes (Schmittou and Logan, 2002). Because the flag was presented as a sacred object to the tribal leaders, they often treated it as such in their long tradition of reciprocity and exchange. Further, when the relationship between the tribes and the U.S. government and military deteriorated, the sense of betrayal the tribes experienced was often manifested in how they subsequently treated the flag. For example, in a Lakota scene of the Battle of Little Bighorn, the flag is drawn upside down, a sign of distress according to the U.S. flag code. Historically it is unlikely that the flag was actually flying upside down in the battle. And it is unlikely that the Lakota were unaware of the basic flag code. The portrayal of the flag in this manner, then, reflects protest and betrayal as well as a symbolic reference to the defeat of the American military at Little Bighorn.

Finally, Schmittou and Logan (2002) argue that during the late 1870s to 1890s the flag represented Native peoples' engagement with the U.S. military in either victory or defeat. However, the flag's symbolic ties to battle began to shift when Native American people began serving in the U.S. Military in World War I. From there, the boundaries between national identity and tribal identity began to blur as the flag began to symbolize service to both tribe and country. The flag, even now, can simultaneously serve as a symbol of protest, military service, peace, reverence to sacred symbols and traditions, and economic growth within the Plains Indians groups (Schmittou and Logan, 2002).

It has occurred to me that the military branches of the U.S. government have, in some ways, inadvertently allowed the warrior tradition to continue within Native cultures. Traditional tribal masculine values have been rearticulated as commitment to national military service since the tribes' own militaries have been disbanded. Additionally, serving in the military has become a source of honor and economic pride on the reservations where there are few opportunities for employment. Finally, the military provides a source of physical pride to societies who are facing severe health crises. The Plains Indians can transform the symbol of the U.S. military into a tribal resource that allows them to continue their warrior traditions. Ironically, they leave their own trace upon the very military that used to oppress them and, in many cases, attempted to annihilate them, by serving honorably and memorably. The reappropriation of the American flag into Cheyenne and Arapaho tribal rituals and practices that blend contemporary military traditions with older paramilitary traditions, suggests that the flag does not belong to a single ideological framework or predominant ethnic interpretation. If America is to be truly inclusive, the flag can be used in sovereign and autonomous respects by the Cheyenne and Arapaho people. The American flag can be incorporated and blended into Cheyenne and Arapaho traditions in a way that neither degrades the flag nor accedes to its potential power as a non–Indian symbol of patriotic unity.

This paradoxical use of the American flag both as a (sometimes simultaneous) symbol of protest and patriotic reverence mirrors the paradoxical qualities of American exceptionalism. At Sand Creek, the use of the flag discloses the moral failings of a nation mandated to be morally exceptional. Additionally, by adopting the American flag as their own symbol, the American Indians embody the difference that the original settlers sought to identify with. American Indians themselves symbolized the ultimate freedom and uniqueness that the early colonials sought to embody. Yet, historically they were not included as official members of the nation and in many cases were pushed out, massacred, and otherwise violently excluded from the nation. Their use of the flag in ritual functions as a critical commentary on both the questionable moral certitude of the American national identity and its uniqueness as a nation-state that pursues democratic principles. Simultaneously, their embracing of the American flag as their own demonstrates the dynamic and unbounded qualities of American national identity, attributes essential to American exceptionalism.

Waving the flag at Sand Creek remembrance rituals allows the Cheyenne and Arapaho to send a sign of peace and allegiance to their fellow Americans. Simultaneously it serves as a communication of protest and betrayal, a reminder to non–Indians that Natives, too, are a permanent part of the sacred symbolic order that betrayed them mercilessly — and that they have survived in spite of it. "Today the American flag represents, for Native peoples, a clear link to their embattled past. It also symbolizes their ongoing tradition as warriors. They let it speak proudly of their bravery, their sacrifices, and their love of land and nation" (Schmittou and Logan, 2002, p. 593).

It should be no surprise, then, that the American flag is an important element of Sand Creek's remembrance. Its symbolic significance to the Plains Indians, including the Cheyenne and Arapaho, makes it a powerful prop in performative scenarios of Sand Creek's remembrance. In the historical narrative of Sand Creek, the American flag is referenced several times, almost as if it is a character in the story. Historical testimony about the events leading up to and taking place on the day of the attack suggests that the Cheyenne and Arapaho tribes were given an American flag and a white flag to be flown in their camp for protection; supposedly, the flag was flying on the day of the attack (Hoig, 1961; Hyde, 1968; Roberts, 1984; Schultz, 1990). Whether this is historically verifiable, the Cheyenne and Arapaho regularly use the 38-star flag as well as the white flag of surrender as part of their Sand Creek memorial ceremonies.

In visual representations of Sand Creek, the American flag and the white flag feature prominently. In an elk-hide painting by the late Eugene Ridgely, Sr., soon to be featured in the Sand Creek Visitors Center in Eads, Colorado, the white flag and American flag are being carried by a man who appears to be a Cheyenne or Arapaho elder as an approaching soldier is shooting him down. The flag, while not hanging upside down, is not displayed in a way that suggests pride or strength, but rather is shown drooping and falling off the pole.

Eugene Ridgely's depiction of the Sand Creek Massacre may reveal much more about the fluidity of meanings when interpreting the past from the Cheyenne and Arapaho perspective. Additionally, Ridgeley's decision to portray White Antelope's martyrdom by showing him waving the American flag at the soldiers as they shot at him challenges notions about America's loyalty to a superior moral framework. Additionally, White Antelope's martyrdom offers up an interpretation of the Christian sacrifice and redemption narrative that is familiar to Americans. At the center of this painting/narrative is the symbol of the Flag, providing both a critique and the possibility of redemption for the viewer as well as locating the flag in a martyrdom narrative that ties into the Christian foundations of American exceptionalism.

At the Spiritual Healing Run every year at Sand Creek, the American flag is used in drumming and prayer ceremonies and is placed at the gravesite of Silas Soule. The American flag and its associated colors and symbols (red, white, blue, the stars and stripes) are also used in the pow-wow held in the evening after the Sand Creek ceremonies are completed. I remember being struck by the patriotism expressed by the tribes both when I went to Lame Deer, Montana, to attend a Sand Creek consultation meeting and pow-wow and when I attended Sand Creek Memorial pow-wows in Denver. It seemed remarkable to me that the tribes could express such a commitment to a symbolic order that held so much pain and anguish for them. I remember the different men who were dressed in accordance with the military societies they belonged to and how service in any of the five military branches played such an important role in the costumes and rituals of the pow-wows.

The dynamic tension between commitment and critique that emerges from the Cheyenne and Arapaho uses of the American flag in Sand Creek ceremonies reveals the paradoxical qualities of the flag itself as a symbol of America. As a paradox, American exceptionalism, the foundational principle of American national identity, attempts to simultaneously uphold both difference and unity, as well as the qualities of sinner and savior, linking it to the Christian framework from which it draws. This paradoxical quality of American exceptionalism is engaged by the Cheyenne and Arapaho people to point out the strengths, weaknesses, and contradictions of the American national character. However, the paradox is what allows for a dynamic exchange between the Cheyenne and Arapaho people and their non–Indian counterparts, allowing them to seek unification with the larger American national identity while still maintaining their autonomy. It also allows them to provide a valid critique and form of resistance to the historical myths of American exceptionalism but to remain tied to American history rather than being alienated from it. While the paradoxical qualities of American exceptionalism are often problematic, it is the enduring tension that makes American exceptionalism so powerful and durable as a national identity framework. It is the paradoxical qualities of American exceptionalism that also make it possible for Americans to be self-reflexive as they consider their own identity in relationship to others, the past, and the future.

Conclusion

The Sand Creek Massacre is memorialized by performances and practices that emerge out of narrative frameworks of American exceptionalism. These are apparent in the current simplified landscape of the Sand Creek site, the Spiritual Healing Run, and other rituals associated with remembering Sand Creek. It is important to emphasize the paradoxical nature of American exceptionalism and how it manifests itself in this particular case. The simultaneous resistance to and reification of American exceptionalism reveals its strength and pervasiveness as a cultural paradigm.

Paradox in American exceptionalism is important to understand because in order for any cultural paradigm to succeed and sustain itself over the long term, it must be able to absorb change and dissent while also enduring and remaining resonant and recognizable to its people. America started by defining itself as a paradox. As Ignatieff (2005) pointed out, even our Bill of Rights begins in the negative, "Congress shall make no law..." Our Declaration of Independence impugns old monarchical governing strategies and denies the political past. This definitive "no" is a reaction to the discursive framework and political identity of Britain, which means that it is also where the new identity had to begin. The old and the new always begin and end in the same place in American identity. The same paradoxical framework applies with regard to Sand Creek. As Deloria (1998) noted, American national identity is predicated on being distinct from, and perhaps even distinctly opposite, its Northern European predecessors. The American Indian provided the perfect foil for European identity. However, in its distinction, the new American identity could never be completely stable and fixed and was always a threat to building a more perfect union, hence the rabid pursuit of the American Indian to near extinction. American Indians, including the Cheyenne and

Arapaho of Sand Creek, know that they were part of the American continent from the beginning. They also know that they are simultaneously included in and excluded from that more perfect national union that Americans are trying to build. Their identities provide much of the distinction necessary to create a history and cultural identity that is founded upon the American continent rather than one imported from abroad and appropriated for cultural use. Therefore, while some minorities may more openly resist identification with a national U.S. identity, many American Indian groups are caught in the paradox. They recognize their essential role in the social construction of American identity while also seeing the tragic consequences of their exploitation. Therefore, American exceptionalism operates at Sand Creek in much the same way it operates more generally, as neither a perfect union nor a disunion, but rather a disjunctive synthesis.

References

Angrosino, M. (2002). "Civil Religion Redux." *Anthropological Quarterly, 75*, 239–67.
Bell, D. (1991). "The 'Hegelian Secret': Civil Society and American Exceptionalism." In B. E. Shafer (Ed.), *Is America Different? A New Look at American Exceptionalism* (pp. 46–67). Oxford: Oxford University Press.
Campbell, K. K., and K. H. Jamieson (2008). *Presidents Creating the Presidency: Deeds Done in Words.* Chicago: University of Chicago Press.
Carpenter, R. H. (1990). "America's Tragic Metaphor: Our Twentieth-Century Combatants as Frontiersmen." *Quarterly Journal of Speech, 76*, 1–22.
Deloria, P. J. (1998). *Playing Indian.* New Haven: Yale University Press.
Dorsey, L. G. (1995). "The Frontier Myth in Presidential Rhetoric: Theodore Roosevelt's Campaign for Conservation." *Western Journal of Communication, 59*, 1–19.
Edwards, J. A. (2008). *Navigating the Post-Cold War World: President Clinton's Foreign Policy Rhetoric.* Lanham, MD: Lexington.
Heitala, T. R. (2003). *Manifest Design: American Exceptionalism and Empire.* Ithaca: Cornell University Press.
Hoig, S. (1961). *The Sand Creek Massacre.* Norman: University of Oklahoma Press.
Hyde, G. E. (1968). *Life of George Bent: Written from His Letters.* Norman: University of Oklahoma Press.
Ignatieff, M. (2005). *American Exceptionalism and Human Rights.* Princeton, NJ: Princeton University Press.
Lipset, S. M. (1991). "American Exceptionalism Reaffirmed." In B. E. Shafer (Ed.), *Is America Different? A New Look at American Exceptionalism* (pp. 1–45). Oxford: Oxford University Press.
_____ (1996). *American Exceptionalism: A Double-Edged Sword.* New York: W.W. Norton.
Lobo, S., and S. Talbot (2001). *Native American Voices: A Reader* (2d ed.). Upper Saddle River, NJ: Prentice Hall.
McCrisken, T. B. (2003). *American Exceptionalism and the Legacy of Vietnam: U.S. Foreign Policy Since 1974.* New York: Palgrave.
McDougall, W. A. (1997). *Promised Land, Crusader State: The American Encounter with the World Since 1776.* New York: Houghton Milton.
McEvoy-Levy, S. (2001). *American Exceptionalism and U.S. Foreign Policy: Public Diplomacy at the End of the Cold War.* New York: Palgrave.

Pohrt, R. A. (1975). *The American Indian, the American Flag.* Flint, MI: Flint Institute of Arts.
Roberts, G. L. (1984). *Sand Creek: Tragedy and Symbol.* Unpublished doctoral dissertation. Norman: University of Oklahoma.
Schmittou, D. A., and M. H. Logan,(2002). "Fluidity of Meaning: Flag Imagery in Plains Indian Art." *American Indian Quarterly, 26,* 559–604.
Schultz, D. (1990). *Month of the Freezing Moon: The Sand Creek Massacre, November 1864.* New York: St. Martin's.
Shafer, B. E. (1991). "Preface." In B. E. Shafer (Ed.), *Is America Different? A New Look at American Exceptionalism* (pp. v-xi). Oxford: Oxford University Press.
Stephenson, A. (1995). *American Expansion and the Empire of Right.* New York: Hill and Wang.
Taylor, D. (2005). *The Archive and the Repertoire: Performing Cultural Memory in the Americas.* Durham, NC: Duke University Press.
de Tocqueville, A. (1975). *Democracy in America.* New York: Vintage. (Original work published 1830.)
Turner, F. J. (1961). "The Significance of the Frontier in American History." In R. A. Billington (Ed.), *Frontier and Section: Selected Essays of Frederick Jackson Turner* (pp. 37–62). Englewood Cliffs, NJ: Prentice-Hall.
Wilson, J. (1998). *The Earth Shall Weep: A History of Native America.* New York: Grove.
Zelinsky, W. (1984). "O Say, Can You See? Nationalistic Emblems in the Landscape." *Winterthur Portfolio, 19,* 277–86.

CHAPTER 10

Those Who Bear the Heaviest Burden
Warfare and American Exceptionalism in the Age of Entitlement

CHRISTINA M. KNOPF

When President Barack Obama addressed Congress on February 24, 2009, he proclaimed, "This is America. We don't do what's easy. We do what is necessary to move this country forward." The line prompted Jon Stewart to ask, on the February 25th episode of *The Daily Show*, "Have you met America? ... Do you know what *E Pluribus Unum* means? Easy and unnecessary.... So in your little plan there, if you're wondering whether to go with necessary or easy, I'd go with easy" (Winstead and Smithberg, 2009). Both opinions are, in fact, expressions of American exceptionalism. Obama's speech alluded to exceptionalist characteristics from the country's history—an independent nation of individuals who had the freedom to achieve whatever they worked for, and the initiative to work toward great things, because they were God's chosen people with a special mission. Stewart's retort indicated exceptionalist characteristics of the country in modern times—a nation of independent individuals who are deserving of great things, because they are special people.

This chapter is about the latter expression of exceptionalism—the notion of American entitlement—and its rhetorical emergence in times of war. My discussion begins with an overview of how American exceptionalism is defined. Special attention is given to the importance of hard work and sacrifice in the formation of the exceptionalist identity—the idea that Americans "don't do what's easy, but what is necessary"—and to the rising value of narcissism in the American ethos since the mid twentieth century — the idea that Americans actually prefer "easy and unnecessary." The chapter continues with an explanation of the significance of war in the creation and maintenance of exceptionalist ideas and identities, and concludes with an analysis of war rhetoric that traces the surfacing of entitlement in the American ethos and discusses its importance in the reshaping of American exceptionalism.

Defining American Exceptionalism: From Hard Work to Easy Money

American exceptionalism, though difficult to define, can be summarized as the notion that the United States was created differently, developed differently, and should be understood differently — on its own terms and in its own context (Carter, 2001; Gutfeld, 2002; Shafer, 1991). Alexis de Tocqueville (1835/2000) was among the first to note "novel" qualities in the American system and the American people (p. 3), contrasting the United States frequently to the antiquated states of Europe. Many basic premises of national uniqueness, however, cannot be proven and are based on impressions more than facts (Gutfeld, 2002). Despite disagreements over definitions, sources, and even the duration of American exceptionalism, it is a "discourse of distinctness," which attempts to characterize a multicultural society as a unified whole (Nayak and Malone, 2009, p. 264; see also Porsdam, 2001).

Exceptionalism has been sought in nearly every institution of the United States, from architecture to art, economics to education, law to literature, popular culture to public policy, and religion to rhetoric. Sometimes it has been found, but sometimes not. Of those who have found it, some say it is essentially unchanged since the first colonists landed on the shores of the New World. Others say new versions have been substituted for old. Most argue that exceptionalism connotes superiority, but critics have also identified America's exceptional failures (Hodgson, 2009). Some scholars, such as Seymour Martin Lipset (1996) and Charles Lockhart (2003), find American exceptionalism in the political structures, practices, and policies of the United States. Others, such as Sacvan Bercovitch (1978, 1993) and Deborah Madsen (1998), recognize American exceptionalism as more of a rhetorical phenomenon. One thing most scholars of American exceptionalism agree upon is that it is a cultural and consensual ideology that creates an American collective identity (Appleby, 2001; Gutfeld, 2002). It is a way of thinking that "imagines the nation as both the surpassing of the past and the hope of the future" in which Americans are different because they believe they are different (Byers, 2001, pp. 45–46; see also Bardaglio, 2001).

The American spirit, the American Creed, the primal meaning of the United States is found in two fundamental documents — the Declaration of Independence and the Constitution, which Arthur Schlesinger, Jr., argues gives America its "extraordinary advantage over most other nations" (1977, p. 521). As Gutfeld (2002) and Hughes (2005) observed, it is reflected in the Declaration's opening line, "We hold these Truths to be self-evident, that all Men are created equal, that they are endowed by their Creator with certain unalienable Rights, that among these are Life, Liberty, and the Pursuit of Happiness." The American ideological experience can, therefore, be understood as a composite of five values: liberty, equality, individualism, populism, and *laissez-faire* (Lipset, 1996), or, alternately as "a triptych" of personal liberty, pluralism, and public order (Kammen, 1975, p. 89).

The exceptionalist ideology has been wrapped in a myth that is America. A central part of this myth, this American story, is that of a Special Destiny — a mission that traces back over 300 years (Gutfeld, 2002; Hughes, 2005; Zarefsky, 2007). In this regard, exceptionalism, whether manifest in policies or in rhetoric, has at least partially referred to the perception of Americans that "they were charged with a special spiritual and political destiny" to create a model society for all nations as they struggled to reform themselves (Madsen, 1998, pp. 1–2). The earliest conceptualization of this "Chosen Nation" myth predates colonization of the Americas, but it is best summarized by the ideals of John Winthrop who in 1630 viewed the American errand as a mission of God in which the colonists would serve as a "model of Christian charity" and America would be "as a city upon a hill" (quoted in Madsen, 1998, p. 18; see also Hughes, 2005). During the eighteenth and nineteenth centuries, this idea evolved from the anticipation of perfecting ecclesiastical institutions to the anticipation of perfecting democratic political institutions, and America became the "global champion of democracy and privileged guardian of political values" (Madsen, 1998, p. 71). Benjamin Franklin, in particular, promoted the American errand as the creation of a secular state, with hopes of a country clean of corruption and hierarchy, which would be a model democratic government for all nations (Madsen, 1998).

Even though Americans always emphasized individualism and personal rights, with individual responsibility and a heightened sense of the self, shaping political, economic, and social institutions, the idea of being a model society imposed a sense of civic responsibility onto American exceptionalism. Americans had to sustain high levels of spiritual, political and moral commitment to their exceptional destiny (Lipset, 1996; Madsen, 1998). The concept of mutual dependence was important to the Puritans because the covenant would work only so long as all members of the community were united in faith; similarly, Benjamin Franklin warned against "immigrating those who seek an easy life, those who are idle or those who expect to be treated according to some inherited rank: these individuals will never make Americans" (quoted in Madsen, 1998, p. 37). Exceptionalism established a reciprocity between America's high moral purpose and its abundance of resources; the belief that they had been blessed with plenty required Americans to act as if they were the world's "best and last hope" (Gutfeld, 2002, p. 205; see also Appleby, 2001).

Hard work was also a central component in the American way in order to reap the blessings God had bestowed on the nation. As Lipset observed:

> Unlike the situation in many European countries [during the nineteenth century], in which economic materialism was viewed by the traditional aristocracy and the church as conducive to vulgar behavior and immorality, in the United States hard work and economic ambition were perceived as the proper activity of a moral person [1996, p. 54].

With westward expansion came opportunity and abundance as well as opportunity *for* abundance, which amplified the significance of hard work and rugged individualism — the pioneer spirit — in shaping the American identity and realizing the American dream (Bacevich, 2008). As Gutfeld noted:

> Only a few innocents thought that one could get rich in the West without hard labor, but many found it easy to deceive themselves that in the West, unlike other places, the effort needed for success was relatively little. The majority believed that the opportunities presented by the West would enable the simple person to gather what nature, in its goodness, had bestowed on all [2002, p. 21; see also Bacevich, 2008].

Frederick Jackson Turner (1893) wrote that Americans' interaction with the wild frontier was at the center of American history and society. The frontier symbolized continuous renewal, new opportunities, the struggle for survival, and American plenty (Gutfeld, 2002), which is what allowed ideals like liberty and equality to be actualized and truly made America unique (Gutfeld, 2002; Potter, 1958; Williams, 1982).

Beginning in the 1960s, however, the necessity of hard work and the sense of responsibility that was tied into American exceptionalism declined. Social psychologists Jean Twenge and Keith Campbell identified the beginning of cultural narcissism in the individual rights and human potential movements of the 1960s. Over the decades that followed they claimed that "American culture's core ideas and values were modified to include the idea of self admiration" (2009, p. 56). Though individualism and self-reliance were always a part of American identity and values, a simultaneous increase in attention to self-esteem and decrease in community orientation has led to what Twenge and Campbell (2009) called a "narcissism epidemic." One result of America's cultural emphasis on self-expression is a sense of entitlement, in which people feel the world owes them more than they contribute (Twenge and Campbell, 2009). Andrew Bacevich has even claimed that "the ethic of self-gratification threatens the well-being of the United States" (2008, p. 17). Entitlement and expectations for a life of privileged ease are arguably central to the modern sense of American exceptionalism, with businesspersons writing that the new American ethos is one of "life, liberty, and the pursuit of balance. Self-actualization and quality time for all" (Hammonds, 2007, para. 4), and educators describing self-esteem as the "national wonder drug" (Kaplan, 1995).

In tracing the roots of American exceptionalism and comparing the U.S. to other industrialized societies, Charles Lockhart concluded that the United States

> has suffered more modestly from economic depression and particularly from war than many other advanced industrial societies. Thus the circumstances under which its citizens have lived have provided more support for the individualistic view that persons are capable of and should be the masters of their own individual fates [2003, p. 161].

Dealing with the social upheaval of the 1960s, the failure of the Vietnam War in the 1970s, the fall of communism in the 1980s, the economic downturn of the 1990s, and the terrorism of the 2000s, therefore, changed America's global position and the identity of Americans. Carol Sarlor, a British writer, posited in *Newsweek* that inflated self-esteem was America's response to biting recession and a replacement for its role as the "world's great defender" against communism (1992, p. 52).

At least since Richard Nixon's 1973 inaugural declaration, "In our own lives, let each of us ask — not just what will government do for me, but what can I do for myself?"— which was itself a self-centered twist on John Kennedy's request of his fellow Americans to "ask not what your country can do for you — ask what you can do for your country," narcissism and entitlement have appeared as components of America's core values throughout U.S. politics. "First, there has been a giant transfer of time, attention, and resources from reality to fantasy. Rather than pursuing the American dream, people are simply dreaming" (Twenge and Campbell, 2009, p. 276). Social capital and community-mindedness have declined, and even voting is now viewed as self-expression rather than as a civic responsibility, as evidenced in the League of Women of Voters slogan, "Express yourself and be heard" (as quoted in Twenge and Campbell, 2009, p. 290; see also Putnam, 2000). The excessive use of credit to attain status, or at least the appearance of status, contributed to the 2008 market crash, and because American domestic political economy cannot keep pace with the demands for oil, credit, and cheap consumer goods, Americans' entitlement has advanced a proclivity for empire in U.S. foreign policy (Bacevich, 2008; Twenge and Campbell, 2009). Leaving behind the old notions of hard work and ingenuity, Americans are now unwilling to deny themselves or sacrifice of themselves (Bacevich, 2008). Nowhere is this new American exceptionalism of privileged entitlement more apparent than in the ritual and rhetoric of warfare — a vital element of American consensus, unity, and identity, and a common place for the language of American exceptionalism, and especially the intertwined notions of global leadership and sacrifice, to be invoked.

The Necessity of War for a Millennial Nation

In widely recognized analyses of American identity, Bercovitch (1993, 1978) described American exceptionalism as the way the people were able to translate sacred ideas and stories into secular directives, providing the nation with a powerful set of symbols. Implicit in America, he said, is a necessity for conflicting points of view; paradoxically, rituals of fear and anxiety about the continuation of the country unite the competing factions. Bercovitch identified those rituals, the rites of consensus and assent, in protest, because when the gap between America's ideal and its reality is emphasized, the people unite in order to make the necessary adjustments to the system. Carolyn Marvin and David Ingle (1999) point to another ritual that is vital to American unity — the ritual of blood sacrifice. They argue that American identity is a ritual system organized around a sacred core myth of sacrifice, that "the nation is the shared memory of blood sacrifice, periodically renewed" (p. 3), and that group solidarity comes from the value of this sacrifice.

> Though the sovereign nation, or nation-state, is an agreement about killing rules that compels citizens to sacrifice themselves for the group, the felt nation makes them want to. Neither the nation or [sic] the nation-state can exist without such memory myths, or not for long. Their maintenance is an ongoing sacred labor shared by rulers and those who grant them authority [p. 4].

Blood sacrifice is closely connected to the religious aspect of America's identity as a Chosen Nation with a manifest destiny, and as such it is an intricate element of American exceptionalism. "Even though Americans prefer to be associated with democracy, freedom, liberty, justice, ingenuity, individualism and destiny, they must face the historical reality that political violence is a major and continuing theme in America's annals and 'as American as cherry pie'" (Gutfeld, 2002, p. 131). As Gutfeld argues, the belief that violence is necessary to end violence, and that violence is a necessary means to fulfill its sacred mission, is a basic axiom of American political culture (2002). Bloodshed and ritualistic sacrifice are symbolized in the American flag and are reenacted every Independence Day and Memorial Day, representing the successful continuation of the nation through those who gave their lives eradicating inferior "others" who would threaten freedom, justice, and liberty (Grundy and Weinstein, 1974; Marvin and Ingle, 1999).

A ritual of heroism and violence has been promoted since the nineteenth century as part of the basis for greatness and morality, and the most powerful enactment of the sacrificial rite is war (Gutfeld, 2002; Marvin and Ingle, 1999; Sternhal and Sznajder, 1994). War has long been at the center of American exceptionalism, ever since Thomas Jefferson called for the tree of liberty to be watered with the blood of tyrants. War is a holistic ritual of radical rebirth with the purpose of causing the warrior (or warrior nation) to return to its origins, which is likely why despite its professed desire for peace, the United States rose to greatness through war in each generation (Murphy, 2003; Rushing and Frentz, 1980). In fact, following the 1890 "closing" of the frontier, warfare became the new wilderness to conquer, a new test of the American spirit (Carpenter, 1990). Substantial attention, resources, and energy are directed to blood sacrifice in war, but for the ritual to be truly transformational and unifying, several factors must be met. Every member of the group must feel the sacrifice; the value of the ritual depends on how many people are affected by the deaths. The sacrificial victims must be willing to die and the cause for their deaths needs to be supported by the group that sacrifices them. Lastly, there must be genuine doubt about the fate and survival of society, and the final outcome must be definite. If these conditions are not met, only another sacrificial ritual can repair the damage done by one that failed (Marvin and Ingle, 1999). Though the sacrifice is real and the body count is material, much of the ritual, especially as it relates to American identity and exceptionalism, takes place rhetorically.

The rhetoric of wars helps elaborate the sacrificial myth for society (Marvin and Ingle, 1999). From providing explanations and justifications for action, to detailing victimage and savagery, presidential war addresses are performative contributions to the construction of acceptable political realities and frequently draw upon the ideals of American exceptionalism (Benjamin, 1991; Bostdorff, 1994; Campbell and Jamieson, 2008; Cherwitz and Zagacki, 1986; Dow, 1989; Heisey, 1986; Ivie, 1974, 1980; Windt, 1983). War and crisis rhetoric is a rhetorical hybrid, combining deliberative uses of argument and epideictic appeals to community, while also seeking to justify military force or to avoid it (Murphy, 2003). As epideictic appeals, exceptionalist ideas may help the rhetor to elucidate the events in relation to America's key values and beliefs and to clarify to the American people who they are in relation to the crisis (Condit, 1985; Murphy, 1990). The myth of manifest destiny can act as a deliberative argument for the need to engage in military struggle, positioning war as a necessary component of America's special mission, and as an unfortunate byproduct of America's moral superiority (Bass and Cherwitz, 1978; Gutfeld, 2002; Hietala, 1985; Hughes, 2005).

The remainder of this chapter considers the expectations for the American people in presidential calls to arms, specifically requests for or admissions of sacrifice, whether of body or of resources. What becomes clear in these speeches is that the new core values of entitlement are appearing not just in the discourses of personal self-expression and the financial marketplaces; rather, they have infused the presidency and the rhetoric underlying the unifying ritual of war, altering the understanding and projection of American exceptionalism.

From Citizen Soldiers to Hired Hands

"As the guardians of freedom charged with saving democracy through eternal vigilance and with providing it protection and sanctuary, Americans customarily have spoken of liberty as a costly struggle" (Ivie, 1987, p. 30). In times of war, presidents present two broad types of challenges to Americans as a result of the U.S.'s military and moral superiority—challenges that are part of the effort to preserve the American way of life and to spread democracy across the globe. These are actual challenges, involving physical resources and bodily risk, and spiritual challenges, which have to do with support, prayer, and resolution. The burdens of these challenges are consigned to, and divided among, three groups: governmental elites (Congress and the president), citizens, and the military. Table 1 provides some concise examples to illustrate the form these assignments take in presidential calls to arms.

The goals of warfare have remained steadily lofty throughout U.S. history. Implicit in the country's role of a "Millennial Nation," destined to "usher in a final golden age for all humankind" of truth, justice, and democracy (Hughes, 2005, p. 91), war was designed to preserve the peace and prosperity of the United States and to bring peace and prosperity to other nations. John Adams and Thomas Jefferson went to war to maintain "this state of general peace with which we have been blessed" (quoted in Buhite, 2003, p. 17). Lyndon Johnson and George H. W. Bush went to war to "strengthen free people

Table 1.
Selected References to Exceptional
War Challenges and Burden Bearers

Year, War
President
Challenge Type
Burden Bearer — *Illustrative Quote*

1797, Quasi-War with France
John Adams
actual (time)
elite (Congress)

"The personal inconveniences to the members and the Senate and of the House of Representatives in leaving their families and private affairs at this season of the year..." (p. 1).

1846, War with Mexico
James Polk
actual (body)
citizens & military

"To this end I recommend that authority should be given to call into the public service a large body of volunteers to serve for not less than six or twelve months unless sooner discharged. A volunteer force is beyond question more efficient than other description of citizen soldiers, and it is not to be doubted that a number far beyond that required would readily rush to the field upon the call of their country" (p. 41).

1861, Civil War
Abraham Lincoln
spiritual (support)
citizens

"I appeal to all loyal citizens to favor, facilitate, and aid this effort to maintain the honor, the integrity, and the existence of our National Union and the perpetuity of popular government and to redress the wrongs already long enough endured" (p. 43).

1917, World War I
Woodrow Wilson
spiritual
elite (President & Congress)

"It is a distressing and oppressive duty, gentlemen of the Congress, which I have performed in thus addressing you. There are, it may be, many months of fiery trial and sacrifice ahead of us. It is a fearful thing to lead this great peaceful people into war..." (p. 154).

1942, World War II
Franklin Roosevelt
actual (body, resources)
citizens

"Production for war is based on men and women-the human hands and brains which collectively we call Labor. Our workers stand ready to work long hours... War costs money. So far, we have hardly even begun to pay for it.... This means taxes and bonds and bonds and taxes. It means cutting luxuries and other nonessentials" (pp. 185–186).

1964, Vietnam War
Lyndon Johnson
spiritual
elite (Congress)

"...I further announced a decision to ask the Congress for a resolution expressing the unity and determination of the United States in supporting freedom and in protecting peace in southeast Asia" (pp. 230–231).

Year, War President Challenge Type Burden Bearer	Illustrative Quote
1990, Persian Gulf War George H.W. Bush actual, spiritual military, citizens	"Standing up for our principles will not come easy. It may take time and possibly cost a great deal. But we are asking no more of anyone than of the brave young men and women of our Armed forces and their families. And I ask that in the churches around the country prayers be said for those who are committed to protect and defend America's interests" (p. 291).

Note: all page numbers refer to Buhite, 2003.

against domination by aggressive foreign powers" (quoted in Buhite, 2003, p. 238). George W. Bush went to war to protect the American way of life and "to defend the world from grave danger" (Bush, 2003a, para. 1). Despite this continuity of purpose, two shifts in the expressed expectations for sacrifice occurred over the years, both revealing diminished wartime effort on the part of the American people. This is the symptom of entitlement: seeking the same, or even greater, rewards for less work (Twenge and Campbell, 2009).

The first shift was that citizens were more likely to be presented with spiritual challenges than actual ones, and were asked to give fewer tangible contributions to the war effort. Presidents Adams, Lincoln, Wilson, Roosevelt, and Truman all detailed the economic burden of war and requested that both the government and the public make sacrifices (see speeches in Buhite, 2003). They warned of supply shortages, increased taxes, possible inflation, and the need for more manpower in both industry and military endeavors. They did this, often, in addition to asking the people to reinforce not only the American economy but also the American spirit. By contrast, Lyndon Johnson did not address the fiscal costs of war in concrete terms, though he spoke of the gratitude and prayers that America was sending its troops, and frequently asked for increased patriotism and concord from the home front (see speech in Buhite, 2003). Similarly, though George H. W. Bush acknowledged that, "at home, the material cost of our leadership can be steep" (quoted in Buhite, 2003, p. 295), his rhetorical emphasis was placed elsewhere, as he claimed Americans would only do their share if others around the world helped. Sacrifice through oil conservation efforts was placed second to increased oil production and the use of petroleum reserves, which would help ensure Americans were not inconvenienced by the war. The economic crisis that Americans faced was to be fixed not through responsible spending by America's people, but by Congress pulling together to "get the job done right" (quoted in Buhite,

2003, p. 297). The American public was primarily responsible for sending prayers and gratitude to the American forces overseas and was otherwise exempt from contributing materially to the exceptionalist mission of the nation.

This trend of decreased civic responsibility in wartime led George W. Bush to distinguish between public and private action in 2001 (Murphy, 2003). As he discussed the military response in Afghanistan to the terrorist attacks of September 11, George W. Bush expected Americans only "to live your lives and hug your children," asking Americans "to uphold the values of America," to support and pray for the terrorist victims, to be patient with increased security measures, and to show "continued participation and confidence in the American economy" (quoted in Buhite, 2003, p. 366). He did not ask Americans to conserve oil, to be careful of their resource usage, to be mindful of their credit, or to buy bonds. He did not ask for military service. Rather, he asked Americans to go shopping and for them to otherwise contribute to the war effort by showing support for the military, law enforcement, and intelligence agencies doing the work (Murphy, 2003; Cole, 2005). Though a stark change from that of the lean war years of a century prior, such a request was not unprecedented. In the midst of the 1979 energy crisis, Jimmy Carter spoke to the American people about the dangers of excess and told them that there was "simply no way to avoid sacrifice" if the country was to regain its energy independence (quoted in Bacevich, 2008, p. 35). Americans were not enthusiastic about the idea of austerity, preferring to maintain their culture of excess; they elected to office Ronald Reagan, the man who told them, "The answer [to the energy crisis], obvious to anyone... is more domestic production of oil and gas..... We must decide that 'less' is not enough" (quoted in Bacevich, 2008, p. 37). George W. Bush was, therefore, continuing the Reaganomics of quantity without the need for sacrifice or self-denial, which some have argued is a mark of the end of American exceptionalism (Bacevich, 2008).

The second shift regarding wartime sacrifice was subtler. Over the generations of U.S. warfare, American citizens and the American military became more distinct and distant entities. During the eighteenth and nineteenth centuries, the military was framed as "citizen soldiers," to use James Polk's words (quoted in Buhite, 2003, p. 41) — courageous American citizens risking their lives on behalf of the whole. When addressing Congress about the War with Barbary States in 1801, Thomas Jefferson described some of the naval skirmishes that had taken place.

> One of the Tripolitan cruisers having fallen in with and engaged the small schooner *Enterprise*, which had gone as a tender to our larger vessels, was captured, after a heavy slaughter of her men, with the loss of not a single one on our

part. The bravery exhibited *by our citizens* on that element will, I trust, be a testimony to the world that it is not the want of virtue which makes us seek their peace, but a conscientious desire to direct the energies of our nation to the multiplication of the human race, and not to its destruction [quoted in Buhite, 2003, p. 18, emphasis added].

Even though it was the American Navy that captured the cruiser, Jefferson did not laud the bravery of "the soldiers" or "the sailors" but rather that of "our citizens."

By the close of the twentieth century, soldiers were framed more as children of America than as its citizens, but they still belonged to the country. The work of warfare, however, belonged solely to the soldiers. George H. W. Bush, who referred to the military as "our sons and daughters" (quoted in Buhite, 2003, p. 306) made this distinction repeatedly in his messages about the Persian Gulf War. Addressing Congress on September 11, 1990, he thanked the military leaders and "every soldier, sailor, marine, and airman serving the cause of peace in the Persian Gulf." He then went on to say,

> I wish I could say *their work* was done. But we all know it's not. So, if there ever was a time to put country before self and patriotism before party, the time is now. And let me thank all Americans, especially those here in this Chamber tonight, for your support of *our armed forces* and for *their mission* [quoted in Buhite, 2003, p. 293, emphasis added].

Such a division may be explained in part because it was an entirely professional military, "an all-volunteer force, magnificently trained, highly motivated," as George H. W. Bush (quoted in Buhite, 2003, p. 306) called it, that was engaged in Kuwait and Iraq in 1990. As Bacevich pointed out,

> To the extent that an army composed of regulars is no longer a people's army, the people have little say in its use. In effect, the professional military has become an extension of the imperial presidency. The troops fight when and where the commander in chief determines [2008, p. 138].

Lyndon Johnson similarly differentiated between American troops and those Americans who were home in the States, despite the fact that Vietnam forces were largely conscripted (see speech in Buhite, 2003).

As the United States entered World War II, Franklin Roosevelt repeated the phrase "We are fighting," six times at the end of his 1942 State of the Union message, in addition to a number of other "we" sentiments, such as "We must guard" and "We will pay" (quoted in Buhite, 2003, pp. 186–189). However, at the start of the twenty-first century, the military was viewed as a group of worker-warriors mostly separate from American citizens.

> Soldiers were now expensive specialists, costly to recruit, costly to maintain, and costly to keep in service. The old concept of a mobilizable force of citizen sol-

diers gradually vanished: this was not merely an All Volunteer Force, as the Pentagon called it, but a professional force, which is not quite the same thing [Cohen, 2008, p. 252].

This new way of understanding American military service was exemplified in George W. Bush's 2003 announcement of the Iraq War, in which he said the following,

> To all of the men and women of the United States armed forces now in the Middle East, the peace of a troubled world and the hopes of an oppressed people now depend on *you*.... I know that the families of our military are praying that all those who serve will return safely and soon. Millions of Americans are praying with you for the safety of *your loved ones* and for the protection of the innocent. For *your sacrifice*, you have the gratitude and respect of the American people and you can know that our forces will be coming home as soon as *their work* is done [para. 4, 10–12; emphasis added].

"We" statements appeared in Bush's declaration only in reference to American ideals as in, "We will bring freedom to others" (2003a, para. 16). The actual sacrifices that needed to be made were entirely those of the troops and their immediate families. Citizens were asked only for prayers and gratitude. Moreover, contrary to the collective and consensual nature of American exceptionalism, the troops were not positioned as either citizen soldiers or as America's children. They were not *our* sons and daughters but the loved ones of *their* families.

Timothy Cole (2005) has suggested that George W. Bush not calling for public sacrifice in wartime was a strategic decision in response to a wary people with limited political tolerance. Whether the shift in rhetoric is a result of the public's changing political sentiments or habits conspicuous consumption, it reinforces the element of entitlement in the new American ethos of exceptionalism. Andrew Bacevich, a political scientist and father of a fallen American soldier, wrote,

> A reliance on professional soldiers eviscerates the concept of civic duty, relieving citizens at large of any obligation to contribute to the nation's defense. Ending the draft during the waning days of the Vietnam War did nothing to heal the divisions created by that conflict; instead, it ratified the separation of army from society. Like mowing lawns and bussing tables, fighting and perhaps dying to sustain the American way of life became something Americans pay others to do [2008, p. 138].

Not only does the separation of the military from American citizens decrease the sense of civic responsibility of those not enlisted, but it may also have an effect on the rites of unification and consensus that contribute to and maintain American exceptionalism.

According to Kathy Roth-Douquet and Frank Schaeffer (2007), yellow ribbons on lapels and "Support Our Troops" magnets on bumpers merely mask the estrangement that many feel toward people in uniform. For war to unify and reinforce national identity, either through the shared sacrifice or through the anxiety of protest, the blood must touch all the people (Marvin and Ingle, 1999), but in the words of George H. W. Bush, "The world is still a dangerous place, and those in uniform will always bear the heaviest burden" (quoted in Buhite, 2003, p. 302). Without claiming that greater numbers of people have to perish in order to ensure a successful blood rite, it is necessary that those who are victims resemble those for whom they die (Girard, 1972/1979); the victims and their community must share a connection or bond. Since the mid-twentieth century, however, war is the industry of the military and the military is not of the people. As George W. Bush said of re-enlistees in July 2003,

> Like many thousands of other soldiers, sailors, airmen, Coast Guardsmen and Marines who will re-enlist this year, these men and women are answering the highest call of citizenship. They have stood *between* the American people and the dangers of the world [2003b, para. 2, emphasis added].

Though the military has long been a specially groomed sacrificial class set apart from the society which sacrifices it, at once representative of and isolated from America, American sentiments tend to rally only around those military heroes that have appeared as common persons — those who were not professional soldiers or who eschewed military trappings (Huntington, 1957; Marvin and Ingle, 1999; Cohen, 2008). In other words, it is important that the American public at large feel connected to those on wars' front lines for their sacrifice to be unifying. The rhetorical disengagement of the troops from their society, therefore, may complicate the rituals of American identity.

When there is too little contact between the victims and those whom the victim represents, when the gap between the sacrificial class and the community grows too wide, all similarity between them is destroyed and the sacrifice loses its power to unify (Girard, 1972/1979), yet unity, or at least the appearance of unity, is at the heart of exceptionalism. Furthermore, military superiority, another aspect of American exceptionalism, has inspired patriotic emotions that reaffirmed the exceptionalist identity and belief in the nation's sacred mission (Cohen, 2008; Schuck and Wilson, 2008). The combination of a professional fighting force and a rhetoric of entitlement, however, have made the public and the one percent who serve it increasingly disparate, "creating a grave risk of mutual incomprehension and disaffection that transcends public attitudes toward any particular way" (Schuck and Wilson, 2008, p. 629). Some, like Bacevich (2008), may argue that this denotes the end of American exceptionalism, but it is really more of a transformation of American exceptionalism — Americans' special situation in the world now being a reason for a lackadaisical attitude.

Conclusion

David Zarefsky (2007) posed the question of why the 300-year old notion of American exceptionalism has only recently received intense criticism, most prominently from overseas. He argued that the increased power of the United States during the twentieth century is to blame, that the relative weakness of the country during the nineteenth century made it easy to ignore America's proclamations of doing holy work. Part of the answer may also be that it is in more recent times that entitlement has become so prominent in the expressions of American exceptionalism, and especially so in foreign policy. During World Wars I and II and the Korean conflict, America's sacred mission was carried out through blood and toil. It was the enterprise of all Americans working in concord with other peoples. In the words of Franklin Roosevelt, "We of the united nations are ... making all this sacrifice of human effort and human lives ... for security, for progress and for peace, not only for ourselves, but for all men" (quoted in Buhite, 2003, pp. 188–189). By the Persian Gulf wars, it was less clear that the U.S. was acting unselfishly and it was very clear that it carried the burden and ramifications of warfare lightly. The narrow purpose and players of the Iraq War were captured in one sentence uttered by George W. Bush: "We will meet that threat now with our Army, Air Force, Navy, Coast Guard and Marines, so that we do not have to meet it later with armies of firefighters and police and doctors on the streets of our cities" (2003a, para. 14). International relations had gone from being the work of dedicated coalitions to the task of small bands of hired guns.

From Max Weber's (1930) study of the Protestant work ethic to Seymour Martin Lipset and Gary Marks's (2001) analysis of why socialism never came to the United States, it is obvious that ingenuity and hard work were central in the creation of American institutions and identities that give foundation and form to the notion of American exceptionalism. Such "rugged individualism" has given way to an individualistic self-centeredness. Now, self-expression and self-admiration are so culturally ingrained that entitlement is part of what it means to be American, as evidenced through countless reality shows that celebrate excess, social networking sites that celebrate self, and political rhetoric that reinforces an ideal of less for more. American exceptionalism is now a right without a responsibility. Hard work is no longer central to the American Dream, thanks to credit, and sacrifice is no longer necessary for the American mission, thanks, in part, to a rhetorical distinction between Americans and American troops, and to a political rhetoric that panders to a people unwilling to deny themselves or to be denied.

References

Appleby, J. (2001). "Recovering America's Historic Diversity: Beyond Exceptionalism." In D. Carter (Ed.), *Marks of Distinction: American Exceptionalism Revisited* (pp. 24–42). Oakville, CT: Aarhus University Press.
Bacevich, A. J. (2008). *The Limits of Power: The End of American Exceptionalism.* New York: Metropolitan.
Bardaglio, P. (2001). "'A Divided Empire'": African Americans, the South, and the Narrative of American Exceptionalism." In D. Carter (Ed.), *Marks of Distinction: American Exceptionalism Revisited* (pp. 167–196). Oakville, CT: Aarhus University Press.
Bass, J. D., and R. Cherwitz (1978). "Imperial Mission and Manifest Destiny: A Case Study of Political Myth in Rhetorical Discourse." *Southern Speech Communication Journal, 43,* 213–232.
Benjamin, J. (1991). "Rhetoric and the Performative Act of Declaring War." *Presidential Studies Quarterly, 21,* 73–84.
Bercovitch, S. (1978). *The American Jeremiad.* Madison: University of Wisconsin Press.
_____ (1993). *The Rites of Assent: Transformations in the Symbolic Construction of America.* New York: Routledge.
Bostdorff, D. M. (1994). *The Presidency and the Rhetoric of Foreign Crisis.* Columbia: University of South Carolina Press.
Buhite, R. D. (Ed.). (2003). *Calls to Arms: Presidential Speeches, Messages, and Declarations of War.* Wilmington, DE: Scholarly Resources.
Bush, G. W. (2003a, March 19). "War Message." *Presidential Rhetoric.* Retrieved from http://www.presidentialrhetoric.com/speeches/03.19.03.html.
_____ (2003b, July 1). "Progress in Afghanistan and Iraq." *Presidential Rhetoric.* Retrieved from http://www.presidentialrhetoric.com/speeches/07.01.03.html.
Byers, T. B. (2001). "A City Upon a Hill: American Literature and the Ideology of Exceptionalism." In D. Carter (Ed.), *Marks of Distinction: American Exceptionalism Revisited* (pp. 45–68). Oakville, CT: Aarhus University Press.
Campbell, K. K., and K. H. Jamieson (2008). *Presidents Creating the Presidency: Deeds Done in Words.* Chicago: University of Chicago Press.
Carpenter, R. H. (1990, February). "America's Tragic Metaphor: Our Twentieth-Century Combatants as Frontiersmen." *Quarterly Journal of Speech, 76*(1), 1–22.
Carter, D. (2001). "Introduction: The Death and Life of an Exceptional Concept." In D. Carter (Ed.), *Marks of Distinction: American Exceptionalism Revisited* (pp. 11–23). Oakville, CT: Aarhus University Press.
Cherwitz, R. A., and K. S. Zagacki (1986, Fall). "Consummatory Versus Justificatory Crisis Rhetoric." *Western Journal of Speech Communication, 50,* 307–324.
Cohen, E. (2008). "The Military." In P. H. Schuck and J. Q. Wilson (Eds.), *Understanding America: The Anatomy of an Exceptional Nation* (pp. 247–274). New York: Public Affairs.
Cole, T. (2005). "The Political Rhetoric of Sacrifice and Heroism and the U.S. Military Intervention." In L. Artz and Y. R. Kamalipour (Eds.), *Bring 'Em On: Media and Politics in the Iraq War* (pp. 139–154). Lanham, MD: Rowman and Littlefield.
Condit, C. M. (1985). "The Functions of Epideictic: The Boston Massacre Orations as Exemplar." *Communication Quarterly, 33,* 284–299.

Dow, B. J. (1989). "The Function of Epideictic and Deliberative Strategies in Presidential Crisis Rhetoric." *Western Journal of Speech Communication, 53*, 294–310.

Girard, R. (1979). *Violence and the Sacred* (Trans. P. Gregory). Baltimore: Johns Hopkins University Press. (Original work published 1972.)

Grundy, K. W., and Weinstein, M. A. (1974). *Ideologies of Violence.* Columbus, OH: Charles E. Merrill.

Gutfeld, A. (2002). *American Exceptionalism: The Effects of Plenty on the American Experience.* Portland, OR: Sussex Academic.

Hammonds, K. H. (2007, December 19). "Balance is Bunk." Fast Company. Retrieved from http://www.fastcompany.com/magazine/87/balance-1.html.

Heisey, D. R. (1986). "Reagan and Mitterrand Respond to International Crisis: Creating Versus Transcending Appearances." *Western Journal of Speech Communication, 50*, 325–335.

Hietala, T. R. (1985). *Manifest Design: American Exceptionalism and Empire* (rev. ed.). Ithaca: Cornell University Press.

Hodgson, G. (2009). *The Myth of American Exceptionalism.* New Haven: Yale University Press.

Hughes, R. T. (2005). *Myths America Lives By.* Urbana: University of Illinois Press.

Huntington, S. P. (1957). *The Soldier and the State: The Theory and Politics of Civil-Military Relations.* Cambridge, MA: Harvard University Press.

Ivie, R. L. (1974). "Presidential Motives for War." *Quarterly Journal of Speech, 60*, 337–345.

_____ (1980). "Images of Savagery in American Justifications for War." *Communication Monographs, 47*, 279–290.

_____ (1987). "The Ideology of Freedom's 'Fragility'" in American Foreign Policy Argument." *Journal of the American Forensic Association, 24*, 27–36.

Kammen, M. (1975). *People of Paradox: An Inquiry Concerning the Origins of American Civilization.* New York: Knopf.

Kaplan, L. S. (1995). "Self-Esteem Is Not Our National Wonder Drug." *School Counselor, 42*, 341–345.

Lipset, S. M. (1996). *American Exceptionalism: A Double-Edged Sword.* New York: W.W. Norton.

_____, and G. Marks (2001). *It Didn't Happen Here: Why Socialism Failed in the United States.* New York: W. W. Norton.

Lockhart, C. (2003). *The Roots of American Exceptionalism: Institutions, Culture, and Policies.* New York: Palgrave Macmillan.

Madsen, D. L. (1998). *American Exceptionalism.* Jackson: University Press of Mississippi.

Marvin, C., and D. W. Ingle (1999). *Blood Sacrifice and the Nation: Totem Rituals and the American Flag.* New York: Cambridge University Press.

Murphy, J. M. (1990). "'A Time of Shame and Sorrow': Robert F. Kennedy and the American Jeremiad." *Quarterly Journal of Speech, 76*, 401–414.

_____ (2003). "'Our Mission and Our Moment': George W. Bush and September 11th." *Rhetoric and Public Address, 6*, 607–632.

Nayak, M. V., and C. Malone (2009). "American Orientalism and American Exceptionalism: A Critical Rethinking of U.S. Hegemony." *International Studies Review, 11*, 253–276.

Porsdam, J. W. (2001). "'They Came to Lawyers, You Know, What Can You Do?' American Exceptionalism and Judicial Activism." In D. Carter (Ed.), *Marks of Distinction: American Exceptionalism Revisited* (pp. 231–256). Oakville, CT: Aarhus University Press.

Potter, D. M. (1958). *People of Plenty: Economic Abundance and the American Character.* Chicago: University of Chicago Press.

Putnam, R. D. (2000). *Bowling Alone: The Collapse and Revival of American Community*. New York: Simon and Schuster.
Roth-Douquet, K., and F. Schaeffer (2007). *AWOL: The Unexcused Absence of America's Upper Classes from Military Service—and How It Hurts Our Country*. New York: Collins.
Rushing, J. H., and T. S. Frentz (1980). "'The Deer Hunter': Rhetoric of the Warrior." *Quarterly Journal of Speech, 66,* 392–406.
Sarlor, C. (1992, February 17). "Stiffen Your Lips. Yanks: No Self-Esteem, Please, We're British." *Newsweek,* p. 52.
Schlesinger, A., Jr. (1977). "America, Experiment or Destiny?" *American Heritage, 28,* 12–17.
Schuck, P. H., and J. Q. Wilson (2008). "Looking Back." In P. H. Schuck and J. Q. Wilson (Eds.), *Understanding America: The Anatomy of an Exceptional Nation* (pp. 627–643). New York: Public Affairs.
Shafer, B. E. (Ed.). (1991). *Is America Different? A New Look at American Exceptionalism.* Oxford: Clarendon Press.
Sternhal, Z., and M. Sznajder (1994). *The Birth of Racist Ideology.* Princeton, NJ: Princeton University Press.
de Tocqueville, A. (2000). *Democracy in America.* (Trans. H. Reeve). New York: Bantam Classic. (Original work published 1835.)
Turner, F. J. (1893). "On the Significance of the Frontier in American History." Retrieved from http://www.learner.org/workshops/primarysources/corporations/docs/turner.html.
Twenge, J. M., and W. K. Campbell (2009). *The Narcissism Epidemic: Living in the Age of Entitlement.* New York: Free.
Weber, M. (1930). *The Protestant Ethic and the Spirit of Capitalism.* (Trans. T. Parsons). New York: Routledge Classics.
Williams, W. A. (1982). *Empire as a Way of Life: An Essay on the Causes and Character of America's Present Predicament Along with a Few Thoughts About an Alternative.* New York: Oxford University Press.
Windt, T. (1983). "The Presidency and Speeches on International Crises: Repeating the Rhetorical Past." In T. Windt and B. Ingold (Eds.), *Essays in Presidential Rhetoric* (pp. 61–70). Dubuque, IA: Kendall Hunt.
Winstead, L., and M. Smithberg (Creators). (2009, February 25). *The Daily Show with Jon Stewart* [Television series episode]. In M. Smithberg (Executive Producer), *The Daily Show with Jon Stewart.* New York: Comedy Central.
Zarefesky, D. (2007). "The U.S. and the World: Unexpressed Premises of American Exceptionalism." *Proceedings of the Sixth Conference of the International Society for the Study of Argumentation* (pp. 1567–1571). Amsterdam: Sic Sat International Center.

CHAPTER 11

Promoting America
U.S. Public Diplomacy and the Limits of Exceptionalism

CRAIG HAYDEN

The rhetorics of American exceptionalism have played a significant role in U.S. strategies of influence abroad, as evidenced in historical policy debates during the Cold War as well the considerable volume of public diplomacy policy recommendations since September 11, 2001. Policy discourse regarding U.S. public diplomacy is illustrative of the persistence of American exceptionalism when conceiving necessary or appropriate strategy, including how aspects of American political culture are assumed to be on face persuasive to foreign publics and how foreign policy requires no explicit deliberative standards of justification. Yet the use of exceptionalist tactics—such as emphasizing the universal values embodied by the United States as evidenced in its actions—has not proven to be an effective strategy of persuasion through the history of U.S. public diplomacy. And political debate over the funding and authorization of public diplomacy has deferred to the supposed power of such rhetorics despite the actual demands of the audience.

Current debate in the United States, however, appears to reflect a shift away from exceptionalist presumptions in international persuasion. After years of struggle to formulate a message strategy that was not tone-deaf to critical foreign audiences, the United States appears to be willing to consider different tactics of persuasion that move beyond the amplification of U.S. values. Nevertheless, the ideological contours of exceptionalism in policy rhetoric has a certain inertia, despite inspiring ineffective messaging strategies and importantly, flawed strategic orientations towards the practice of public diplomacy.

This chapter examines instances of foreign policy discourse, legislation, and historical evidence to chart the implications of American exceptionalism for public diplomacy programs and initiatives since the Cold War. It presents evidence in discourse and program design to suggest that the intrinsic logic of exceptionalism constrained the kinds of programs justified under a policy argument formation that was itself often fraught with exceptionalist rhetoric. The chapter reviews the formative years of U.S. public diplomacy at the dawn of the Cold War as an early example of the difficulties imposed by exceptionalism in strategic discourse. Policy rhetoric in the form of speeches by U.S. government officials and legislators, proposed legislation, and policy scholarship after September 11, 2001 is then examined to illustrate the constraints that exceptionalism imposes on the policy imagination. Finally, the rise of so-called "public diplomacy 2.0" (Glassman, 2008) strategies are discussed as evidence of a shift away from value-centric advocacy as a policy orientation for public diplomacy in the aftermath of the Hughes appointment at the State Department. The chapter concludes with a consideration of diminished exceptionalism in US public diplomacy. Ubiquitous communication technologies, from social networking to regional satellite networks, enable qualitatively new forms of international actorhood, necessitating a revised understanding of *audience* in the strategic calculus of international influence.

Historical Exceptionalism in U.S. Foreign Policy

The record of public discourse amongst legislators, policy-makers, and commentators on public diplomacy discussed in this chapter illustrates how influence is perceived and translated into the U.S. foreign policy strategy. This evidence reveals that elements of American exceptionalism — in particular the presumption that information about American values will translate into measurable gains or contribute to tangible foreign policy objectives for the United States — has left an indelible imprint on formation of public diplomacy strategy and thus, the available tools of influence and persuasion implemented by the United States.

Recent studies suggest that years of exposure to the domestic political rhetoric of American exceptionalism have impacted foreign audience perception of the United States — the crucial context for public diplomacy programs and initiatives (Kohut and Stokes, 2006; Sweig, 2006). This chapter, however, looks to the impact of such rhetoric on the policies of influence themselves. It is a critique of the policy arguments — the discourse — that reflect the policy imagination about a necessary and at times, ethically proper public diplomacy strategy.

The themes of American exceptionalism have been a staple of political rhetoric since 1630, when Massachusetts Colonial governor John Winthrop described the new Puritan colony as a "city on a hill" (McEvoy-Levy, 2001, p. 24). Since then the tropes of American exceptionalism have functioned as a kind of "foundational narrative" that represent the mythic portent of the nation's founding and distinction from Europe (Nayak and Malone, 2009, p. 254). Exceptionalist rhetoric expressed a "God-given" destiny that provided the world with a moral compass embodied in its values and political system (Lipset, 1996). Michael Adas (2001, p. 1702) identifies the "essence" of American exceptionalism identified across historical and political scholarship as an unwavering belief in the "uniqueness" of the United States and an obligation to transform the rest of the world based upon its providential mandate. This framework provides a crucial shared discursive context for future policy arguments — a scaffold for the boundaries of public argument over necessary — strategies and policies.

Although these ideas predated the founding of the Republic, American exceptionalism would surface to inform pivotal policy and strategic motivations for U.S. foreign policy in the ensuing centuries. In the 1840s, John Sullivan's notion of the "manifest destiny" of westward expansion drew upon attempts to distinguish the United States from other countries and to be a "natural" extension of the nation's character (Horsman, 1981, pp. 219–220). Theodore Roosevelt would later reframe the Monroe Doctrine as an extension of the arguments used to justify the "manifest destiny," in order to suggest that the mythical frontier was in fact *international* (Nayak and Malone, 2009). Senator Albert Beveridge in 1899 justified U.S. imperial acquisitions, arguing that "God has not been preparing the English-speaking and Teutonic peoples for a thousand years for nothing but vain and idle self-admiration. No! He has made us the master organizers of the world to establish system where chaos reigns" (quoted in Nayak and Malone, 2009, p. 267).

Such responsibility for global stewardship was invoked in arguments for Wilson's "Fourteen Points" at the end of World War I, and yet again to pursue involvement in World War II. Henry Luce declared in 1941 that it was the right of the United States to manage the course of international events, "to accept wholeheartedly our duty and our opportunity as the most vital nation in the world" (McEvoy-Levy, 2001, p. 26). These ideas would subsequently animate Cold War rhetoric by infusing an intrinsic status of legitimacy and inevitability to the "truth" of U.S. positions, and inform attempts by the U.S. to reach out to audiences barraged by Soviet propaganda.

Public Diplomacy: Constraints on the Policy Imagination

To understand the nature of the relationship between exceptionalism and public diplomacy, it is first necessary to establish a working definition of the sometimes ambiguous concept of public diplomacy. American exceptionalism is argued here as having impacted the vocabularies and positions that frame debate over an ideal public diplomacy policy for the United States. The term *public diplomacy* is used in this chapter as an inclusive term to capture the range of communication practices and interventions that aim to influence foreign publics. "Public diplomacy" has come to reflect a range of policies that collapse the distinctions and cross-purposes of international broadcasting, education, and dialogue (Brown, 2002). It includes "the direct advocacy of specific policies to the more 'noble' pursuits of cultural diplomacy and the use of the arts [in order to gain] sympathizers abroad" (Scott-Smith, 2008, p. 51). In the U.S. context, public diplomacy serves as both a euphemism for propaganda and an institutional arrangement of responsibility for various communication and cultural exchange programs.

Diplomacy scholar Paul Sharp (2007) describes public diplomacy as "the process by which direct relations with people in a country are pursued to advance the interests and extend the values of those being represented" (p. 106). Public diplomacy include programs and initiatives that aim to provide information or cross-cultural exchange activities, such as the International Visitor Leadership Program, the *Al-Hurra* satellite television channel, or the *America.gov* web presence, but the justification remains grounded in the influence that these programs will accrue. As Kristin Lord states, public diplomacy, broadly conceived, aims to "engage, persuade, and attract the cooperation of foreign publics" (2008, p. 3). It is ultimately an instrumental set of activities and initiatives that must deploy some sort of communication — through direct messaging or some other symbolic activity — that is thought to achieve a policy end.

Yet public diplomacy is often a controversial term that has no normative referent in international relations; i.e., there is no theory of public diplomacy as a distinct form of international communication (Gilboa, 2008; Kelley, 2008; Melissen, 2007). Consequently, it is as much a rhetorical construction as it is a historical reflection of policy innovation. Understanding the components of policy rhetoric about public diplomacy can thus yield insight into the subsequent problems stemming from the conception of persuasion that is derived from policy debate (Goodnight, 1998). The rhetoric of policy arguments that create a reservoir of terms, expressions, and characteristics used to justify, observe and induce specific policy articulations may thus be useful for unpacking the elements of exceptionalism that undergird arguments for how the U.S. should communicate to the rest of the world (Hayden, 2007).

Siobhan McEvoy-Levy (2001) claims that exceptionalism has been a defining component of foreign policy discourse in the United States, and that this in turn functions as a kind of public diplomacy in its own right to foreign audiences. She states explicitly that the rhetoric used domestically to justify, promote, and define foreign policy represents the "basic driving forces and motivating ideas, myths, and ideals of different administrations ... and a consideration of constraints and possibilities of future US policy" (2001, p. 4). Policy rhetoric in this view is a repertoire from which arguments can be crafted to devise, adapt, or propose foreign policy. McEvoy-Levy's rhetorical analysis illustrates themes and trends in policies over time; rhetoric is as much an instrument of political actors as a persistent discursive framework from which to articulate necessary policy.

McEvoy-Levy (2001) identifies exceptionalism as "para-ideological" within foreign policy discourse in the United States, creating "a climate of belief, a consensus on broad values, which supports and enables the contingent use of rhetoric for addressing specific foreign policy issues and international events" (p. 3). It manifests across what she describes as a "sympathetic ecology of experts, commentators, and [the] general public" (McEvoy-Levy, 2001, p. 4). The persistence of such rhetoric sustains the assumptions of exceptionalism across successive administrations and the sphere of public argument that surrounds foreign policy. The "felt historicity" of exceptionalism, however, takes on new meaning outside the context of the American experience (McEvoy-Levy, 2001, p. 44). The relatively closed system of U.S. public argument about foreign policy may limit the imagination of what is required to adequately address foreign audiences, and more generally may constrain the strategic formulations about the *global* ecology of opinion about the United States.

Yet a logic of exceptionalism is imbricated at a fundamentally strategic level prior to the formation of specific information or advocacy campaigns. Exceptionalism is translated into the very assumptions about what is persuasive for foreign audiences. And, exceptionalism leads to a particularly simplistic and cybernetic model of communication that is increasingly problematic in global communications. As Rhonda Zaharna (2004, 2005) argues, contemporary public diplomacy requires relationship-building and a network orientation to audiences in order to garner influence, not simply to offer a volume of communication that overwhelms the messages of your adversary. Nevertheless, much of what counts as U.S. public diplomacy since the Cold War outside of exchange programs reflects an implicit assumption that exposing foreign audiences to U.S. values will illuminate a shared identification with U.S. motives and policies. For example, Anne-Marie Slaughter (2004) argues,

> Our shared values are essential because they link America to the world. The belief that American values are universal values — that all men and women are created equal, that all are entitled to life, liberty, and the pursuit of happiness, regardless of race, creed, or nationality — connects us to other nations [p. 7].

Such arguments for public diplomacy efforts presuppose that influence is accomplished in the revelation of shared values and, in particular, that the United States embodies universal values. In this view, all audiences are assumed to aspire to these abstractions of political and social values.

Yet when values are represented as both universal and distinct to the United States, they may become less effective as a route to persuasion. Pedantic reminders of the special providence of U.S. political culture does not, as it turns out, generate copious support for the United States (Kohut and Stokes, 2006). More generally, using exceptionalism as a master frame for messages to promote the United States suffers from very basic argument context problems. Put another way, exhorting U.S. exceptionalism as a means to cultivate influence relies on an enthymeme that is, as McEvoy-Levy (2001) argues, profoundly dependent on the diachronic dimension of U.S. political rhetoric. Foreign audiences may share some premises, but the patchwork of experience and exposure to potentially competing justificatory arguments means that finding a perfect message is probably impossible in a complex, immersive global media environment (Corman, 2008).

The presumption of exceptionalism becomes a strategic problem of the policy discourse that generates public diplomacy programs — coloring the formulations and expectations that justify influence programs — when the value-centric assumptions that support claims to exceptionalism are assumed to be universally comprehensible and indeed rational. While exceptionalism may "work" as an acceptable set of arguments to frame policy debate within the United States, it runs aground when translated into actionable policy prescriptions. This problem is both tactical and strategic. Tactically, exceptionalist rhetoric may justify failed programs like the "Shared Values" campaign of advertisements highlighting Muslim integration into American culture in 2002. Strategically, exceptionalism sets up unrealistic expectations for what kind of communication interventions may influence foreign publics.

One example of a strategic problem with exceptionalism is its implicit function as a currency of "soft power," a notion which asserts the supposed non-coercive power of ideas, which can be cultivated as part of a nation-state's foreign policy. Joseph Nye's (2004) notion of soft power suggests that cultural attraction should be considered alongside traditional metrics of material power in international affairs. Nye (2008) explicitly identifies public diplomacy as a means to cultivate and highlight soft power as an asset for nation-states. Soft power may be augmented through efforts to amplify cultural and other social or political values, often represented in the cultural products of a state as well as their social institutions. Soft power is not synonymous with public diplomacy, but rather provides a justificatory template for communication policies to achieve foreign policy objectives (Snow, 2008).

For Nye (2008), strategic attention to soft power is increasingly necessary in a world awash in communication content; the relative decline of identification with the United States is in part due to the rise of other outlets and efforts to frame U.S. actions negatively. To reinforce soft power is to remind foreign audiences of values shared with the United States, which in turn increases the relative attractiveness of the United States and lends credibility to its policies. Public diplomacy's charge is thus to cut through the information surplus (and negative framing) in order to highlight values presumptions that foreign audiences already share. Public diplomacy's purpose is then to reinvigorate the U.S. enthymeme: its status as specially representative of universal values. Soft power ultimately works to build a kind of enthymematic understanding of the United States, where audiences come to conclusions about U.S. intentions in a way that affords legitimacy and credibility to U.S. actions.

The strategic problem of exceptionalism is evident, albeit indirectly, in Janice Bially-Mattern's (2005) critique of soft power. For Bially-Mattern, the logic of soft power as articulated by Nye (2004, 2008) is incomplete and ultimately, recursive. This is because the dynamic of influence within soft power — the force of attraction — is laced with an internal contradiction. Bially-Mattern argues that soft power operates through a kind of Habermasian form of communicative action, whereby soft power is actively constructed through the act of argumentation. For public diplomacy to be an effective instrument of soft power, it must engage foreign publics through communicative acts of persuasion. Yet under the standards of idealized argumentation, both parties in the argumentative exchange must share some basic premises that constitute a shared lifeworld — such as fundamental or indeed, universal values. Under this concept, soft power and its attendant public diplomacy of promoting U.S. values would be unnecessary, for Nye (2004, 2008) argues that such shared values function naturally as attractors.

As historical episodes reveal, when values-promotion is the articulated objective, public diplomacy strategy has failed to achieve significant shifts in public opinion (Fullerton and Kendrick, 2006; Green, 1988). Even if one does not accept the preconditions for rational argument that Bially-Mattern (2005) suggests renders soft power as redundant, the promotion of values simply cannot be *sold* through communication campaigns because they are ultimately "public goods," not goods for private consumption (Wolf and Rosen, 2004). Democracy, tolerance, and the rule of law are not easily reduced to something that can be marketed as distinct qualities of the United States to be emulated or to sanction positive disposition to the United States.

As Wolf and Rosen suggest,

> Acceptance and support for public goods depend on other means: namely, on endorsement by a *constituent group*… whose members collectively share in the benefits of the collective goods and (directly or indirectly, and sooner or later) can accept the burden and responsibility of their attendant costs [2004, p. 6].

The persuasive function of public diplomacy depends profoundly on the constituent acceptance of premises and accordingly the risks and costs that they incur for the audience. As Wolf and Rosen (2004) note, the rhetorical successes of transformative social entrepreneurs have historically depended on linking the construction of audiences with the values to be marketed, an idea well-established in the rhetorical tradition (see also McGee, 1975; Perelman and Olbrechts-Tyteca, 1969).

Yet even this conceptual shift does not necessarily negate the effect of exceptionalism as contradictory to identification as a rhetorical strategy idealized in soft power. In promoting distinct social and political values that are framed as essentially American *and* universal, one forecloses on the shared lifeworld that soft power seeks to cultivate. For Nayak and Malone (2009), American values are simultaneously universal yet unattainably American in their embodiment: "The United States, on account of its special values, has a superiority that is "self-evident" and beyond reproach; at the same time, the United States is divinely ordained to serve as the only political, cultural, and economic model for the rest of the world" (Nayak and Malone, 2009, p. 260). As a persuasive strategy, highlighting the purported "truths" of American exceptionalism appears to be problematic as successive attempts to invigorate American engagement with international opinion has demonstrated.

Early Cold War Public Diplomacy: From Truman to Eisenhower

The term "public diplomacy" was not explicitly used until 1965 (Cull, 2008a), when it was coined to characterize the range of communication efforts engaged by the United States Information Agency as something other than propaganda. Yet U.S. public diplomacy's history goes back farther than the common use of the term, as does its reliance on the tropes of American exceptionalism.

President Truman's efforts to justify and design an effective counter-propaganda strategy is illustrative of the exceptionalism problem within U.S. public diplomacy. Truman's efforts laid the groundwork for institutions of U.S. public diplomacy, such as the Voice of America, which later become part of the United States Information Agency established in the Eisenhower administration (Cull, 2008b). After World War II, President Truman sought to continue wartime propaganda efforts in order to counter the growing influence (and influence operations) of the Soviet Union. Yet as demonstrated by Shawn Parry-Giles's (1993, 1994) analyses of foreign policy rhetoric at the time, Truman faced considerable resistance to a continued propaganda effort on the grounds that propaganda was antithetical to the values of the United States. Truman's plans were constrained by the accepted outlines of terms, values, and descriptions within policy argument, or what Goodnight (2006) referred to as an argument formation. To argue for an aggressive propaganda capability would mean to confront the ideological and cultural framework of the time, or as Goodnight describes "the limits and inventive possibilities of the cultural, social, practical contexts within which actions and judgments are contested" (1998, para. 15). Parry-Giles (1993) argues that Truman was forced to reconcile the implications of propaganda with the values representative of democracy.

Parry-Giles claims "because of the restrictive nature of ideological commitments, rhetors are often confined with ideological frameworks predating them" (1993, p. 119). She describes what transpired during Truman's administration as a situation where policymakers "worked predominantly from a pool of pre-existing arguments and conceptions of propaganda and democracy" (1993, p. 119). While Truman was successful in the passage of the Smith-Mundt Act (Public Law 402), creating the impetus and funding for international advocacy programs, the kind of persuasion programs justified under the terms of his strategy failed to gain traction in international audiences (see Cull, 2008b, pp. 68–80).

Truman's difficulties were not just bureaucratic, but also a consequence of exceptionalism influencing strategic discourse and resultant policies. To make propaganda palatable to lawmakers, the Truman administration argued for a propaganda program that would both "mirror" and "showcase" the United States (Parry-Giles, 1993, pp. 119–120). The success of U.S. democracy would be reflected as a compelling representation of American values. Programs would inevitably "showcase" certain aspects of the United States in a positive light, while still providing news and facts in the face of Soviet propaganda.

Early programs, such as the *Know North America* films, highlighted the relative prosperity and abundance of the United States, which unwittingly played into the depictions in Soviet influence campaigns of the United States as a greedy imperialist power and fostered resentment in certain audiences (Green, 1988). Truman's subsequent "Campaign of Truth" was a tacit recognition that simply providing the "truth" in depictions of the United States was not sufficient in countering Soviet efforts. Truman was forced into a paradoxical quandary of suggesting that "truth" was the most effective propaganda, yet acknowledged that the Soviets remained more successful in their own programs. President Eisenhower's Jackson Committee, formed in 1953 to review flagging U.S. propaganda efforts, found that "the note of self-praise and the emphasis on material achievements by the United States frequently created envy and antagonism" (Parry-Giles, 1993, p. 125). Recommendations by the Committee led to the formation of the clandestine U.S. broadcasting efforts to supplement international broadcasting outlets such as the VOA and other programs affiliated with the nascent public diplomacy structure (Cull, 2008b).

Parry-Giles's (1993) analysis implicates the exceptionalist tenor of policy argumentation in hampering Truman's initial efforts to implement an effective propaganda strategy. She argues that "because of the perceived normative power of democracy and its ideological force domestically, these political actors assumed that democracy could be exported with ease" (p. 121). She later describes how "justificatory arguments and America's propaganda were... driven by a belief in the inherent naturalness of democracy" (Parry-Giles, 1994, p. 450). The persuasive power of this form of propaganda was assumed to be inherent in the message itself.

In these early days of Cold War public diplomacy, the routes to persuasion were depicted as relatively straightforward. Audiences merely needed to be aware of the benefits of democracy to be persuaded. In a 1953 address to the United States Information Agency, Eisenhower claimed that when given a choice between governments, the American system had "greater appeal to the human soul" (Bogart, 1995, p. xxvii). This echoed the early implications of the Smith-Mundt Act authorizing attempts at international influence. As Parry-Giles interprets, under its logic "foreign audiences would naturally believe the "truth" disseminated by America and naturally reject the principals of communism" (1994, p. 451). In his own historical account, former Assistant Secretary of State Edward Barrett reflected that the United States was well positioned to be effective in a propaganda war with the Soviets because "in the contest for men's minds... truth can be a peculiarly American weapon" (Barrett, 1953, p. ix).

The beginnings of a communication strategy directed more by persuasive necessity (rather than an ideological commitment to exceptionalism) were articulated in the Eisenhower Administration's Committee on International Information Activities findings. This group, also known as the "Jackson Committee," was broadly tasked with reviewing the earlier efforts of the Truman administration's propaganda programs, and concluded that psychological operations were just as crucial to economic as to military efforts (Hixon, 1998). The committee reviewed the previous programs to match Soviet propaganda and found them lacking, concluding that the information provided in the Truman campaigns was of "little use ... for foreign audiences" (quoted in Parry-Giles, 1994, p. 457). It argued for a tighter integration of propaganda with foreign policy planning and objectives, and suggested that propaganda should "harmonize" the interests of foreign audiences with those of the United States — meaning that messages should be tailored to the specific needs and cultural sensitivities of the specific audience. The Eisenhower Administration later pursued a more pragmatic approach to propaganda that integrated the use of journalism in international broadcasting outlets with clandestine information operations — representing a departure from the confines of exceptionalism. Yet the constraints of exceptionalism's "sympathetic ecology"— the argument formation inherited from the Cold War for policy debate — would resurface again as the United States faced a renewed crisis of international communication in the wake of September 11, 2001.

Post 9/11— Repairing the Arsenal of Persuasion

The significant decline of positive opinion about the United States in the years leading up to the events of 9/11 was at some level largely ignored by the U.S. government, in part because the United States Information Agency (USIA) had been eliminated, with its remaining assets folded into the State Department or divested to the authority of the Broadcast Board of Governors in 1999. Arguments for dismantling the USIA were framed around cost, but also because it was assumed by Congress that the cultural products that represented the United States would be sufficient to carry the burden of promoting the U.S. style of market-democracy (Snow, 2002). The events of September 11, 2001, however, forced serious scrutiny on the instruments of public diplomacy available to the United States that could somehow address its increasing unpopularity.

Yet the incredulity among the lawmakers was revealing. Then Chairman of the House International Relations committee Henry Hyde asked, "How is it that the country that invented Hollywood and Madison Avenue has such trouble promoting a positive image of itself overseas?" (2001, p. 1). As the

Congress deliberated over the allocation of resources to communication interventions, elements of exceptionalism appeared again in the course of arguments. One possible reason for a reliance on the historical tropes of exceptionalism: there simply wasn't a compelling set of paradigmatic arguments; i.e., justificatory statements, terms, or indeed a grammar with which to resolve an obvious policy solution. The argument formation remained mired in elements of persisting Cold War rhetoric, something rhetorical scholars predicted soon after end of the Cold War (Kane, 1991).

Representative Howard Berman, describing the necessity of funding international broadcasting efforts to the House Committee on International Relations in 2001, referenced the words of famed U.S. journalist and USIA director Edward R. Murrow, to proclaim the future of U.S. public diplomacy, declaring "fortunately, we have the acts on our side, and in the end, the truth will prevail" (2001, p. 6). As the legislators sought answers from existing tools, then Under Secretary of State for Public Diplomacy, Charlotte Beers, a successful U.S. advertising industry executive, reminded the House Committee on International Relations that foreign audiences may not know the values and motivations of the United States.

> The burden is on us to act as if no one has ever understood the identity of the United States, to redefine it for audiences who are, at best, cynical. It is a war about the way of life and fundamental beliefs and values. We did not expect to ever have to explain and defend concepts like freedom and tolerance [2001, p. 15].

Beers's remarks acknowledge the incredulity of Hyde, but also imply that the abstractions of democracy are by necessity coterminous with the United States. This kind of argument framing would fuel the nascent "War on Terrorism" as an existential struggle of competing ideological formations.

The nature of the conflict prompted some legislators to question the viability of *any* attempts at public diplomacy, if the conflict really was between two vastly divergent rationalities. Representative Tom Lantos considered the possibility by asking: "Is it feasible to conduct the rational and patient and compromise-prone approach which has characterized, obviously, all of our domestic dialogue, but which is so totally inappropriate in dealing with the virulently hostile segment of the world?" (2001, p. 18). One problem with Lantos's characterization of the challenges to public diplomacy is that it assumed a monolithic and powerful enemy, conflating Muslim extremists with both Arabs and the global Muslim community. The "problem" of public diplomacy was not about finding the right message, but the ability of other audiences to recognize the "truth" of America's "rational" set of arguments.

The initial response of the Bush administration implemented by Charlotte Beers was the now maligned "Shared Values" campaigns, a series of advertisements, documentaries, and pamphlets designed by the United States to show how Muslims were treated in the United States (Fullerton and Kendrick, 2006). The documentaries failed to reach the majority of their intended audience, and the content of the programming was later derided as profoundly unpersuasive. As Rampton and Stauber observed, the content failed to address the "core of Muslim resentment of the United States," the scope of U.S. policies in the Middle East and the continued handling of the Israeli/Palestinian crisis (2003, p. 31). They cited an Indonesian student who had watched the TV advertisements: "We know that there's religious freedom in America, and we like that. What we're angry about is the arrogant behavior of the U.S. in the rest of the world" (p. 31). Charlotte Beers resigned in March 2003 as internal criticism of U.S. public diplomacy mounted (Defense Science Board Report, 2004; Wolf and Rosen, 2004).

The first definitive statement during the Bush administration arguing for a significant policy change was the "Changing Minds, Winning the Peace" report of the U.S. Advisory Group on Public Diplomacy for the Arab and Muslim World, chaired by Edward Djerejian in 2003. The report identified how the gap between U.S. policies and their value-centric rhetoric created a "reinforcing cycle of animosity" in the Arab world (p. 17). The hypocrisy of the "say-do" gap fueled growing resentment against the United States and suspicion over its intentions, sentiments that were only compounded by the 2003 invasion of Iraq.

In 2005, the Bush administration appointed Karen Hughes, a trusted insider to the post of Under Secretary of State for Public Diplomacy. Yet her inaugural appearance as the new Under Secretary appeared to reflect a continued reliance on exceptionalism as compass for public diplomacy. Secretary of State Condoleezza Rice seemed to acknowledge the predicament of the United States in arguing for its policies and values with audiences skeptical or hostile foreign audiences.

> I know that sometimes it is difficult to see that this is a history that is moving in the right direction but I think as long as we remain true to our values and true to our belief that democracy and freedom and liberty are the birthright of every living human being, that we will one day stand here and see that the world has been transformed, indeed, for the better [Rice, 2005, para. 5].

For Rice, a refocus on more audience-centric strategies of influence seemed outside the realm of speculation, something evident in the moral obligations of promoting U.S. values that laced the Bush administration's 2007 U.S. National Strategy for Public Diplomacy and Strategic Communication. Perhaps not surprisingly, Karen Hughes's tenure failed to dramatically improve the standing of the United States in the eyes of foreign audiences crucial to U.S. national interests. Her "listening tour" of Arab countries was roundly criticized by journalists and public diplomacy experts, and was symbolic of the "tone-deaf" characterization of the Bush administration's public diplomacy strategy (Brown, 2007).

One critic in the Arab media, however, highlights the consequences of the U.S. approach to public diplomacy that relies on the higher priority given to values than to addressing the substantive grievances most important to audiences in the Arab and Muslim World. Rami Khouri, an Arab journalist and media scholar, used the occasion of Hughes's resignation in 2007 to sum up the impact of her stewardship of U.S. public diplomacy. In a cross-posted editorial on the Al-Arabiya network's website and the Lebanese *Daily Star* paper, Khouri writes that Hughes's time at the State Department was "a political catastrophe in all respects" (2007, para. 6). The irony of Khouri's critique is that it acknowledges the exceptionalism of American values.

Indeed, Khouri (2007, para. 6) uses American values as a standard to judge the U.S. actions negatively. He describes Hughes's method of public diplomacy as

> not only ineffective and probably counter-productive; it is also very un–American. She rejected the honesty, humility and realism that define the values of most Americans, and instead opted to live in a dream world in which America was perfect, and foreigners who thought badly of it needed to be lectured about American values and policies.

Khouri's arguments depict U.S. public diplomacy as patronizing, with elements of Orientalist framing. He bluntly characterizes as unreflexive the nature of Hughes and the Bush administration's brand of public diplomacy: "She never understood that her brand of moralizing and arrogant cultural cheerleading—'Go Muslims, go! Reach for the sky! You can be modern and democratic, if you really try!'—was part of the problem, not part of the solution" (Khouri, 2007, para. 8). After Hughes's departure, significant changes to U.S. public diplomacy strategy idled in anticipation of the forthcoming 2008 presidential election.

Retreat from Exceptionalism: Public Diplomacy 2.0 and Open Source Diplomacy

Despite the apparent failures of the Bush administration's value-centric stance towards public diplomacy strategy, proposed fixes to U.S. public diplomacy still were framed within the parameters of an exceptionalist discourse.

In September of 2008, legislation was proposed to rebuild an institutional structure to coordinate public diplomacy and so-called "strategic communication" programs. Senator Sam Brownback's proposed bill, the "Strategic Communication Act of 2008" (S 3546), outlined a series of arguments framing the necessity of a centralized institution to coordinate public diplomacy activities in response to the perceived threat of Islamic extremists. The draft legislation explains that "the United States, out of a decent respect to the opinions of mankind, owes an explanation of its founding principles and the purposes of democratic, constitutional, and political order" (sec. 3, p. 3).

The Brownback bill echoes burdens that hearken back to Senator Beveridge's apology for imperialistic expansion at the dawn of the twentieth century. There is an obligation in the bill to promote and defend the political values embodied by the United States. Yet this mandate shares space in the bill with the argument that such engagement with foreign audiences will lead to the "advancement of the national interests of the United States" (S 3546, sec. 2, p. 3). Interestingly, the document elaborates how U.S. interests will be facilitated not only by explaining U.S. policies, but in particular by "advancing understanding and appreciation for the founding principles of the United States and ... defeating ideas that are inimical to the founding principles of the United States" (S 3546, sec. 3, p. 4). The Brownback bill depicted a public diplomacy that defends the narrative legacy of U.S. political values, while at the same time discouraging foreign audiences from the lure of anti–American sentiment.

The Brownback bill did not, however, represent the last statement of the Bush administration on public diplomacy. James Glassman, a publisher and journalist, was the last Under Secretary of State for Public Diplomacy to serve in the Bush administration. His appointment was short, yet he managed to articulate a strategic vision for public diplomacy that was relatively unfettered by exceptionalist rhetoric. While Glassman somewhat problematically described the context of U.S. public diplomacy as a "war of ideas" (2008, para. 9) his main emphasis for retooling U.S. public diplomacy was to abandon efforts to craft a more perfect message designed to move opinion or cultivate identification with U.S. values. Instead, Glassman argued for public diplomacy that would facilitate "conversation" in foreign audiences. In a speech to the New America Foundation in 2008, Glassman laid out the basic premises of what he called "public diplomacy 2.0."

In Glassman's words, public diplomacy 2.0 is "an approach, not a technology" (2008, para. 24). As he describes it, public diplomacy should strive to discourage participation in extremist movements and, importantly, encourage active and deliberative participation in the public sphere. It is not democracy promotion *per se*, but a strategic framework of facilitation, where "interactivity" and "conversation" define the "ideal of the many" (2008, para. 22) embodied in social networking technologies and modes of interaction that lend credibility. For Glassman, nation-states not embracing the implications of how new media platforms both enable political action and engender credibility "risk being ignored" (2008, para. 35).

Glassman's "ideal of the many" represents a significant departure from the received exceptionalism tropes because the basis of the strategy is to *de-emphasize* the primacy of the United States in the construction and promotion of the "message." Public diplomacy 2.0 would build credibility by demonstrating openness to other opinions, and by facilitating direct engagement through recognized social media platforms, on top of existing efforts in cultural diplomacy and international broadcasting. Rather than be a "broadcaster" in what Zaharna has called "information battle" (2005, p. 1), Glassman's approach would position the United States as a "convener" of global dialogue between foreign stakeholders that would be able to effect the desired foreign policy outcomes of the administration.

Former diplomat and consultant Ali Fisher has described this approach as a form of "open source" diplomacy (2008, p. 2), where the lack of control over the "message" of the United States is acknowledged and indeed embraced. An open source "ethic" would allow for direct participation across levels of international actors, and capitalize on the legitimacy accorded to specific forms of communication. Early attempts by the United States to embrace this form of public diplomacy include deploying so-called digital outreach teams in foreign language websites to explain U.S. policy views, and also to convene social organizers and activists seeking alternatives to extremism. For Glassman, the role of the United States in facilitative public diplomacy constitutes an indirect route to influence, if not necessarily persuasion towards specific attitudes about the United States.

It is, of course, important to contextualize the more modest ambitions of Glassman's public diplomacy strategy. "Public Diplomacy 2.0" was articulated at the end of an unpopular U.S. presidency which had soured public opinion around the world (Pew Research Center, 2008). The legacy of the broader exceptionalist policy framework of the Bush administration's "War on Terror" is a diminished international credibility to leverage public argument, let alone cultivate soft power through communicative action like public diplomacy.

The retreat from exceptionalism extends beyond public diplomacy to the rhetoric of the president himself. When asked in April 2009 if he subscribed to a "school of American exceptionalism," President Obama responded by denying that exceptionalism is distinctly American: "I believe in American exceptionalism, just as I suspect that the Brits believe in British exceptionalism and the Greeks believe in Greek exceptionalism. I'm enormously proud of my country and its role and history in the world" (para. 47). Yet Obama (2009) was also forced to reconcile exceptionalism with the diminished capacity of the U.S. to operate as an unilateral global power.

> I see no contradiction between believing that America has a continued extraordinary role in leading the world towards peace and prosperity and recognizing that that leadership is incumbent, depends on, our ability to create partnerships because we create partnerships because we can't solve these problems alone [para. 50].

Conclusion: Thinking Beyond the Promotion of American Exceptionalism

In devising a new formulation for public diplomacy, the Obama administration contends with both a legacy of exceptionalism in the arguments for an ideal communicative strategy, but also with a complex global communication environment that works against monological attempts at amplification of U.S. values and their distinct qualities. Moreover, the policy arguments intended to devise a strategic framework are further hampered by the inertia of the policy imagination still persisting nearly two decades after the end of the Cold War. The U.S. Department of Defense's Defense Science Board in 2004 noted how the Bush administration's foreign policy strategy was "reflexively inclined toward Cold War-style responses to the new threat" (Defense Science Board, 2004, p. 42). As Zaharna (2005) observed, the promotion of American values soon after 9/11 merely prompted other international actors to defend and reassert their own values.

More fundamental strategic arguments for public diplomacy are similarly lacking. As Bially-Mattern (2005) argues, the notion of "soft power" does not provide a sufficient strategic template to conceive of an influence strategy that transcends the enthymemes of arguments that American values are universally shared. Soft power does not suggest what an ideal public diplomacy praxis should look like; rather, it assumes a register of influence through the act of presentation. This assumption pervades the history of U.S. public diplomacy and underscores a persistent attended belief in a "magic bullet" theory of communication. Bially-Mattern's ultimate critique notes that attempts to persuade are framed by the context of the material power and add to the representational force of the communication. Soft power is not, in her view, a measure of positive acceptance of American exceptionalism, but a consequence of insecurity in the face of threat.

The move to embrace a more facilitative public diplomacy strategy as evidenced in the rhetoric of James Glassman (2008) suggests that both a more modest set of objectives of public diplomacy and quite possibly a different kind of exceptionalism lie at the heart of public diplomacy 2.0's strategic assumptions. By embracing what Fisher (2008, p. 2) calls an "open source ethic" in defining the motives and ambitions of public diplomacy, Glassman seemingly aligns U.S. international communication strategy with what Manuel Castells (2004) has described as a kind of "network" value that is emergent across audiences linked through ubiquitous communication technologies). Castells argues that if there is a common value to what he calls the "network society," it is a respect for the act of communication itself, the shared immersion in the spaces of connectivity — including networks of social capital and people (2004, pp. 38–39).

Glassman (2008) implicitly argues that the facilitative ambitions of public diplomacy 2.0 represent ideals congruent with this broad perspective; that the "ideal of the many" is a viable communication strategy, but that it is also *American*. For Glassman claims that the goals of public diplomacy 2.0 are rooted in the promotion of ideals of civic participation, freedom of speech, and democratic governance — shared aspects of both the American political heritage and also of the "open source" ethics that inspire scholars like Castells. Perhaps the new exceptionalism is an abandonment of the City on a Hill, in order to stake a claim in the Network Society.

Put another way, the logic of this view of public diplomacy has shifted from message management to communication as *communitas*, where efficiency is considered not in the advertisement of an exceptional America, but of a networked global community emboldened by its horizontal, communicative capacity to reject conflict and embrace cooperative networks of affiliation. Glassman's arguments lay claim to this vision as both vital to U.S. security, and as an outgrowth of the values embodied in the American system. This distinction may serve as a basis from which to elaborate a new set of terms and oppositions to assemble an argument formation for public diplomacy strategy that is relevant in a complex global communication infrastructure.

The implication is not, however, that future policy debate will simply lead to a better argument strategy or message waiting to be discovered within a presumed logic of international persuasion. Admittedly, a shift away from exceptionalism may be necessary for policy-makers and legislators to recognize how arguments about the United States circulate in an ecology of global discourse. As public diplomacy planners struggle to reconcile the goals of promoting the United States amidst an incredibly diverse, pluralistic mediapshere of competing opinions, they have turned towards new modes of outreach, recognizing that the previous tropes of American exceptionalism do not cultivate influence by themselves, regardless of context. And yet the imperatives of public diplomacy, and thus the promotion of the United States, have not disappeared. If anything, the need for public diplomacy is heightened.

As public diplomacy planners reach for new modes of outreach, they reveal in the process something about the rhetoric of American exceptionalism itself. An argument formation of U.S. foreign policy is ultimately refracted through a prism of relationships, practices, and networks that condition the legitimacy of claims: value, policy, or otherwise. When policy-makers recognize the limits of exceptionalism, they are not necessarily rejecting the premises of exceptionalism, or perhaps even the need for an exceptionalist impulse to communicate about the United States. Rather, efforts to define a "public diplomacy 2.0" work to embody American exceptionalism in a kind of universalist ethic of communication. Exceptionalism, in this incarnation, does not suggest a bold arc of history culminating in American global dominance through some kind of virtuous predestination, but rather an America playing the role of benefactor and patron of dialogue, cooperation, and democratic empowerment. This conception retains a distinctive vision for the U.S. on a global stage, but reflects a slightly more humble attitude towards global leadership. Public diplomacy, as is argued here, provides a measure of how American exceptionalism functions within the confines of debate about U.S. foreign policy, and perhaps signals a broader shift in how it is rhetorically constituted in political discourse.

References

Adas, M. (2001). "From Settler Colony to Global Hegemon: Integrating the Exceptionalist Narrative of the American Experience into World History." *American Historical Review, 106*, 1692–1720.
Barrett, E. (1953). *Truth Is Our Weapon.* New York: Funk and Wagnalls.
Beers, C. (2001, October 10). *The Role of Public Diplomacy in Support of the Anti-Terrorism Campaign: Hearing Before the Committee on International Relations.* House Committee on International Relations, 107th Congress, 1st Session, serial number 107–47.
Berman, H. (2001, October 10). *The Role of Public Diplomacy in Support of the Anti-Terrorism Campaign: Hearing Before the Committee on International Relations.* House Committee on International Relations, 107th Congress, 1st Session, serial number 107–47.
Bially-Mattern, J. (2005). "Why 'Soft Power' Isn't So Soft: Representational Force and the Sociolinguistic Construction of Attraction in World Politics." *Millennium — Journal of International Studies, 33*, 583–612
Bogart, L. (1995) *Cool Words, Cold War: A New Look at the USIA's Premises for Propaganda.* Washington, DC: American University Press.

Brown, J. (2007). "The Second Coming of Karen Hughes." *The Huffington Post*. Retrieved from http://www.huffingtonpost.com/john-brown/the-second-coming-of-kare_b_59851.html.

Castells, M. (2004). "Informationalism, Networks, and the Network Society: A Theoretical Blueprint." In M. Castells (Ed.), *The Network Society: A Cross-Cultural Perspective* (pp. 3–45). Northampton, MA: Edward Elgar.

Cull, N. (2008a). "Public Diplomacy: Taxonomies and Histories." *Annals of the American Academy of Political and Social Science*, 616, 31–54.

―――― (2008b). *The Cold War and the United States Information Agency: American Propaganda and Public Diplomacy, 1945–1989*. Cambridge, UK: Cambridge University Press.

Fisher, A. (2008). "Music for the Jilted Generation: Open Source Public Diplomacy." *Hague Journal of Diplomacy*, 3, 1–24.

Fullerton, J., and A. Kendrick (2006). *Advertising's War on Terrorism: The Story of the U.S. State Department's Shared Values Initiative*. Spokane: Marquette.

Gilboa, E. (2008). "Searching for a Theory of Public Diplomacy." *Annals of the American Academy of Political and Social Science*, 616, 55–77.

Glassman, J. (2008, December 1). *Public Diplomacy 2.0: A New Approach to Global Engagement*. Address to the New America Foundation, Washington, DC.

Goodnight, G. T. (1998, Summer). "Public Argument and the Study of Foreign Policy." *American Diplomacy*. Retrieved from http://www.unc.edu/depts/diplomat/AD_Issues/amdipl_8/goodnight.html.

Goodnight, G. T. (2006). *The Nuclear Age as Argument Formation: On Rhetorical Construction and Epochal Change*. Working paper for the University of Southern California International/ Interdisciplinary Discourse Analysis Series. Los Angeles: University of Southern California.

Green, F. (1988). *American Propaganda Abroad*. New York: Hippocrene.

Hayden, C. (2007). "Arguing Public Diplomacy: The Role of Argument Formations in U.S. Foreign Policy Rhetoric." *Hague Journal of Diplomacy*, 2, 229–254.

Hixon, W. (1998). *Parting the Curtain: Propaganda, Culture, and the Cold War, 1945–1961*. New York: St. Martin's.

Horsman, R. (1981) *Race and Manifest Destiny: The Origins of American Racial Anglo-Saxonism*. Cambridge, MA: Harvard University Press.

Hyde, H. (2001, October 10). *The Role of Public Diplomacy in Support of the Anti-Terrorism Campaign: Hearing before the Committee on International Relations*. House Committee on International Relations, 107th Congress, 1st Session, serial number 107–47.

Kane, T. (1991). "Foreign Policy Suppositions and Commanding Ideas." *Argumentation and Advocacy*, 28, 80–90.

Kelley, R. (2008). "Between 'Take-Offs' and 'Crash Landings': Situational Aspects of Public Diplomacy." In N. Snow and P. Taylor (Eds.), *The Routledge Handbook of Public Diplomacy* (pp. 72–85). New York: Routledge.

Khouri, R. (2007, November 3). "Karen Hughes's Two-Year Halloween." *The Daily Star*. [Lebanon]. Retrieved from http://www.dailystar.com.lb/article.asp?edition_id=1&categ_id=5&article_id=86476.

Kohut, A., and B. Stokes (2006). *America Against the World: How We Are Different and Why We Are Disliked*. New York: Macmillan.

Lantos, T. (2001, October 10). *The Role of Public Diplomacy in Support of the Anti-Terrorism Campaign: Hearing Before the Committee on International Relations*. House Committee on International Relations, 107th Congress, 1st Session, serial number 107–47.

Lipset, S. M. (1996). *American Exceptionalism: A Double-Edged Sword*. New York: W.W. Norton.

Lord, K. (2008). *Voice of America: U.S. Public Diplomacy for the 21st century.* Washington, DC: Brookings Institution.
McEvoy-Levy, S. (2001). *American Exceptionalism and U.S. Foreign Policy.* London: Palgrave.
McGee, M. C. (1975). "In Search of 'the People': A Rhetorical Alternative." *Quarterly Journal of Speech, 61,* 235–249.
Melissen, J. (2007). "The New Public Diplomacy: Between Theory and Practice." In J. Melissen (Ed.), *The New Public Diplomacy: Soft Power in International Relations* (pp. 3–27). New York: Palgrave Macmillan.
Nayak, M., and C. Malone (2009). "American Orientalism and American Exceptionalism: A Critical Rethinking of U.S. Hegemony." *International Studies Review, 11,* 253–256.
Nye, J. (2004). *Soft Power: The Means to Success in World Politics.* New York: Public Affairs.
_____ (2008). "Public Diplomacy and Soft Power." *Annals of the American Academy of Political and Social Science, 616,* 94–109.
Obama, B. (2009, April 4). "News Conference by President Obama." Retrieved from http://www.whitehouse.gov/the_press_office/News-Conference-By-President-Obama-4-04-2009/.
Parry-Giles, S. (1993). "The Rhetorical Tension Between Propaganda and Democracy: Blending Competing Conceptions of Ideology and Theory." *Communication Studies, 44,* 117–131.
_____ (1994). "Rhetorical Experimentation and the Cold War, 1947–1953: The Development of an Internationalist Approach to Propaganda." *Quarterly Journal of Speech, 80,* 448–467.
Perelman, C., and L. Olbrechts-Tyteca (1969). *The New Rhetoric: A Treatise on Argumentation.* Notre Dame, IN: University of Notre Dame Press.
Pew Research Center (2008, December 18). *Global Public Opinion During the Bush Years (2001–2008).* Retrieved from http://pewresearch.org/pubs/1059/global-opinion-bush-years.
Rampton, S., and J. Stauber (2003). *Weapons of Mass Deception: The Uses of Propaganda in Bush's War on Iraq.* Madison, WI: Tarcher/Penguin.
Rice, C. (2005, September 8). "Remarks with Under Secretary for Public Diplomacy and Public Affairs Karen Hughes at Town Hall for Public Diplomacy." Retrieved from http://www.state.gov/secretary/rm/2005/52748.htm.
Scott-Smith, G. (2008). "Exchange Programs and Public Diplomacy." In N. Snow and P. Taylor (Eds.), *The Routledge Handbook of Public Diplomacy* (pp. 50–56). New York: Routledge.
Sharp, P. (2007). "Revolutionary States, Outlaw Regimes and the Techniques of Public Diplomacy." In J. Melissen (Ed.), *The New Public Diplomacy: Soft Power in International Relations* (pp. 106–123). New York: Palgrave Macmillan.
Slaughter, A.-M. (2007). *The Idea that Is America: Keeping Faith with Our Values in a Dangerous World.* Cambridge, MA: Basic.
Snow, N. (2002). *Propaganda, Inc.: Selling America's Culture to the World.* New York: Seven Stories.
_____ (2008). "Rethinking Public Diplomacy." In N. Snow and P. Taylor (Eds.), *The Routledge Handbook of Public Diplomacy* (pp. 3–11). New York: Routledge.
Sweig, J. (2006). *Friendly Fire: Losing Friends and Making Enemies in the Anti-American Century.* New York: Public Affairs.
Wolf, C., and B. Rosen (2004). *Public Diplomacy: How to Think About It and How to Improve It.* RAND Occasional Paper. Santa Monica, CA: RAND.
Zaharna, R. S. (2005). "The Network Paradigm of Strategic Public Diplomacy." *Foreign Policy in Focus, 10,* 1–4.

About the Contributors

Lindsay R. Calhoun is an assistant professor of communication studies at Marshall University. Her research focuses on intercultural and international communication, critical/cultural studies, and ethnography. Her essays have appeared in *The Howard Journal of Communications* and *Text and Performance Quarterly*. Her monograph on the memories and memorialization of the Sand Creek Massacre is forthcoming.

Kevin Coe is an assistant professor in the Department of Communication at the University of Arizona. His research and teaching focus on the interaction of American political discourse, news media, and public opinion. His scholarship has appeared in such journals as *Journal of Communication, Political Communication, Presidential Studies Quarterly*, and *Rhetoric & Public Affairs*. He is the coauthor, with David Domke, of *The God Strategy: How Religion Became a Political Weapon in America*.

Jason A. Edwards is an assistant professor of communication studies at Bridgewater State University. His research interests lie at the intersection of presidential communication, American foreign policy rhetoric, and international political discourse. He is the author of *Navigating the Post-Cold War World: President Clinton's Foreign Policy Rhetoric*, as well as two dozen articles, book chapters, and book reviews. He is working on a monograph exploring the rhetorical and historical contours of American exceptionalism as it relates to debates over America's role in the world.

David Charles Gore is an assistant professor in the Department of Communication at the University of Minnesota Duluth. His research interests address the interrelationships between religion, politics, and economics. His work has been published in the *International Journal of Listening*, *White House Studies*, the *KB Journal*, and various edited volumes.

Craig Hayden is an assistant professor in the international communication program at American University's School of International Service. His research focuses on the discourse of public diplomacy, the rhetoric of foreign policy related to media technologies, and the impact of global media and media convergence on international relations. He is a member of the Public Diplomacy Council. His blog is the International Media Argument Project (intermap.org). His new book is *The Rhetoric of Soft Power: Public Diplomacy in Global Contexts*.

About the Contributors

Arthur W. Herbig is an assistant professor at Indiana University–Purdue University, Fort Wayne, where he teaches courses in media production, rhetoric, and popular culture. His research interests include heroism, gender studies, and political discourse. He is working on several studies about the discursive existence of Pat Tillman and plans to continue to examine the existence of public characters.

Michael J. Hostetler is a professor in and chair of the Department of Rhetoric, Communication and Theatre at St. John's University in New York. He is a former Fulbright Teaching Fellow who specializes in the history and criticism of American public address and the rhetoric of religion and politics. His research has appeared in many communication journals including *Rhetoric & Public Affairs*, *Quarterly Journal of Speech*, and *Rhetorica*.

Christina M. Knopf is an assistant professor of communication at the State University of New York at Potsdam, where she teaches in the Speech Communication, Women's and Gender Studies, and Africana Studies programs. Her scholarship is in the area of civil-military dialectics.

Katherine L. Lavelle is the director of forensics and an assistant professor of communication studies at the University of Northern Iowa. Her research program emphasizes connections between sports, rhetoric, race, and masculinity. Her work has been published in *The Howard Journal of Communications*, *Contemporary Argumentation and Debate*, *International Journal of Sport Communication*, and the collection *Sports Mania: Essays on Fandom and the Media in the 21st Century* (McFarland, 2008).

Brett Lunceford is an assistant professor of communication at the University of South Alabama, where he serves as the head of the interpersonal communication/rhetoric track. His research focuses on social movements, technology, and democratic practice. In addition to other scholarly collections, his work has appeared in *American Communication Journal*, *Communication Teacher*, *ETC: A Review of General Semantics*, *Explorations in Media Ecology*, *Media History Monographs*, *Northwestern Journal of Technology and Intellectual Property*, *Review of Communication*, and *Theology and Sexuality*.

Rico Neumann works for the Human Rights Center at the Universidad para la Paz in Costa Rica, a UN–mandated institution with a focus on peace and conflict research. His academic interests include political communication and public opinion with an emphasis on strategic presidential discourse, international political rhetoric, and media performance during wartime.

Burton St. John, III, is an assistant professor of communication at Old Dominion University. He is author of *Press Professionalization and Propaganda: The Rise of Journalistic Double-Mindedness, 1917–1941*, and he coedited *Public Journalism 2.0: The Promise and Reality of a Citizen-Engaged Press*. His work has appeared in *Journalism Studies*, *Journalism Practice*, *Journalism History*, *Public Relations Review*, *The Communication Review*, *American Journalism* and the *Journal of Mass Media Ethics*.

M. Karen Walker is a Ph.D. candidate in the Department of Communication at the University of Maryland College Park. Her dissertation research focuses on the rhetorical dimension of soft power as evinced through public-private partnerships in international diplomacy. She has served as a Franklin Fellow at the U.S. Department of State, informing regional and departmental strategies for Diaspora community engagement, and managing policy planning and programs to support democratic development in Iraq.

David Weiss is an assistant professor of media studies and political communication at Montana State University–Billings. His research interests include critical media discourse, representations of "culture war" issues in popular culture, and religious communication in the political and public sphere. A former advertising and marketing executive, he is the coauthor of *Streetwise Sales Letters* and the editor of *What Democrats Talk About When They Talk About God: Religious Communication in Democratic Party Politics*. His research has appeared in *Popular Communication, The Howard Journal of Communications, Theory in Action*, the *SAGE Encyclopedia of Communication Theory*, and numerous edited collections.

Index

ABC *see* television
activism *see* government activism; *see also* statism
Adams, Henry 121
Adams, John 37, 42, 45, 178–180
Adams, John Quincy 41
addresses *see* inaugural addresses; State of the Union addresses
Afghanistan 4, 14, 18, 20, 133–134, 139, 143–144, 149, 181
America-centrism 16, 20; *see also* nationalism; patriotism
American character *see* character; *see also* values
American continent 2, 32, 35, 48–51, 54, 56–57, 60, 114–115, 118–119, 124–126, 129, 158, 169; *see also* geography; land; New Israel/Jerusalem/Zion; New World; Promised Land
"American Creed" 13, 36, 66, 173
American dream 56, 133, 174–175, 185
American exceptionalism, definitions of *see* definitions
American flag *see* flag
American genius 31, 37, 44–46, 74
American history *see* history
American identity *see* identity
American Indians *see* Native Americans
American land *see* chosen land; geography; land; Promised Land
American Revolution 2, 13, 43, 54, 104, 136; *see also* founding fathers
American values *see* values
American way of life 70, 74, 174, 178, 180, 183
Americanism 63, 68, 75, 76, 136
Arabs 95, 200–202; *see also* Iraq; Middle East; Muslims and Islam
army *see* military
athletics and athletes *see* sports
Atlantic Ocean 31, 34, 126, 156; *see also* Pacific Ocean
autonomy 82–83, 87, 91, 141, 168; *see also* freedom; independence; self-determination

Bacevich, Andrew 3, 174–176, 181, 182, 184
basketball *see* sports
beacon (of light) 1–3, 43, 46, 48, 155–157; *see also* "city on a hill"
Bell, Daniel 2, 13, 154–155
Bible 49, 50, 52, 54, 57, 60, 104, 107, 111, 112, 115; *see also* Gospel; Matthew; New Testament
blessings 31, 41, 67, 73, 103, 130, 141, 160–161, 174, 197; *see also* divine providence; God; prayer
Book of Mormon 49–52, 54, 56–60, 101–104, 111–112, 115; *see also* Bible; Lehi; Mormons and Mormonism; Smith, Joseph
bravery 37, 41, 142, 166, 180, 182; *see also* courage
Britain and the British 11, 23, 36, 37, 56, 127, 168, 205; *see also* Europe and Europeans
broadcasting *see* media; television
burden 178–185, 196, 199, 200, 203; *see also* sacrifice
Bush, George H.W. 14, 20, 22, 24, 178, 180, 182, 184
Bush, George W. 3, 14, 17, 18, 20, 31–32, 36, 44, 78, 87–88, 132–135, 143–147, 180–181, 183–185, 200–205
business 5, 63–65, 67–70, 72, 74–79, 86, 175, 180, 184, 200; *see also* capitalism; economics and economic issues; free market

capitalism 5, 8, 67, 78, 83, 119; *see also* economics and economic issues; free market; industry
Carter, Jimmy 19–22, 27, 181
Catholics and Catholicism 53; *see also* Christians and Christianity
character 31, 33–34, 36–38, 41, 44–45, 129, 156, 167, 171–172, 191; *see also* uniqueness
China 5, 82, 85–95
chosen land 34, 48, 50, 53, 55–56, 59–60, 173, 176; *see also* chosen people; New Israel/Jerusalem/Zion; Promised Land
chosen nation *see* chosen land; *see also* chosen people; Promised Land

215

chosen people 2, 5, 31, 42, 46, 56, 58–59, 107, 171; *see also* chosen land; Promised Land
Christ *see* Jesus Christ
Christians and Christianity 54, 56–58, 103–104, 115, 157–158, 160, 162, 167, 173; *see also* Bible; faith; God; Jesus Christ; Mormons and Mormonism; Puritans; religion
Church of Jesus Christ of Latter-day Saints *see* Mormons and Mormonism
"city on a hill" 2, 3, 12, 26, 46, 191, 206; *see also* beacon (of light); Matthew, Book of; Puritans; Reagan, Ronald; Winthrop, John
civil religion 114, 115, 163; *see also* religion
civil rights *see* rights
Civil War 153, 157, 179; *see also* wars and warfare
civilization 45, 69, 107, 121, 126, 129, 156–157, 160–162
class *see* social class
Cleveland, Grover 42
Clinton, William Jefferson (Bill) 14, 20, 24, 25, 45
CNN *see* television
Cold War 7, 14, 19–20, 22, 31, 189–191, 193, 196, 198–200, 205
colonialism and colonization 6, 34, 46, 120–121, 123–126, 129–130, 157–160, 172–173; *see also* imperialism; Manifest Destiny
Columbus, Christopher 54, 57, 104
communism 13, 18, 64, 115, 175, 198; *see also* socialism
competition 5, 84–95, 163, 176, 200, 207; *see also* inferiority; sports; superiority
Congress 133, 154, 168, 171, 178–182, 199–200; *see also* House of Representatives; Senate
Constitution 20, 25, 27, 37, 41, 45, 53–55, 57–58, 60, 74, 104–106, 108, 110–114, 119, 122, 123, 136–137, 168, 173, 203; *see also* First Amendment; freedom of religion; rights
constitutional rights *see* rights
Coolidge, Calvin 38, 41, 64
courage 36, 107, 135, 139, 141, 149, 181; *see also* bravery
covenant 5, 31, 35, 38, 40, 42, 46, 66–68, 70, 73, 75–78, 102–104, 106, 111, 115, 173; *see also* divine providence; God

Declaration of Independence 54, 57, 115, 168, 173; *see also* independence
definitions 1, 2, 11–13, 14, 17, 26, 32–33, 36, 65–66, 82–84, 87, 114, 136, 154–157, 171–173, 191, 193
democracy, democratization, and democratic movements 2, 11–13, 24, 32, 40, 44–45, 48, 52–53, 65–66, 73, 76, 85, 115, 137, 155, 166, 173, 176, 178, 196–203, 206–207, 212, 213; *see also* American way of life; myth
Democrats and the Democratic Party 3, 18, 20, 22, 24–25, 123–124
the Depression 63, 65, 69, 71, 73, 175; *see also* recession
destiny 1, 2, 6, 39, 41, 45, 48, 55, 67, 104, 114, 119–121, 125–129, 155–157, 162, 173, 176, 191; *see also* mission
de Tocqueville, Alexis *see* Tocqueville, Alexis de
devotion to nation 37, 135, 139–141, 148, 150, 183, 191; *see also* love of country; loyalty; nationalism; patriotism; responsibility
diplomacy 7, 41, 84, 86, 95, 126, 189–190, 192–207, 211, 213; *see also* foreign policy; international relations; public diplomacy; public policy
divine destiny *see* destiny; God; Manifest Destiny
divine providence 4, 31, 33–34, 38, 39, 41, 43, 119, 155; *see also* blessings; covenant; God
domestic policy 3, 4, 14, 16, 19–20, 26–27, 31, 40, 42, 122, 127, 176, 190, 193, 198, 200; *see also* diplomacy; foreign policy; public policy
domination 3, 41, 84–87, 90–91, 95, 137, 180; *see also* imperialism; power
Douglass, Frederick 130, 136; *see also* Lincoln, Abraham
duty *see* devotion to nation; *see also* love of country; nationalism; obligation; patriotism

economics and economic issues 3, 4, 13, 18, 32, 36, 41, 46, 63–66, 69, 71–72, 74–76, 78–79, 82, 85, 86, 95, 107, 154, 157, 160, 165, 172–176, 178, 180–181, 196, 199; *see also* capitalism; free market
Eden, Garden of 50, 52, 57
education 13, 23, 43, 172, 192
egalitarianism 13, 36, 65–66, 75, 77, 155
Eisenhower, Dwight 19–22, 24, 27, 43–44, 196–199
empire *see* imperialism
entitlement 3, 7, 171–172, 174–176, 178, 180, 183–185, 194
equality 13, 32, 36, 55, 65, 69, 74, 101, 110–111, 136, 142, 173–174, 194; *see also* egalitarianism
equality of opportunity *see* opportunity
Europe and Europeans 6, 12, 18, 24, 26, 31–32, 48, 51, 59, 66–67, 84, 95, 103–104, 118–119, 121, 125–130, 168, 172, 174, 191
exceptionalism, definitions of *see* definitions
exemplar and exemplarism 5, 12–18, 23–24, 26, 32, 39–40, 43–46, 55, 66–67, 83, 110, 155–156, 173, 193, 196; *see also* intervention and interventionism; leadership role; specialness
expansion and expansionism 2, 6, 106, 109, 119–130, 156, 174, 191, 203; *see also* American continent, frontier; Manifest Destiny

fairness 36, 142; *see also* values
faith 39, 42, 52, 54, 55, 60, 67, 174; *see also* religion
financial issues *see* economics and economic issues; *see also* business; capitalism; free market
First Amendment 53, 56, 109, 112; *see also* Constitution; freedom of religion
flags 159, 161, 163–167, 177; *see also* symbols and symbolism

Index 217

football *see* sports
Ford, Gerald 19–22
foreign countries 3, 17–27, 105, 180, 189, 192, 194–195, 198–204
foreign entities *see* foreign countries; *see also* foreign policy
foreign policy 3, 4, 6, 7, 12, 14, 16, 17, 27, 31–32, 40, 45, 120–128, 134, 176, 180, 185, 189–195, 197, 203–205, 207, 211; *see also* diplomacy; domestic policy; international relations
founders *see* founding fathers
founding fathers 3, 40, 54–55, 57–58, 60, 105, 112, 136, 157
Fox News Channel *see* television
free enterprise *see* free market
free market 5, 7, 13, 64–65, 68–76, 78–80, 199; *see also* capitalism; economics and economic issues; industry
freedom 3, 5, 18, 24, 31–32, 41, 43–45, 50, 55, 64, 71–73, 76–77, 105, 109, 111, 125, 127, 136, 139, 141–142, 153, 162–163, 166, 171, 176–179, 183, 200–201, 206; *see also* autonomy; Constitution; Declaration of Independence; First Amendment; independence; rights; self-determination
freedom of religion 53, 56, 72, 76–77, 101–103, 105–106, 108, 110–115, 201; *see also*; Constitution; First Amendment; rights
frontier 119–120, 129–130, 156–162, 174, 177, 191; *see also* American continent; geography; land; Manifest Destiny; westward expansion

Garden of Eden *see* Eden, Garden of
genius *see* American genius
geography 31, 34–35, 45, 51, 58, 60, 115, 118–120, 123–124, 126–129; *see also* American continent; land; nature; Promised Land
global leadership *see* exemplarism; intervention and interventionism; leadership role
God 1, 4, 5, 34, 38–39, 41–43, 48–50, 52–59, 66–67, 73, 103–107, 109–113, 116, 125, 147, 171, 173–174, 191; *see also* belief; blessings; covenant; divine providence; Jesus Christ; religion
Gospel 12, 49, 53, 57, 58; *see also* Bible; New Testament
government 34, 37, 39–41, 45, 48–49, 52–60, 63–72, 75–80, 106, 108–114, 130, 133–134, 136–137, 143, 147–148, 153, 155, 161, 164–165, 173, 175, 178–180, 190, 198, 199; *see also* Congress; House of Representatives; law; legislation and legislators; presidents and the presidency; Senate
government activism 14, 46, 64, 68, 70–72, 75, 77, 79, 203, 204; *see also* statism
Grant, Ulysses 43, 60, 61
Gulf War *see* Persian Gulf War

Harding, Warren 35, 40–41
Harrison, Benjamin 39, 41

heaven 38, 39, 54–55, 57, 110–112; *see also* God
heroism 6, 94, 132–134, 141, 143–146, 148–149, 177, 184, 212
history 1, 2, 4, 12–16, 56–59, 77, 83, 104, 109, 114, 118–120, 122–124, 126–129, 136, 154–159, 162, 165, 166, 168–171, 174, 176, 178, 189–191, 193, 195, 196, 200, 201, 205, 207, 212; *see also* American Revolution; Civil War; founding fathers
House of Representatives 121, 130, 133–134, 148, 179; *see also* Congress; Senate
human rights *see* rights

identity 1, 4, 5, 7, 12, 15, 31–34, 58, 83, 84, 153–154, 156–160, 163, 165–169, 171–172, 174–177, 184, 200; *see also* character
ideology 13, 43–44, 65, 67, 77, 121, 133–140, 148–150, 155, 157, 160, 165, 172–173, 189 193, 197–198, 200; *see also* myth; values
imperialism 3, 41, 122–126, 130, 136, 157, 176; *see also* colonialism and colonization; domination; Manifest Destiny; world order
inaugural addresses 5, 33–46, 175; *see also* presidents and the presidency; State of the Union addresses
independence 36–37, 39, 41, 62, 75, 171; *see also* Declaration of Independence; freedom
Indians *see* Native Americans
individual rights *see* rights
individualism 5, 13, 36, 64–66, 68–71, 73, 74, 76–80, 155, 173–175, 185
industry *see* business *see also* capitalism; economics and economic issues; free market
inferiority 85, 90, 93, 177; *see also* competition; superiority
international relations 4, 5, 12, 14, 16, 19, 22, 26, 27, 32, 33, 46, 82, 84–95, 122, 185, 189–200, 204–206, 211, 212; *see also* diplomacy; foreign policy
intervention and interventionism 3–6, 14, 22, 38, 40, 44–46, 69, 71–74, 78–79, 192, 194, 200; *see also* exemplar and exemplarism; leadership role; mission
Iran 18, 19; *see also* Middle East; military; Muslims and Islam; Persian Gulf War; wars and warfare
Iraq 4, 6, 14, 20, 134, 139–140, 142–149, 182, 183, 185, 201, 213; *see also* Middle East; military; Muslims and Islam; Persian Gulf War; wars and warfare
Iraq War *see* Iraq
Islam *see* Muslims and Islam

Jackson, Andrew 40, 44
Jefferson, Thomas 34–35, 39–40, 177–178, 181–182
jeremiad 5, 42–43, 46, 63–68, 70, 73–77, 79, 103–104
Jesus Christ 49–50, 53–55, 57, 59, 103; *see also* God
Jews and Judaism 53, 102
Johnson, Lyndon Baines 19–22, 35, 178–180, 182

Kennedy, John Fitzgerald 19–23, 45, 53, 138, 175
Korea 18, 22, 51, 185
Korean War *see* Korea

laissez-faire 13, 36, 63–65, 155, 173
land 5, 31–32, 34–35, 38–40, 42, 45–46, 48–60, 69, 73, 101–108, 110, 118–119, 125, 129, 150, 156–157, 166; *see also* American continent; geography; nature; Promised Land
Latter-day Saints *see* Mormons and Mormonism
law 52, 55, 64, 71–72, 75, 105, 107–108, 110–111, 123–126, 136, 168, 172, 181, 196–197; *see also* government; legislation and legislators
leadership role 3–5, 17, 21–26, 32, 43, 46, 85, 86, 176, 180, 205, 207; *see also* policeman role
League of Nations 6, 120–122, 125–128
legislation and legislators 36, 53, 72, 79, 190, 200, 203, 206; *see also* government; law
Lehi 49–50, 54, 102–103; *see also* Book of Mormon; Mormons and Mormonism; Nephi
liberty 13, 35–36, 39, 53, 55, 65, 68, 71–72, 75–77, 101–106, 108, 110–115, 123, 129, 136, 148, 155, 173–178, 194, 201; *see also* freedom; freedom of religion
Lincoln, Abraham 136, 141, 179, 180
Lipset, Seymour Martin 1, 2, 11–13, 17, 27, 36, 64–66, 75, 83, 114, 155, 172–174, 185, 191; *see also* definitions
Lodge, Henry Cabot 6, 118, 120–130
love of country 73, 141, 166; *see also* devotion to nation; nationalism; patriotism
loyalty 136, 142, 164, 167, 179; *see also* devotion to nation

Madison, James 37, 39
Manifest Destiny 2, 122, 156–159, 176, 178, 191; *see also* colonialism and colonization; destiny; expansion and expansionism; frontier; imperialism
market *see* free market; *see also* capitalism
marketplace *see* free market; *see also* capitalism
mass media *see* media
Matthew, Book of 12, 49; *see also* Bible; "city on a hill"; New Testament
McCain, John 6, 135, 138–143, 146, 148–150
McKinley, William 41
media 4–6, 14, 17, 32, 75, 83–95, 109, 133, 139, 143, 153–154, 158–159, 194, 202, 204, 207, 211, 212; *see also* newspapers; television
Middle East 24, 183, 201; *see also* Iran; Iraq; Muslims and Islam
military 4, 14, 36, 106, 108, 112, 125, 132–134, 140–149, 164–165, 177–185, 199, 212; *see also* soldiers; wars and warfare
mission 3, 6, 22–23, 39, 42, 46, 85, 87–89, 105, 122, 125, 155–156, 171, 173, 177–178, 181–186; *see also* destiny; ideology; intervention and interventionism; myth

Missouri 50–51, 53, 60, 101–102, 104, 106–108, 112, 113, 115; *see also* Mormons and Mormonism
model *see* exemplar and exemplarism
Monroe, James 34–35, 37
morality 2, 14, 32, 36, 83, 105, 119, 122, 124–125, 130, 149, 157, 162, 164, 166–167, 173–174, 177–178, 191, 201
Mormons and Mormonism 5, 6, 48–60, 101–116; *see also* Book of Mormon; Smith, Joseph
MSNBC *see* television
Muslims and Islam 7, 95, 194, 200–203
myths and mythologies 1, 4, 13, 15, 19, 26, 33–34, 36, 56, 58, 66, 79, 82–84, 87, 91, 119, 130, 132, 149, 168, 173, 176–178, 191, 193; *see also* American dream; American way of life; destiny; mission

NAM *see* National Association of Manufacturers
National Association of Manufacturers 5, 63–65, 67–79
national identity *see* identity; *see also* American way of life
national pride *see* pride of nation; *see also* nationalism; patriotism
nationalism 85, 122, 128, 130, 136; *see also* America-centrism; love of country; patriotism
Native Americans 7, 103, 153–154, 156–169; *see also* Manifest Destiny
nature 34–35, 39, 109–111; 118, 124, 174; *see also* geography; land
NBC *see* television
Nephi 49–50, 54, 59, 102–104, 115; *see also* Book of Mormon; Lehi; Mormons and Mormonism
New Deal 5, 71, 72, 79
New Israel/Jerusalem/Zion 2, 5, 48–51, 104; *see also* New World; Promised Land
New Testament 12, 49, 51, 54; 57; *see also* Bible; Gospel; scripture
New World 57, 119, 172; *see also* American continent; New Israel/Jerusalem/Zion; Promised Land
newspapers 2, 11, 14, 32, 51, 78, 134, 140, 144, 202; *see also* media
Nixon, Richard 19–22, 24–25, 27, 175
North America *see* American continent; *see also* geography; land; Manifest Destiny; westward expansion

Obama, Barack 11–12, 27, 32, 171, 204–205
obligation *see* responsibility; *see also* devotion to nation
Olbermann, Keith 6, 135, 138–139, 143–150
Old Testament *see* Bible; *see also* New Testament; scripture
Olympic Games 5, 82, 84–95
opportunity 32, 36, 41, 65–66, 69, 71, 73–74, 79, 174, 191
origins 12–13, 34, 36, 65–66

Index 219

Pacific Ocean 102, 120, 124–126, 129, 156; *see also* Atlantic Ocean
patriotism 36, 127, 133–134, 142, 146, 155, 165–167, 180, 182, 184; *see also* America-centrism; love of country; nationalism
peace 18, 24, 35, 40, 43, 126–128, 153, 165–166, 177–179, 182–183, 185, 201, 205, 212; *see also* wars and warfare
Persian Gulf War 180, 182, 185; *see also* wars and warfare
personal rights *see* rights
persuasion *see* rhetorical strategy
Philippines 6, 120–130
Pierce, Franklin 35, 40
policeman role 5, 17, 25; *see also* leadership role
policy *see* domestic policy; foreign policy; public policy
politics and political discourse 1–8, 12–13, 16, 25–26, 32–33, 36, 39, 41, 46, 53, 59, 67–69, 77–78, 82, 84–85, 95, 104, 107, 110, 112–115, 118–121, 123, 124, 127, 129, 133–139, 142–145, 147–149, 154–157, 168, 172–177, 183, 185–186, 189–196, 198, 202–204, 206, 207, 211, 212
Polk, James Knox 39, 44, 45, 179, 181
populism 13, 36, 155, 173
post–Cold War *see* Cold War
power 3, 4, 5, 15 31, 39, 41–42, 45, 63, 68–70, 78–79, 82, 84, 85, 95, 111, 114, 120, 129, 157, 168, 185, 194–198, 204–207, 211, 212; *see also* domination; soft power; world order
prayer 158, 161, 167, 178, 180, 181, 183; *see also* blessings; spiritual components
presidential campaigns, candidates, and elections 3, 7, 32, 36, 53, 113, 134, 139, 141, 147, 202; *see also* presidents and the presidency
presidents and the presidency 5, 11–27, 32–37, 40, 42, 44–46, 52–55, 64, 87–88, 111, 113, 123, 126, 130, 132, 133, 135, 138, 143, 145–146, 148, 155, 171, 177–180, 197–198, 202, 204, 211, 212; *see also* Adams, John; Adams, John Quincy; Bush, George H.W.; Bush, George W.; Carter, Jimmy; Cleveland, Grover; Clinton, William Jefferson (Bill); Coolidge, Calvin; Eisenhower, Dwight; Ford, Gerald; government; Grant, Ulysses; Harding, Warren; Harrison, Benjamin; inaugural addresses; Jackson, Andrew; Jefferson, Thomas; Johnson, Lyndon Baines; Kennedy, John Fitzgerald; Lincoln, Abraham; Madison, James; Monroe, James; Nixon, Richard; Obama, Barack; Pierce, Franklin; Polk, James Knox; presidential campaigns, candidates, and elections; Reagan, Ronald; Roosevelt, Franklin Delano; Roosevelt, Theodore; State of the Union addresses; Taylor, Zachary; Truman, Harry; Van Buren, Martin; Washington, George; Wilson, Woodrow
pride of nation 5, 14, 26, 31, 42, 86, 139, 149, 153, 164–165, 167; *see also* America-centrism; nationalism; patriotism

private enterprise *see* capitalism; free market
progress 1, 24, 36, 39–40, 42, 48, 64–67, 71, 126, 129, 136, 156–157, 185
Promised Land 48, 50, 53, 55, 56, 58, 101–102, 104; *see also* American continent; chosen land; chosen people; New Israel/Jerusalem/Zion; new world
propaganda 63, 65–68, 75, 77, 80, 191–192, 196–199; *see also* rhetorical strategy
prophets and prophetic discourse 43, 49–51, 53–57, 60, 101–104, 107, 109, 112–113, 116
prosperity 18, 24, 37, 39, 45, 56, 58, 59, 64, 73–76, 129, 178, 197, 205; *see also* success; wealth; well-being
protest 108, 113–114, 164–166, 176, 184; *see also* resistance
providence *see* divine providence; *see also* God
public diplomacy 7, 8, 189–207, 211; *see also* diplomacy; domestic policy; foreign policy
public policy 39, 154, 172; *see also* diplomacy; domestic policy; foreign policy
Puritans 2, 12, 14, 36, 43, 65, 67, 103, 173, 191; *see also* Winthrop, John

Reagan, Ronald 18–23, 42–43, 181
recession 65, 78, 175; *see also* the Depression
redemption 5, 54, 86–89, 94–95, 104–105, 109, 154–155, 157–164, 167; *see also* sin
religion 4, 13, 48–49, 51–53, 56–60, 74, 101, 104, 107, 110–112, 114–115, 171–172; *see also* Bible; Christians and Christianity; civil religion; faith; First Amendment; freedom of religion; Mormons and Mormonism; theology
religious liberty *see* freedom of religion; *see also* freedom; liberty
Republicans and the Republican Party 3, 18, 20, 22, 24–25, 121, 123–124, 127, 139, 143
resistance 84, 129, 159–164, 168–169; *see also* protest
responsibility 14, 37, 40, 110–111, 120, 128, 173–175, 181, 183, 185, 191, 192, 196, 201, 203; *see also* devotion to country; sacrifice
Revolutionary War *see* American Revolution
rhetorical strategy 7, 14, 26, 46, 65, 75, 80, 130, 183, 189–199, 201–206, 212, 213
rights 1, 6, 35, 44–45, 66, 68, 71, 77, 85, 101–102, 105–114, 136–137, 164, 173, 181–182, 212; *see also* freedom
rituals 158, 160, 164–168, 176–178, 184; *see also* sacrifice
role model *see* exemplar and exemplarism
Romney, Mitt 53
Roosevelt, Franklin Delano 15, 17–19, 20–24, 27, 63–64, 68, 71, 75, 179, 180, 182, 185
Roosevelt, Theodore 42, 121, 191

sacrifice 7, 42, 133–134, 138–142, 145–146, 149, 157–158, 152, 164, 166–167, 171, 176–181, 183–185; *see also* burden; redemption; responsibility; rituals; sin
salvation 58, 158; *see also* redemption; sin

Sand Creek Massacre 7, 153–154, 157–164, 166–169, 211
scripture 49, 51, 56, 60, 101–106, 112–115; *see also* Bible; Book of Mormon
self-determination 40–41, 72, 74, 163; *see also* autonomy; independence
self-reliance 35, 67, 174
self-sacrifice *see* sacrifice
Senate 53, 121–126, 179; *see also* Congress; House of Representatives
service to nation 140–142, 144, 165, 167, 179, 181–183
sin 59, 105, 157–158, 162, 164, 167; *see also* redemption; religion; theology
Smith, Joseph 6, 49–53, 56–57, 60, 101–105, 107–116; *see also Book of Mormon*; Mormons and Mormonism; Young, Brigham
social class 4, 13, 66, 68–69, 71, 74–75, 77, 111, 121, 184
socialism 13, 64, 185; *see also* communism
soft power 194–196, 204–205; *see also* diplomacy
soldiers 132–133, 139–147, 161, 167, 178–184; *see also* military; wars and warfare
Spanish-American War 2, 122–123, 128
specialness 1, 32, 46, 48, 67, 83, 115, 119, 120, 142, 155–156, 171, 173, 178, 185, 194–196; *see also* character; destiny; exemplar and exemplarism; uniqueness
spiritual components 8, 43, 66–67, 76, 105, 109, 115, 154, 160–164, 167–168, 173, 178–180; *see also* religion; theology
sports 2, 4–6, 83–95, 133, 140–141, 148, 154, 162, 212
State of the Union addresses 17–26, 35, 136, 182; *see also* inaugural addresses
statism 68–70, 77
strategy *see* rhetorical strategy
success 16, 32, 36–37, 42, 70, 74–75, 88–93, 133, 140, 168, 174; *see also* prosperity; wealth
superiority 1–2, 6, 23, 83, 87, 89–92, 94–95, 155–156, 167, 172, 178, 184, 196; *see also* competition; inferiority; nationalism; sports
symbols and symbolism 18, 25, 33, 129, 134, 138–141, 147–149, 159–167, 174, 176–177, 192, 202; *see also* flag

Taylor, Zachary 39, 45
technology 3, 23, 43, 203, 204, 206, 211, 212
television 2, 5, 6, 82–95, 133, 135, 138–139, 143–150, 192, 198–200, 204; *see also* media
territory *see* land
terror and terrorism 32, 132, 175, 181, 200, 204
theology 5, 48–49, 52, 54–59, 104; *see also* religion
Tillman, Pat 6, 132–135, 137–150, 212
Tocqueville, Alexis de 2, 12, 13, 52, 56, 83, 155, 172
tribes *see* Native Americans
"tripod of freedom" 76–78; *see also* freedom
Truman, Harry 18–20, 22, 24, 27, 180, 196–199
truth 40, 50, 55, 58, 59, 68, 75, 111–113, 126, 142, 144–145, 173, 178, 191, 196, 198, 200; *see also* propaganda; rhetorical strategy
TV *see* television

unification 36, 168, 183
uniqueness, 1, 2, 5, 7, 11, 27, 31, 33, 38, 48, 50, 58, 66, 68, 73–74, 77, 83, 101, 103–105, 113–114, 135–137, 155–157, 166, 172, 174, 191; *see also* character; specialness
United States Constitution *see* Constitution

values 3, 5, 12–14, 32, 33, 36, 64–66, 68, 75–77, 80, 133–137, 139–143, 146–150, 158, 173–175, 178, 181, 189–197, 200–203, 205–206; *see also* democracy; fairness; freedom; ideology; independence; morality; myth
Van Buren, Martin 39, 45, 53, 60, 111, 113
Vietnam 2–4, 14, 19, 20, 24, 175, 179, 182, 183; *see also* wars and warfare
Vietnam War *see* Vietnam
violence 56–57, 60, 106, 161–162, 166, 176–177; *see also* protest; resistance; wars and warfare

"War on Terror" *see* terror and terrorism
wars and warfare 2, 3, 6, 7, 14, 19, 22–23, 25, 35, 39, 41, 43, 46, 50, 54, 67, 75, 79, 102, 106, 108, 115, 120, 122–123, 126, 128, 132, 134–136, 139–149, 153, 157, 165–166, 171–172, 175–185, 191, 197, 212; *see also* Afghanistan; American Revolution; Civil War; Iraq; military; peace; soldiers; Spanish-American War; Vietnam; violence; World War I; World War II
Washington, DC 111, 113, 153
Washington, George 38
wealth 41, 66, 69, 74; *see also* prosperity; well-being
well-being 3, 42, 68, 74, 175; see also prosperity; wealth
westward expansion *see* expansion and expansionism; *see also* American continent; frontier; Manifest Destiny
the White House 133, 135, 139, 211; *see also* government; presidents and the presidency
Wilson, Woodrow 6, 38, 42, 126, 128, 179, 180, 191
Winthrop, John 2, 12, 34, 173, 191; *see also* "city on a hill"; Puritans
world order 5, 16–17, 21–22, 25–27; *see also* domination; imperialism
World War I 41, 67, 120, 126, 165, 179, 185, 191; *see also* wars and warfare
World War II 22, 46, 75, 79, 179, 182, 185, 191, 197; *see also* wars and warfare

Young, Brigham 55, 60; *see also* Mormons and Mormonism; Smith, Joseph

Zion *see* New Israel/Jerusalem/Zion

www.ingramcontent.com/pod-product-compliance
Ingram Content Group UK Ltd.
Pitfield, Milton Keynes, MK11 3LW, UK
UKHW041918140426
5217IPUK00013B/212